Perverse Feelings

Perverse Feelings

Poe and American Masculinity

Suzanne Ashworth

LEXINGTON BOOKS
Lanham • Boulder • New York • London

Published by Lexington Books
An imprint of The Rowman & Littlefield Publishing Group, Inc.
4501 Forbes Boulevard, Suite 200, Lanham, Maryland 20706
www.rowman.com
86-90 Paul Street, London EC2A 4NE

British Library Cataloguing in Publication Information Available

Library of Congress Cataloging-in-Publication Data Available

ISBN 978-1-7936-2652-3 (cloth)
ISBN 978-1-7936-2654-7 (paper)
ISBN 978-1-7936-2653-0 (electronic)

Contents

Acknowledgments

I have found meaning and purpose in the classrooms of a liberal arts university in Columbus, Ohio. Like many of my counterparts, I teach a seven-course load, often juggling seven distinct "preps," for English and women's gender & sexuality studies students as well as undergraduates across all disciplines. Teaching in topical, culturally relevant curricula requires steady new course development. Most recently, this innovation has extended to LGBTQ memoir, gothic literature, contemporary masculinities, sexual violence, true crime media, and more. In addition, my institutional service work is labor-intensive and mission driven. Faculty at small colleges chair programs and committees; advise students and student organizations; coordinate speakers and events; and contribute to shared governance. It is an invigorating, gratifying, and at times exhausting existence.

My teaching and scholarship nourish one another. I have designed courses informed or inspired by many of the writers and thinkers that populate this project. And my classes consistently deepen my scholarly fascinations. That said, a teaching life like this one can mean working in relative isolation and obscurity. Thus, I first want to acknowledge the wonder of my Otterbein colleagues. I teach alongside incredibly talented and devoted faculty. Their work often goes unseen and unsung. Especially in an era increasingly defined by neoliberal education, vocational degrees, and anti-intellectualism.

I want to thank the English Department at Otterbein University. My chair, Dr. Margaret Koehler, enabled this project with her conscientious stewarding of my teaching schedule and support for an early sabbatical. Margaret, Dr. Karen Steigman, and Dr. Tammy Birk restored my spirit again and again with sincere friendship—and a group text—that I would be lost without. I hope we are drinking cocktails—wearing kaftans and smoking cigarettes—in this life and the next. Dr. Shannon Lakanen is one of the most creative and generous teachers I have ever known, an incomparable essayist and poet, and a true-hearted friend. Dr. Paul Eisenstein is a teacher-scholar for the ages, embodying everything admirable in academic excellence. Jeremy Llorence resists cynicism and embraces optimism in every facet of this profession. Dr. Phyllis Burns encourages me to speak—and teach—honestly and bravely even when it's hard. Dr. Jeremy Smith affirms that the ideals of a liberal education can become an ethic and conviction. And Drs. Alison Prindle, Patti Frick, and Beth Daugherty welcomed a novice faculty member into a new world and mentored me with wisdom and care.

I want to thank the Humanities Advisory Committee at Otterbein University, and its summer writing grant support, chaired by Dr. Amy Johnson as this project evolved. Her position—colliding unexpectedly with a pandemic and fiscal crisis—called her to an urgent advocacy for the relevance of the Humanities to academic, professional, and human learning. She proved an eloquent and courageous force.

I want to thank Dr. Judith Lakamper, acquisitions editor, for her responsiveness and guidance. The copy editing team at Lexington Books for their blue-pencil precision. And Allen Reichart, librarian and comrade, for his agile and meticulous indexing.

I want to thank my students. Dear ones, you nurtured this book in countless ways. As I taught to—and through—these ideas, you lived the questions with me. You made me a more thoughtful and attuned scholar. You remind me, always, that knowledge isn't just power; it is also liberation. And some of you gave me the privilege and pleasure of deeper dives into queer theory or the gothic in your senior writing projects, especially Rachel Stonebrook, Wes Jamison, Katy Major, Jess Bryant, Josh Brandon, Gretchen Heisler, and Lucy Clark.

I want to thank my mom for "rabbit rabbit rabbit," "onward and upward," and unwavering belief in me. My dad for showing me that Marcums are made of mountains, half-runners, and unconditional love. I want to thank Brian. You are laughter and ease in the sunshine; you are my keep calm and carry on. I want to thank Laura, for connecting me to earth and trees; for turning up the music; and for nesting with me. You are a gentle breeze and a summer evening on the porch. And Tam. Twin flame. My soul's society. You brilliantly edited every chapter of this book. It is more lucid, more insightful, and blessedly more Virgo for your feedback. We are predestination. You got me, and baby, I got you. Each of you—one and all—are essential to me. I would not have survived without you.

Finally, my boys, sweet boys, Jacob and Samuel, thank you for the most happiness and continuity I have ever known. You made my life, you are my heart.

Introduction

Perverse Feelings

" . . . to those who feel rather than to those who think . . . "[1]

—Poe, "Eureka," 1848

With the publication of "The Black Cat" in 1843, Poe identified a psycho-somatic force he believed inherent to the human condition: "the SPIRIT of perverseness." First explored in the *Narrative of Arthur Gordon Pym* five years earlier, perverseness is the "wild, indefinable emotion" that Pym experiences as he descends a cliff. Staring into the chasm beneath him, Pym feels an irresistible attraction to his own death: "*a longing to fall*; a desire, a yearning, a passion utterly uncontrollable."[2] In "The Black Cat," perverseness extends beyond Pym's suicidal urge, driving the narrator to defy social and moral law: to kill what he loves and what loves him, to commit unforgivable sin. As the narrator explains, he feels compelled by "this unfathomable longing of the soul *to vex itself*—to offer violence to its own nature—to do wrong for the wrong's sake only."[3] In Poe's imagination, perverseness is an obstinate commitment to trespass and transgression, even if the violation destroys the sacred, the other, or the self.

By 1845, the image of the subject at the edge of death, flirting with his own annihilation, comes to epitomize the perverse. In the "Imp of the Perverse," Poe positions us all at "the brink of a precipice," staring "into the abyss," shuddering with "horror" and "delight" at the prospect of our fall. He defines perverseness as a "*prima mobilia* of the human soul," a "paradoxical something," a "*mobile* without motive." The perverse propels unintelligible actions, including inexplicable violence and self-injury. Here, Poe calls perverseness "a strongly antagonistical sentiment" as well as "a maddening desire." The perverse seduces us into destruction against our better will and better judgment. "Through its promptings we act without comprehensible object," Poe contends, "through its promptings we act, for the reason that we should *not*." Indeed, reason magnifies and intensifies a perverse fixation. Poe

1

emphasizes: "Because our reason violently deters us from the brink, *therefore*, do we the more impetuously approach it."[4] As his theory of the perverse evolved, Poe explicated its tangled relationship with moral or logical prohibitions, arguing that ethical and rational constraint only makes a perverse affect that much more enticing.

In "Imp of the Perverse," Poe also describes what it is like to *feel* perversely. It begins with a "single thought: to deliberately provoke another person, to procrastinate an essential labor, to confess to a murder committed with perfect impunity." Thought turns to impulse, and an affective acceleration begins: "impulse increases to a wish, the wish to a desire, the desire to an uncontrollable longing." Eventually, the perverse becomes "craving," an insatiable need. Internally, we war against our hunger: "We tremble with the violence of the conflict within us." To finally gratify the perverse is an act of "consummation," an ecstatic release.[5]

Critics have analyzed perverseness as a narrative strategy, a psychological drive, a philosophical concept, and the tragic principle that ravaged Poe's own life and psyche.[6] In this book, I return the perverse to Poe's insistence on *feeling*. For Poe, the perverse was a "sentiment," a "faculty," and a "longing." I revive the perverse in these terms: as an emotion, a power of mind, and a desire. I read it as an *affect* and as a way to understand a nexus of affiliated affects.

I understand the affect as a psychosomatic experience, a cultural construction, and a political apparatus. My conception of affect is deeply informed by queer and feminist scholarship that examines the intricate relationships between affects, personhood, and power. With Ann Cvetkovich, I see the affective as "a category that encompasses affect, emotion, and feeling, and that includes impulses, desires, and feelings that get historically constructed in a range of ways."[7] Affects reach into the sensation and expression of an emotion, and they tangle with the cultural paradigms that enable us to name or know a feeling, like anger, fear, or pleasure. Affects are historical, located in place, time, and culture; and they have distinct histories of their own, histories that push us to interrogate the official memory a culture creates. With Sara Ahmed, I recognize that emotions resonate with "about-ness": They are *about* a person, an event, the self. As such, emotions are relational and motile, circulating through dynamics of attraction, attachment, repulsion, and estrangement. With Ahmed, I recognize, too, that emotions map onto existing power differentials. Western cultures suppress emotion, subordinating it to thought and reason. As Ahmed writes, "To be emotional is to have one's judgment affected: it is to be reactive rather than active, dependent rather than autonomous." Cultures also create hierarchies of emotion, promoting "good" feeling and stigmatizing marginalized others as "the source of bad feeling."[8]

We pursue happiness, for example; we cherish contentment, gratitude, and forgiveness; and we assume that oppressed populations are irrationally angry, hostile, or depressed. Finally, with Ahmed, I recognize that feeling infiltrates being. Emotions inform social ontologies, including ontologies of gender, race, sexuality, and nation.

FEELING MASCULINITY

This book examines white masculinity and affect in Poe's short fiction. It tracks the feelings that propel Poe's writing and distort American manhood. Poe's men are tormented by chronic illness, deviant attachments, and ugly emotions. As I analyze these afflictions, the book illuminates the pathologies of American masculinity that emerged in a terrible history of imperialism, capitalism, racism, misogyny, and homophobia. One of its central contentions is that we can better understand a past and present American masculinity through a reckoning with its "perverse feelings."

More pointedly, this book asks: *What does masculinity feel?* What does masculinity feel in the temporal and cultural scene that Poe and his victim-heroes occupy? What does white American masculinity feel in the first decades of nation formation? What does it feel in the crucible of its revolution, its slave system, its democracy, its nascent capitalism, and its quest for happiness? What affects besiege and beleaguer Poe's men? And what can they teach us about the antagonisms of contemporary white American masculinity?

Scholarly studies of nineteenth-century masculinity implicitly reinforce how much white American manhood defines itself through feeling and unfeeling. As Michael Kimmel details the rise of the "self-made man" in the new republic, he identifies the affects of a manhood animated by economic uncertainties and westward expansion: "Mobile, competitive, aggressive in business, the Self-Made Man was temperamentally restless, chronically insecure, and desperate to achieve a solid grounding for a masculine identity."[9] In the nineteenth century, manhood was increasingly solidified—and proven—by emotional regulation. The self-made man transcended psychosocial precariousness and became invulnerable. "A man was independent, self-controlled, [and] responsible," Kimmel writes. Boys and enslaved men, in contrast, were unreliable, careless, and volatile. Enslaved black masculinity represented a formative antithesis to the command of white manhood, personifying a terrifying vector of powerlessness.[10] A "real" man remained emotionally autonomous, mastering feeling, thought, and action. According to Kimmel, "native-born white men" secured their manhood through disciplines of the body and the passions, rejecting idleness, sensuality, and excess. Nineteenth-century manhood also required an aggressive "repudiation of the feminine," including any emotional tenderness or fragility. Capitalism and imperialism pushed men to extremes of "calculation, self-control and unremitting effort."[11] In this America then, white men gave freest expression to ambition, rivalry, and entitlement.[12] The self-made man was simultaneously a gender ideal and an affective Pandora's box. Self-made masculinity required combustible extremes of emotional regulation, economic accretion, and social supremacy. Its repressions and yearnings created a shadow manhood that was hostile, anxious, and rapacious.

Andrew Jackson personified the affective preoccupations—and disturbances—of self-made manhood, including conquest, acquisition, and violence.[13] In the years of his ascendancy, Jackson was a metonym for American liberty, self-reliance, and audacity. Michael Rogin observes, "Born on the farthest frontier, lacking the advantages of birth and family connections, he seemed entirely responsible for his own life." Yet Jackson was volatile and hot tempered, "as famous for his violence as for his independence." He "had moods of manic omnipotence, paranoid rage, and occasional deep depression." He struggled for the affective control that defined self-made masculinity, but "he gained his mature political power from his ability to sublimate" his anger and appetites. Although he drank, gambled, and caroused with abandon, he sought to purify the republic of its dissipations. In his personal relationships, Jackson was suspicious, mistrustful, and wary of attachment: "He imagined domination and submission only, not mutuality." He settled grievances through a lifetime of dueling, believing death more tolerable than dishonor. In his commitments to Indian removal, slavery, and empire building, he personified both "the imperial" and the xenophobic "paranoid style" of American politics.[14] His victories made the American national psyche seem strong and viable. He came to symbolize the ruthless, calculated vitality of white masculine supremacy and manifest destiny. As a man and an icon, Jackson was combative, merciless, and voracious.

These are the predilections of perverse feelings. First and foundationally, I define perverse feelings as affects of white masculine domination. Perverse feelings are the emotive constructs of privilege, entitlement, and hegemony. In the chapters that follow, I analyze emotions that rely on a capacity for violence or violation that fascinates Poe. To be acculturated to patriarchal supremacy requires an openness and even an attraction to perverse feelings. White nineteenth-century manhood established itself through assertions of power and desire. Men were "men" when they subdued a rival, took what they wanted, owned people and property. Indian genocide, slavery, the subjugation of women, and capitalist accumulations necessitated certain forms of domestic violence: violence in the home, in the marketplace, and in the nation. To survive and thrive, white men had to cultivate a willingness to brutalize an other or do unpardonable wrong, even when it meant psychological torment, moral condemnation, or their own death. The perversity that Poe's men feel cannot be understood apart from the affects of national, racialized, and gender primacies.

The annals of nineteenth-century literature attest to the emotional prerogatives—and troubles—of white masculinity. Seminal texts bear witness to its monopoly on the affects that this book investigates. Herman Melville's Ahab, for instance, feels "all the general rage and hate felt by his whole race from Adam down," inspiring sympathetic "oaths of violence and revenge" from his crew. And he also closets a "direful madness" in his "hidden self."[15] Henry David Thoreau likewise seethes with indignation and combativeness. "I was not born to be forced. I will breathe after my own fashion," Thoreau insists.[16] And he also laments that "the mass of men lead lives of quiet desperation."[17] Ralph Waldo Emerson rails against the world with paranoid resentment, "Society everywhere is in conspiracy against the manhood of everyone of its members."[18] And he also struggles to make sense of sadness and loss: "I grieve that grief can teach me nothing. . . . Nothing is left us now but death."[19] Perhaps most ominously, Frederick Douglass describes the cold violence of white men. His overseer, Mr. Gore, whips enslaved people "from a sense of duty, and feared no consequence," punishing defiance with methodical precision. "He was, in a word, a man of the most inflexible firmness and stone-like coolness," Douglass writes, "His savage barbarity was equaled only by the consummate coolness with which he committed the grossest and most savage deeds upon the slaves under his charge."[20] Such literature contributes to the history of unquiet feelings that this book interrogates.

Poe populates his fictions with kindred men: white men angry, aggrieved, and vindictive. Hence, this book chronicles an astonishing accumulation of white male torment. Each chapter centers on a select short story and a perverse emotion that propels the narrative: hate, melancholia, disgust, revenge, and resentment. Chapter 1 analyzes "William Wilson" as a chronicle of nihilistic self-hatred. I argue that the story grapples with the humiliations that often instigate hate. And, more fundamentally, I argue that the narrator embodies his culture's scorn for psychosomatic states of white male bondage. Chapter 2 examines "The Tale of the Ragged Mountains" as a study of white masculine melancholia. I read "Ragged Mountains" as a tale of white men sick with loss and subsumed in each other's pain. In the process, I trace the crises of feeling and attachment—predicaments of both desire and grief—that hold white men in networks of reoccurring trauma across time, place, and bodies. Chapter 3 centers on the disgust the white male body provokes in "The Facts in the Case of M. Valdemar." This fiction registers the grip of a lethal homophobia on American masculinity and adds to a literary necropolis of gender and sexual deviants. Chapter 4 excavates the etiology of resentment in the letters between Poe and his foster father, John Allan. I argue that the letters illuminate the significance of injury, grief, and grievance in the persistence of resentment, as well as the reparations Poe discovered in victimization. Chapter 5 situates "The Cask of Amontillado" in the brutalities of the insult for white American men and the redemptive effects of retaliatory violence. In his murderous revenge, Montresor bends time, alters memory, and resurrects his masculinity. All told, this is canon of abuse and affliction. It penetrates the affective shadows of white manhood, exposing its anguish and ugliness.

In answering the question "what does white nineteenth-century American masculinity feel?" then, more haunting questions emerge for me. How does this masculinity live with what it feels? How does it bear the affects of its dominance? How does it survive the force of its own animus? What do perverse feelings do to the subject and subjectivity experiencing them?

FEELING GOTHIC

To reckon with the effects of perverse affects, I turn to the gothic. In other words, I read perverse feelings as an affect of white nineteenth-century masculinity *and* as a gothic feeling. This interpretive concurrence seems salient for two reasons. First, critics laud Poe as a progenitor of the American gothic; and second, the gothic vividly illuminates the psychosocial implications of distressing emotional states.[21] A number of scholars emphasize the gothic's preoccupation with precarities of body, mind, self, and sensation. Jefferey Weinstock notes that the gothic consistently depicts disordered minds addled by "irrational compulsions" and "immoderate, ungovernable passions."[22] David Punter underscores the gothic's investment in "prohibited desires" and "emotional extremes": the illicit internal forces "with which we find it difficult, if not impossible, to come to terms." Fred Botting summarizes the gothic's penchant for the disturbed and the disturbing: "Ill-formed, obscure, ugly, gloomy and utterly antipathetic to effects of love, admiration or gentle delight, gothic texts register revulsion, abhorrence, fear, disgust, and terror."[23] The gothic repeatedly enacts perplexing encounters with sinister feelings. In the process, the gothic reveals that the center of modern subjectivity—including rational, post-Enlightenment masculinity—cannot hold. As Brian Baker explains, the gothic presents us with "a radically disrupted masculine subject," a subject "fractured or divided," a subject occupied by alterities it cannot escape.[24] The gothic disaggregates coherent masculinity, confounding it with doubt, unreason, and otherness. In Cyndy Hendershot's words, "the Gothic exposes the others within and without that give the lie to the notion of such a category as stable masculinity."[25] And Botting affirms, the gothic "leaves no one and no thing safe from an awful dissolution of boundaries, meanings and identities"[26]

This "awful dissolution" of masculinity is, for my purposes, one of the impacts of the perverse feelings that unsettle Poe's men. According to Alfred Bendixen, a disintegrated masculinity is a distinct characteristic of Poe's storytelling. "If the Gothic's chief purpose in a democratic culture is to warn that identity can be lost, then Poe's repeated treatment of the dissolution of the self in tales narrated by murderers and others who fail to understand the meaning of their own stories constitutes the most American version of that mode."[27] These lost selves—Poe's baffled protagonists—are men, *white men* like William Wilson, Montresor, and a cast of unnamed narrators that feel perversely, hurt themselves, or hurt others. They rank among what Poe called "the many uncounted victims" of the perverse.[28] As Botting states, Poe's "characters manifest a predilection for mental states that are disturbed, drugged or diseased, delusional or pathological states from which neither they or the tales recover." Indeed, Poe never reconciles these affective derangements. More than his contemporaries, he "leaves boundaries between reality, illusion, and madness unresolved."[29] He leaves his men anguished, psychopathic, or dead.

The whiteness of this masculinity is pivotal to the expression and implications of its perverse feelings. A number of critics affirm Teresa Goddu's conviction that "the American gothic is haunted by race."[30] Goddu notes that the American gothic "emerged simultaneous to and in dialogue with the rise of New World slavery and the construction of racial categories."[31] Ellen Weinaur argues that the gothic "tells the 'true' story of race in America—a story that points not only to the existence of a substantive national 'unfreedoms' but also of the strenuous effort to create racial categories that distinguish free from unfree, civilized from savage, white from black."[32] In the United States, the gothic's fixations on dark feelings, historical hauntings, and ruptured identities are refracted through the horrors of racist violence and exploitation. And Poe's work is considered central to a racialized American gothic. Toni Morrison holds that Poe, more than any other early American writer, captures white culture's contested relationship with race, including its fears, longings, and fantasies.[33] Bendixen reinforces that "Poe's almost relentless obsession with absurd acts of violence and self-destruction stems from the evils of racism and slavery."[34] In Poe's America and his fiction, lethal cruelties were the prerogatives of white men. Their perverse feelings—their contempt, revulsion, depression, and bitterness—thrived in the torrent of their racialized dominance.

As a gothic feeling then, a perverse feeling may be aberrant, abnormal, or criminal. It is an affect of the evildoer or evil doing. In other words, a perverse feeling can incite deviance or it emerges in the deviant act. A perverse feeling may be ugly, grotesque, or monstrous. It is feeling that white masculinity wants to repudiate. It is a feeling that terrifies, distorts, or repulses the subject experiencing it. A perverse feeling forces the subject to endure an awful mortification *about feeling itself.* A perverse feeling may activate temporal disruptions or hauntings. It refuses to go gently into memory, history, or death. Instead, it reorganizes time, insisting on its inexorable presence and vitality. Finally, a perverse feeling may shatter subjectivity itself. It disrespects the organizing boundaries and dualities of personhood: inside and outside, body and mind, self and other. And thus it dismantles the normal and the normalizing distinctions of gender, sexuality, and race.

FEELING QUEER

Given this dismantling—given the power of the perverse to unravel identity, even the most privileged identity—I also read it as a queer feeling. I understand queer as Carla Freccero explains it, queer as "that which deviates from the norm . . . [and] the force of that deviation."[35] And I read queer as Ahmed posits, queer as "discomfort," queer as an unease that exposes the unfitness of a norm. Ahmed writes that a queer feeling is *"about inhabiting norms differently."* It suggests that something in "the available scripts for living and loving" is fallacious, incomplete, not quite right.[36] A perverse feeling registers a kindred discomfort with white masculinity.

Perverse feelings are also queer in the sense that Judith Butler suggests with her reconsideration of Freudian melancholia in the constitution of gender and sexual identity. Freud maintained that certain desires, especially incest and homosexuality, must be repressed in the Oedipal process of ego formation. Yet repression is never complete. A heterosexual, gendered ego emerges through disavowal. And it preserves its lost erotic objects in the abiding tenacity of shame, aversion, and yearning. As a result, heterosexuality sustains an intractable hold on the rejected and refused. Butler contends that these repeated renunciations leave heterosexuality with an unexpressed grief for its disowned desires.[37] In other words, attractions to forbidden behaviors and intimacies haunt the heterosexual subject. My contention is that other feelings—perverse feelings—likewise emerge in the trauma of compulsory losses. The repudiations that create a viable manhood—repudiations of the feminine and the homoerotic—also fester primal angers, aversions, and grievances. Poe's men are alive with animosity, sorrow, and rage. They are both made and mangled by perverse feelings.

Finally, a perverse feeling is queer in the sense that Jose Munoz describes: It is "the thing that lets us feel that this world is not enough, that indeed something is missing"; and it is a "longing that propels us onward." Queer is a dissatisfaction, an unease that registers a desire for—and a belief in—an alternative present and a different reality. As Munoz states, a queer feeling is "about the rejection of a here and now and an insistence on potentiality or concrete possibility for another world." A perverse feeling betrays a similar opposition to time, place, and culture, insisting on an elsewhere that is not (yet) here. Although Munoz valorizes hope—"hope in the face of hopeless heteronormative maps of the present"—the darker affects of Poe's fiction can also reverberate with transformative promise.[38]

Poe acknowledges that the perverse might do right by us somehow. He explicitly states that perverseness can "occasionally . . . operate in the furtherance of good."[39] Most critics, if they observe any "good" in perverseness, argue that it brings a few of Poe's criminals to justice. Perversely compelled to confess their undetected crimes, some of Poe's men go to prison or the gallows. I am not convinced, however, that this is the potential "good" Poe discerns in the perverse. Instead, I hold that whatever "good" the perverse tenders, comes from the vitality of its queer negativity. The "antisocial turn" in queer theory illuminates my contention here. This scholarship advocates for a sociopolitical commitment to queer modes of pessimism, hostility, and alienation. Articulated most notably by Lee Edelman, antisociality conjures a queerness that embraces its historical alliance with the death drive. As a result, it refuses fidelity to the false promises of any present or future "good." For Edelman, queerness exercises its most radical energy when it channels the nihilism and regression that it already represents.[40] This scholarly trajectory has inspired a substantial reconsideration of "bad" feelings, including affects like shame, grief, unhappiness, and depression. Jack Halberstam, for example, elucidates the anarchic power these affects can release into the world. Such "undisciplined" responses agitate a political negativity that "promises, this time, to fail, to make a mess, to fuck shit up, to be loud, unruly, impolite, to breed resentment, to bash back, to speak up and out, to disrupt, assassinate, shock, and annihilate." When the world and time we occupy punishes, marginalizes, or rejects certain identities, the prospect of annihilation seems more arresting. "[I]t is here that the promise of self-shattering, loss of mastery and meaning, unregulated speech and desire are unloosed," Halberstam writes. The antisocial proposition holds that "bad" feelings can deliver on this promise of shattering, and "may in fact offer more creative, more cooperative, more surprising ways of being in the world."[41] Such thinking maintains that bad feelings can nurture more liberatory politics and practices.

Certainly, Poe's fictions reverberate with this potentiality. With perverse agencies, Poe's men let go into the abyss, and they allow the abyss to infiltrate the psyche and self. In addition, Poe's men open themselves, however fleetingly, to complex affinities with other men. This book attends closely to those relationships. As we shall see, Poe's men persist in relationships of interest, curiosity, and attraction, as well as relationships of dread, malice, and horror. These texts proffer odd couples and couplings, including William Wilson's inescapable bond with his double; P's devoted yet medicalized watch at Valdemar's bedside; Bedloe's felt experience of Templeton's memory of colonial warfare; and Montresor's intimate claim to Fortunato's death and his dead body. Drawing on histories of sexuality and gender, as well as queer and feminist theory, I read these relationships as queer attachments. Whatever else they feel, Poe's men express the grief of homoerotic loss through their bodies and sensations.

Like other subjects of queer history, Poe's men also materialize the disfiguring impacts of patriarchal, capitalist, and imperial violence. They remind us that some men die, self-destruct, go mad, or kill others in the nucleus of normative masculinity. Nevertheless, these are the affects of a conquering race, sexuality, gender, and nation. A significant critical tradition documents the oppressions of Poe's canon: its racism, misogyny, and homophobia.[42] Yet an abundance of scholarship also shows that Poe's work vigorously critiques the abuses of power and the powerful.[43] Certainly, Poe and Poe's men are answerable for their despotisms and damage. This book does not attempt to redeem historical white masculinity or advocate for a sentimentalized sympathy with its pain. Still, one of the pressures of a project like this arises from the question of its "use" in the world. How might it be enlisted in a feminist or queer politic? How might it serve the aspirations of scholarly activisms that grapple with the urgencies of social justice and social change?

Heather Love articulates one of the critical temptations such work might confront: the desire to alchemize negativity, to ensure that "bad" feelings help us make things "better." "Given the scene of destruction at our backs," Love writes, "queers feel compelled to keep moving on toward a brighter future."[44] Often that obligation produces a scholarship that wants to replace despair with resilience, agency, and optimism. Even Edelman writes with a hope for the queer negativity he theorizes: "Such queerness proposes, in place of the good, something I want to call 'better,' though it promises, in more than one sense of the phrase, absolutely nothing." We stay beholden to the hope for a compensatory present or reparative future.

Do I write with hope? Do I write with the same confidence that enables Love to suppose we can "make a future backward enough that even the most reluctant of us might want to live there"? Love believes that if we "feel backwards"—if we embrace a "history of marginalization and abjection"—we can make "visible the damage that we live with in the present." In the process, we can "develop a vision of political agency that incorporates the damage that we hope to repair."[45] My study attends to a history of injury in the ways that Love recommends. It stays with antecedent rage, shame, betrayal, hurt, and loss. It makes visible the ruin that haunts a past masculinity. Is this visibility enough? And what will this visibility do in this present, in the next future, and to the subjects newly exposed?

Judith Butler analyzes the perils of visibility, contending with the intricacies of recognition for modern subjectivity. Through recognition, we access personhood: a "socially viable" identity and a place inside the human. But "the terms by which we are recognized as human are socially articulated and changeable."[46] We can only be seen through the prisms of a place, time and culture, if we get seen at all, and the legibility of race, gender, and sexuality are pivotal to recognition. As Butler contends, limited, mistaken, or refused forms of recognition "undo" the subject and make for "unlivable" or "ungrievable" lives.[47] There is no *person* in the errata of recognition. In Butler's thinking, recognition constitutes a horizon of both vitality and vulnerability. We live or die there.

In an act of historical recognition then—with figures that come to us through violence and harm done—how do we hold vigil for liveable and grievable lives? Butler indicates that this proposition is "about distinguishing among the norms and conventions that permit people to breathe, to desire, to love, and to live, and the norms and conventions that restrict or eviscerate the conditions of life itself."[48] This work is always dangerous and unpredictable. Butler cautions, "The question most central to recognition is a direct one, and it is addressed to the other: 'Who are you?'"[49] We cannot predict an other's answer, and the question itself changes us. As Butler affirms, "in the asking, in the petition, we have already become something new. . . . " Nobody stays the same in this mediation. And although we may not survive without it, we risk our lives to be seen. "To ask for recognition, or to offer it, is precisely not to ask for what one already is. It is to solicit a becoming, to instigate a transformation. It is also to stake one's own being, and one's own persistence in one's own being, in the struggle for recognition."[50] In recognition, we summon a mutual and uncertain becoming.

Poe's perverse first-person narrators—speaking to undesignated listeners and unknowable futures—beckon us into the channels of recognition. What we see and what we become remains unmapped. But the change, and its strange new freedoms, is already arriving. As if Poe had this premonition, his narrator in "The Imp of the Perverse" leaves us with this avowal: "But why shall I say more? To-day I wear these chains, and am *here*. To-morrow I shall be fetterless!—*but where?*"[51] Why say more? We have his story. He is already becoming otherwise. He is already going elsewhere.

METHODOLOGY

I read Poe's work as part of an "archive of feelings."[52] I investigate the feelings that Poe's writing names, describes, and represents. I follow the feelings a text assigns to character, event, time, or place. I analyze feelings that seem to permeate identity and masculinity in a text. I try to make sense of affects through historical and theoretical inquiry. I ask and answer questions like: what defines a feeling? How did the nineteenth century understand it? What distinguishes a specific feeling from kindred affects? How does an affect reverberate through the cultural constructs of gender, race, sexuality, and nation? What can it teach us about the psychosomatic experience of white American masculinity—its fears, sorrows, and regrets; its pleasures, freedoms, and appetites; and its failures and atrocities?

This archive reaches into nineteenth-century medicine, psychology, and philosophy—discourses that illuminate the extant conception of a feeling. It includes Poe's letters, biographies of Poe, and records of relevant events in Poe's affective history. It integrates scholarly studies of nineteenth-century men and masculinity. And it draws on contemporary theory, particularly queer, feminist, and psychoanalytic thought. As I have already indicated, these theories help clarify the relationships between affects and other organizing structures of human experience, including identity, power, perception, memory, and time.

In this interplay between history and theory, I recognize that I open myself to allegations of dehistoricization. Three decades ago, gender and sexuality studies committed to historicist methodologies that prohibit the imposition of modern concepts on historical bodies and desires. Historicist readings insist on the precedence of temporal contingency, specificity, and alterity. They also proceed through linear timeframes. By this logic, Poe and Poe's men must be read "in their own terms," only through ideologies and discourses that were "present" in their time. Such a method prizes a strict inventory of historical source material and the writer's mind, preferably the books on Poe's shelves; his letters, diaries, and other writings; and discursive evidence of Poe's familiarity with any phenomenon under study. This method may reach into the immediate present of a literary text or its documented past, but some critics assume it goes rogue if it borrows anachronistically from the future or from too distant antecedents.

A recent generation of scholars interrogate the misapprehensions of this methodology. Valerie Rohy asserts that allegations of historical impropriety can "obscure the difference between a neglect of history and a violation of chronology." It is hubris to presume that scholarship can reliably reinhabit the past if it stays inside temporal parameters or follows sequential time.

Such historicism "upholds the illusion of a true, unidirectional history, whose effect of veracity and realism is in fact sustained by the very retroaction it condemns." When we look backwards, adhering to sequential chronologies, we may recreate a progressive—and fictional—history. We may discern false historical causes, effects, and advances. In addition, Rohy observes, "the practice of historical criticism is impossible *on its own terms*. Historical alterity is, after all, a recent invention; the conviction that past ages are non-continuous with modernity is a hallmark of modernity."[53] How we do history matters as much as the history we discover, and we cannot know any past before we find it.

An uncritical devotion to linear time is especially incompatible with my project, given its investment in histories of race, gender, sexuality, nation, and affect. In the nineteenth century, gender and sexual deviance foretold "the corruption of history, the retroactions of anachronism and arrested development, and all that violates the developmental chronology we might call *straight time*."[54] Just as importantly, Dana Luciano's notion of "affective timekeeping" in the nineteenth century reinforces the ways that affects take their own time.[55] A feeling like grief or anger may phenomenologically stop time, slow time, fracture time, propel us forward or back in time. A queerer, more feminist, and more historical history then, "might mean a turn away from the discipline of straight time."[56] It might mean a different conception of timeliness and temporal relevance. As Carla Freccero elucidates, such "analyses proceed otherwise than according to the presumed logic of cause and effect, anticipation and result; and otherwise than according to a presumed logic of the 'done-ness' of the past, since queer time is haunted by the persistence of affect and ethical imperatives in and across time."[57] Such analyses heed the vagaries of time.

I am deeply attentive to Poe's own time; to his lived experience; to the discourses he directly engaged; to the historical realities that pervade the lives of his men. I carefully investigate cultural allusions and autobiographical connections. Simultaneously, I read over and through time as well. My methods reflect Freccero's contention that "the possibility that reading historically may mean reading against what is conventionally referred to as history." Like Freccero, I "make use of intertexuality, a mode of figural intra- and intertemporal articulation that might be called 'literary' rather than historical. . . . "[58] In this articulation, I am especially intrigued by temporal adjacencies and proximities. I make connections between texts that seem portentously close in time, texts published in a timely vicinity with Poe's fictions. And I investigate the times that a text makes proximate through setting, historical inferences, and affective reorganizations.

My interest in temporal nearness resonates with Carolyn Dinshaw's vision of more tactile histories. Dinshaw imagines a "touch across time" as the basis of an alternative historiography. She calls this "a queer historical impulse," one that wants to make connections between past and present alterities. Her work seeks "to demonstrate the simultaneous copresence of different chronologies at any moment."[59] As Nicholas Reich explains it, this method "is about establishing an affective relationship with subjects and situations that resonate meaningfully with current understandings of gender, sex, and sexuality."[60] The value of such an approach comes in recognitions that can likewise happen over and through time. It allows us to see fragments of past and present masculinities that resonate in other contexts.

That said, we should not overestimate the ease of temporal or affective symmetries. Heather Love wonders if Dinshaw's touch can accommodate a past that remains untouchable, arguing that "untouchability runs deep in the queer experience." And, I would add, so does ambivalence. In the end and for now, Poe and Poe's men leave a legacy of ambivalence. Poe's fictions contribute to timeworn worries about sick, weak, disturbed, and failing men. They press the same questions that agitate the current moment: What do we do with the shattered patriarchs that ghost our culture? How should we feel about their pain and perdition? In response, this book warns against an uncritical relationship with white masculine injury. The history I enter is a cautionary tale, one that reveals our culture's contradictory attachments to wounded white men. Like Poe, our culture persists in a vexed relationship with white masculine violence, imperialism, racism, sexism, and homophobia. We may condemn the patriarch's past transgressions, but we are nostalgic for his dominance. We may disparage an unfeeling masculinity, but we still want the love and approbation of the impassive forefather. We may fear the lethal impacts of violent masculinity, but we revel in the wantonness of violent men. There is no simple, unconflicted way to reencounter this manhood. As Love affirms, "Taking care of the past without attempting to fix it means living with bad attachments, identifying through loss, allowing ourselves to be haunted."[61] I write from this haunted place. I write with the knowledge that we are haunted by the men—and the masculinity—in this study. This past abides. We live with ghosts. In this haunting, we are in relationship with stark symmetries between Poe's men and our own. We are in relationship across misapprehensions and difficulty. We are in relationship across time.

NOTES

1. Edgar Allan Poe, "Eureka: A Prose Poem" (New York: Geo. P. Putnam, 1848), www.eapoe.org/works/editions/eurekac.htm.

2. Edgar Allan Poe, *The Narrative of Arthur Gordon Pym*, in *The Selected Writings of Edgar Allan Poe*, ed. G. R. Thompson (New York: W.W. Norton & Co, 2004), 553.

3. Edgar Allan Poe, "The Black Cat," in *Edgar Allan Poe Tales & Sketches Volume 2: 1843–1849*, ed. Thomas Ollive Mabbot (Urbana: University of Chicago Press, 2000), 852.

4. Edgar Allan Poe, "The Imp of the Perverse," in *Edgar Allan Poe Tales & Sketches Volume 2: 1843–1849*, ed. Thomas Ollive Mabbot (Urbana: University of Chicago Press, 2000), 1222, 1220, 1221, 1225, 1220, 1223.

5. Ibid., 1222.

6. Louise J. Kaplan analyzes the perverse as a series of textual tactics that rely on "mystification and concealment," an "ambiguous relationship to the moral order," and a "fundamental antagonism to representational reality" ("The Perverse Strategy in 'The Fall of the House of Usher,'" in *New Essays on Poe's Major Tales*, ed. Kenneth Silverman [Cambridge: Cambridge University Press, 1993], 47). Leland S. Person understands the perverse as a narrative manipulation that "encourages readers to identify with the criminal and to participate more intimately in their crimes" ("Outing the Perverse: Poe's False Confessionals," in *The Oxford Handbook of Edgar Allan Poe*, eds. J. Gerald Kennedy and Scott Peeples [Oxford: Oxford University Press, 2019], 253). Frank Pisano sees the perverse as a "theory of irrational motivation" that can illuminate the actions of arch villains in other nineteenth-century fictions ("Dimmesdale's Pious Imperfect Perverseness: Poe's 'Imp of the Perverse' and *The Scarlet Letter*, in *Poe Writing/Writing Poe*, eds. Richard Kopley and Jana Argersinger [New York: AMS Press, Inc, 2013], 144). Russell Sbriglia argues that "Poe's use of perversity to overthrow the reign of reason . . . constitutes an even more radical overthrowing of liberal subjectivity itself—a subjectivity that, from Descartes and Locke in the seventeenth century to Kant and Hegel in the eighteenth and nineteenth centuries, was thought to be constituted, first and foremost, by reason" ("Feeling Right, Doing Wrong: Poe, Perversity, and the Cunning of Unreason," *Poe Studies* 26 [2013]: 8). Clark T. Moreland and Karime Rodriguez read the perverse as a catalyst of gender reversals that feminize and unman Poe's narrators ("'Never Bet the Devil in Your Head': Fuseli's The Nightmare and Collapsing Masculinity in Poe's 'The Black Cat,'" *The Edgar Allan Poe Review* 16, no. 2 [2015]: 204–20.). And Jeffrey Meyers deems it the "fatal principle" that destroyed Poe (*Edgar Allan Poe: His Life and Legacy* [New York: Charles Scribner's Sons, 1992], 58).

7. Ann Cvetkovich, *An Archive of Feelings: Trauma, Sexuality, and Lesbian Public Cultures* (Durham: Duke University Press, 2003), 4.

8. Sara Ahmed, *The Cultural Politics of Emotion* (New York: Routledge, 2004), 7, 3, 4.

9. Michael Kimmel acknowledges that other ideals of manhood were extant in the nineteenth century, including the Genteel Patriarch, a "dignified aristocratic manhood," and the Heroic Artisan, a "virtuous, honest" laboring manhood. But Kimmel maintains that the self-made man dominates the era until the final decades of the century until a more muscular, primitive masculinity takes hold (*Manhood in America: A Cultural History*, 3rd edition [Oxford: Oxford University Press, 2012], 13). Amy S. Greenburg introduces another taxonomy, arguing that "restrained manhood" competed with "martial manhood" in this historical interval. Restrained manhood centered itself in faith, family, and professional success. Martial manhood reveled in

its toughness, aggression, and bravery. More holistically, Greenburg argues that in the mid-nineteenth century, before industrialization and class stratifications solidified, "gender norms were in flux" (*Manifest Manhood and the Antebellum American Empire* [Cambridge: Cambridge University Press, 2005], 12, 13, 9). Certainly, there were multiple archetypes of manhood in the nineteenth century. My study centers on the affects of dominance that white patriarchal masculinity nurtured in men, even as its norms or paradigms evolved. In addition, with Lorien Foote, I recognize that there are other ways to consider manhood that do not rely on types and categories: "Men chose from a spectrum of options when they pieced together the component parts of their manly identities." More importantly, men shared the same hope or expectation: that "others would recognize and respect their manhood" (*The Gentleman and the Roughs: Manhood, Honor, and Violence in the Union Army* [New York: New York University Press, 2010], 4).

10. Paul Gilmore reinforces the "centrality of race to the construction of white manhood across class lines" and throughout the nineteenth century. Gilmore further argues that Poe "appropriates mass cultural racial difference" to establish his own white literary manhood (*The Genuine Article: Race, Mass Culture, and American Literary Manhood* [Durham: Duke University Press, 2001], 7, 100).

11. Kimmel, *Manhood in America*, 14, 24, 35, 44, 33.

12. E. Anthony Rotundo confirms, "Ambition, rivalry, and aggression drove the new system of individual interests, and a man defined his manhood not by his ability to moderate the passions but by his ability to channel them effectively. . . . In this world where a man was supposed to prove his superiority, the urge for dominance was seen as a virtue" (*American Manhood: Transformations in Masculinity from the Revolution to the Modern Era* [New York: Basic Books, 1993], 3–4). David G. Pugh reinforces, "If any single trait characterized the struggling American male in the first half of the nineteenth century, it was a certain restlessness, a free-floating anxiety, in the conduct of his affairs that, paradoxically, caused him to fight for economic progress as a way of asserting his individuality even as he ached for . . . a peaceful, subsistence life" (*Sons of Liberty: The Masculine Mind in the Nineteenth-Century* [Westport, CN: Greenwood Press, 1983], 13).

13. Michael Kimmel likewise notes that "The emotions that seem to have animated Jacksonian America were fear and rage. . . . Here was the fatherless son, struggling without guidance to separate from the mother and, again, for adult mastery over his environment. Terrified of infantilization, of infantile dependency, his rage propelled the furious effort to prove his manhood against those who threatened it, notably women and infantilized 'others'" (*Manhood in America*, 25).

14. Michael Paul Rogin, *Fathers & Children: Andrew Jackson and the Subjugation of the American Indian* (New Brunswick: Transaction Publishers, 2006), 39, 41, 45, 48, 59, 46.

15. Herman Melville, *Moby-Dick,* ed. John Bryant and Haskell Springer (New York: Pearson Longman, 2007), 176, 172, 177.

16. Henry David Thoreau, "Resistance to Civil Government," in *The Norton Anthology of American Literature,* Volume B 1820–1865, 7th edition, ed. Nina Baym (New York: W. W. Norton & Co, 2007), 1867.

17. Henry David Thoreau, "Walden," in *The Norton Anthology of American Literature*, Volume B 1820–1865, 7th edition, ed. Nina Baym (New York: W. W. Norton & Co, 2007), 1875.

18. Ralph Waldo Emerson, "Self-Reliance," in *The Norton Anthology of American Literature,* Volume B 1820–1865, 7th edition, ed. Nina Baym (New York: W. W. Norton & Co, 2007), 1165.

19. Ralph Waldo Emerson, "Experience," in *The Norton Anthology of American Literature,* Volume B 1820–1865, 7th edition, ed. Nina Baym (New York: W. W. Norton & Co, 2007), 1197.

20. Frederick Douglass, "Narrative of the Life of Frederick Douglass," in *The Norton Anthology of American Literature*, Volume B 1820–1865, 7th edition, ed. Nina Baym (New York: W. W. Norton & Co, 2007), 2081.

21. G.R. Thompson argues that Poe is a "stunningly complex psychological and philosophical writer in the dark tradition" of the Gothic (*Poe's Fiction: Romantic Irony in the Gothic Tales* [Madison: University of Wisconsin Press, 1973], 68). George E. Haggerty maintains that "Edgar Allan Poe was the first American to write truly sophisticated Gothic fiction" (*Gothic Fiction/Gothic Form* [University Park: The Pennsylvania State University Press, 1989], 81). And Bendixen notes that "As theorist, poet, and master of the short story form, Edgar Allan Poe made the Gothic into a central part of American literary romanticism" ("Romanticism and the American Gothic," in *The Cambridge Companion to American Gothic*, ed. Jeffrey Andrew Weinstock [Cambridge: Cambridge University Press, 2017], 34). As Catherine Spooner defines it, the Gothic relentlessly reinforces "the legacies of the past and its burdens on the present; the radically provisional or divided nature of the self; the construction of peoples or individuals as monstrous or 'other'; the preoccupation with bodies that are modified, grotesque, or diseased" ("Introduction: A History of Gothic Studies in the Twentieth and Twenty-First Centuries," in *The Cambridge History of the Gothic*, Volume 3, eds. Catherine Spooner and Dale Townshend [Cambridge: Cambridge University Press, 2021], 14).

22. Jeffrey Andrew Weinstock, "Introduction: The American Gothic," in *The Cambridge Companion to American Gothic*, ed. Jeffrey Andrew Weinstock (Cambridge: Cambridge University Press, 2017), 4, 1.

23. Fred Botting, *Gothic*, 2nd edition (New York: Routledge, 2014), 2.

24. Brian Baker, "Gothic Masculinities," in *The Routledge Companion to the Gothic*, eds. Catherine Spooner and Emma McEvoy (New York: Routledge, 2007), 164, 167.

25. Cyndy Hendershot, *The Animal Within: Masculinity and the Gothic* (Ann Arbor: University of Michigan Press, 1998), 1.

26. Fred Botting, "Reviews," *Erudit* 10 (May 1998), www.erudit.org/en/journals/ron/1998-n10-ron422/005797ar/.

27. Alfred Bendixen, "Romanticism," 35.

28. Poe, "Imp," 1224.

29. Botting, *Gothic*, 110, 111.

30. Teresa A. Goddu, *Gothic America: Narrative, History, and Nation* (New York: Columbia University Press, 1997), 4. In Weinstock's words, the American gothic "draws much of its energy from anxieties over racial difference" ("Introduction," 3).

31. Teresa A. Goddu, "The African American Slave Narrative and the Gothic," in *A Companion to the American Gothic*, ed. Charles L. Crow (Hoboken, NJ: John Wiley & Sons, 2014), 71.

32. Ellen Weinauer, "Race and the American Gothic," in *The Cambridge Companion to American Gothic*, ed. Jeffrey Andrew Weinstock (Cambridge: Cambridge University Press, 2017), 86.

33. Toni Morrison writes, "No early American writer is more important to the concept of American Africanism than Poe." Morrison defines American Africanism as: "the denotative and connotative blackness that African people have come to signify, as well as the entire range of views, assumptions, readings, and misreadings that accompany Eurocentric learning about these people." In addition, Morrison reinforces the ways that such an inquiry simultaneously reveals the composition of whiteness: "through a close look at literary 'blackness,' the nature—even the cause—of literary whiteness.' What is it for? What parts do the invention and development of whiteness play in the construction of what is loosely described as 'American'?" (*Playing in the Dark: Whiteness and the Literary Imagination* [New York: Vintage Books, 1992], 31, 6, 9).

34. Bendixen, "Romanticism," 35.

35. Carla Freccero, *Queer/Early/Modern* (Durham: Duke University Press, 2006), 18.

36. Ahmed, *Cultural Politics*, 154, 155.

37. In other words, Butler reinforces heterosexuality's melancholic relationship with homosexuality: It is an identity based on "a double disavowal, a never having loved, and a never having lost." It is an identity formed through "ungrieved and ungrievable loss" ("Melancholy Gender/Refused Identification," in *The Judith Butler Reader*, ed. Sarah Salih [Malden, MA: Blackwell Publishing, 2004], 250, 248).

38. Jose Esteban Munoz, *Cruising Utopia: The Then and There of Queer Futurity* (New York: New York University Press, 2009), 1, 28.

39. Poe, "Imp," 1223.

40. As Lee Edelman writes, "The ups and downs of political fortune may measure the social order's pulse, but *queerness*, by contrast figures, outside and beyond its political symptoms, the place of the social order's death drive: a place, to be sure, of abjection expressed in the stigma, sometimes fatal, that follows from reading that figure literally, and hence a place from which liberal politics strives. . . . More radically, though, as I argue here, queerness attains its ethical value precisely insofar as it accedes to that place, accepting its figural status as resistance to the visibility of the social while insisting on the inextricability of such resistance from every social structure" (*No Future: Queer Theory and the Death Drive* [Durham: Duke University Press, 2004], 3).

41. Judith Halberstam, *The Queer Art of Failure* (Durham: Duke University Press, 2011), 110, 2–3.

42. Terry Whalen holds Poe's fiction accountable for the "average racism" essential to a white nineteenth-century mainstream that was deeply ambivalent about slavery and blackness. Whalen also recognizes that Poe contributed to American culture's romance with xenophobic narratives of white, male exploration (*Edgar Allan Poe and the Masses: The Political Economy of Literature in Antebellum America* [Princeton: Princeton University Press, 1999], 112). Leland S. Person argues that Poe's representations of race in his fiction "turns on a psychology of white male racism, but it turns out to produce a perverse, topsy-turvy reversal of racial differences—a nightmare of amalgamation, reversed racism, and ironic vigilante justice" ("Poe's Philosophy of Amalgamation: Reading Racism in the Tales," in *Romancing the Shadow: Poe and Race*, eds. J. Gerald Kennedy and Liliane Wiessberg [Oxford: Oxford University Press, 2001], 221).With generations of feminists, J. Gerald Kennedy interrogates "the problem of dying women" in Poe's canon, reinforcing "Poe's tortured thinking about women" ("Poe, 'Ligeia,' and the Problem of Dying Women," in in *New Essays on Poe's Major Tales*, ed. Kenneth Silverman [Cambridge: Cambridge University Press, 1993], 114). Joan Dyan argues that "Poe dwells repeatedly on [racialized] extremes of savagery and cultivation, brute possession and tender affection in his depictions of heterosexual romance" ("Amorous Bondage: Poe, Ladies, and Slaves," in *The American Face of Edgar Allan Poe*, eds. Shawn Resenheim and Stephen Rachman [Baltimore: Johns Hopkins University Press, 1995],189). Leland S. Person reminds us "that Poe's tales typically end in [homoerotic] failure—often with violent foreclosure on male-to-male intimacy," arguing that they participate in "the inception of a powerful homophobia in the middle of the nineteenth century" ("Queer Poe: The Tell-Tale Heart of His Fiction," *Poe Studies* 41, no. 1 [2008]: 8).

43. Dana D. Nelson contends that Poe exposes "the rupture in an emerging form of U.S. manhood that stakes its privileged status not just through race but through gender, class, and political exclusions" ("The Haunting of White Manhood: Poe, Fraternal Ritual, and Polygenesis," *American Literature* 69, no. 3 [September 1997]: 518). Matt Sandler shows how Poe frames "moments of jeopardy and survival in fragments of historical narrative to question both the potential of the United States as rising empire and the importance of the individual in US ideology" ("Poe's Survival Stories as Dying Colonialism," in *The Oxford Handbook of Edgar Allan Poe*, eds. J. Gerald Kennedy and Scott Peeples [Oxford: Oxford University Press, 2019], 271). Thomas Peyser maintains that Poe dramatizes the "nightmare of equality" in American democracy that turns "every citizen into a potential competitor and makes the individual . . . declare war on his own desires—if, that is, they are at odds with the will of the majority" ("Poe's 'William Wilson' and the Nightmare of Equality," *The Explicator* 68, no. 2 [2010]: 103). Peter Jaros explores Poe's interrogation of "the legal doctrine of artificial personhood" that emerged in an era of enslavement, corporate fraud, and capitalist expansion ("A Double Life: Personifying the Corporation from *Dartmouth College* to Poe," Poe Studies 47 [2014]: 4).

44. Heather Love, *Feeling Backward: Loss and the Politics of Queer History* (Cambridge: Harvard University Press, 2007), 162, 5.

45. Love, *Feeling Backward,* 163, 29, 151.

46. Judith Butler, *Undoing Gender* (New York: Routledge, 2004), 2. In Butler's words, "I may feel that without some recognizability I cannot live. But I may also feel that the terms by which I am recognized make life unlivable." This is the paradox of recognition. "The 'I' becomes, to a certain extent unknowable, threatened with unviability, with becoming undone altogether" when it exceeds recognition. And yet, in some circumstances, recognition will destroy the "I." "There are advantages to remaining less than intelligible," Butler explains, if a normative recognition "will only do me in from another direction" (*Undoing Gender*, 4, 3).

47. For Butler, the prospect of the "grievable life" is just as critical to the negotiations of recognition as the liveable life. "The matter is not a simple one," Butler states, "for, if a life is not grievable, it is not quite life; it does not qualify as a life and it is not worthy of note. It is already the unburied, if not the unburiable" (*Precarious Life: The Powers of Mourning and Violence* [London: Verso, 2006], 34).

48. Butler, *Undoing Gender*, 9.

49. Judith Butler, *Giving an Account of Oneself* (New York: Fordham University Press, 2005), 31.

50. Butler, *Precarious Life*, 44.

51. Poe, "Imp," 1226.

52. Ann Cvetkovich defines an archive of feelings as "an exploration of cultural texts as repositories of feelings and emotions which are encoded not only in the content of the texts themselves but in the practices that surround their production and reception." This definition recognizes that affect—particularly trauma—can challenge scholarly assumptions about what constitutes an archive (*Archive of Feelings*, 7).

53. Valerie Rohy, "Ahistorical," *GLQ* 12, no. 1 (2006): 67, 70, 68.

54. Rohy, 68. Elizabeth Freeman implicates straight time in the machinations of "chrononormativity": orchestrations of time that "organize individual human bodies toward maximum productivity" and that make people seem "coherently collective" (*Time Binds: Queer Temporalities, Queer Histories* [Durham: Duke University Press, 2010], 3). Chrononormative scholarship might likewise maneuver people and bodies toward something more productive and coherent than queer historiography. Similarly, African and indigenous people have been imperiled by linear time, deemed primitive, backward, uncivilized, or destined for extinction. Thomas M. Allan shows that early American nationalism relied on "conquering" time. Imagining itself as an "empire of time," the United States quested to "dominate world history" and colonize future time (*A Republic in Time: Temporality and Social Imagination in Nineteenth-Century America* [Chapel Hill: University of North Carolina Press, 2008], 13).

55. Dana Luciano, *Arranging Grief: Sacred Time and the Body in Nineteenth-Century America* (New York: New York University Press, 2007), 5.

56. Rohy, "Ahistorical," 70.

57. Freccero, *Queer/Early/Modern*, 5.

58. Ibid., 4, 4–5.

59. Carolyn Dinshaw, *Getting Medieval: Sexualities and Communities, Pre- and Post-modern* (Durham: Duke University Press, 1999), 71.

60. Nicholas Tyler Reich, "Bottom Terror in Poe's 'William Wilson,'" *The Edgar Allan Poe Review* 21, no. 1 (2020): 89.

61. Heather Love, *Feeling Backwards: Loss and the Politics of Queer History* (Cambridge: Harvard University Press, 2007), 40, 43.

Chapter One

Hate

In 1829, George Washington Adams, the eldest son of John Quincy Adams, drowned himself. George had studied law at Harvard and served in the Massachusetts House of Representatives, but he struggled with drinking, gambling, and depression for much of his life. After an illicit affair with a young servant woman produced an illegitimate child, his parents called him home, hoping to interrupt his ruin. On the steamboat to Washington, George became delusional and paranoid. He hurled himself into the river waters, and his body was found a month later in the Long Island Sound. He was twenty-eight years old. His death represents a bleak nineteenth-century reality: Three out of every four completed suicides in Europe and the United States were committed by men. Physicians believed that men were more vulnerable to lethal despair because they were more exposed to the world's caprices—to financial precarity or thwarted ambition—and because men had the courage and fortitude to die.[1]

Like the men of his time, Poe knew suicidal extremes of desolation. He threatened suicide more than once,[2] and, in the fall of 1848, Poe tried to kill himself. He took an ounce of laudanum, a solution of powdered opium and alcohol. It was a fatal hit: The equivalent to 300 milligrams of morphine, almost thirty times the average dose. But Poe vomited, a friend intervened, and he was saved.[3] In July 1849, he yearned for death again: "It is no use to reason with me *now*," he wrote to his mother-in-law, Muddy, "I must die."[4] Scholars have long speculated that Poe's death a few months later was a passive suicide: death by chronic drinking and drug use. Charles Baudelaire said that his last alcoholic relapse was "almost a suicide[,] a suicide prepared from an early period."[5] Poe lived the nihilistic despondency that the nineteenth century believed afflicted its men.

Intriguingly, however, Poe's death-obsessed short fictions rarely represent suicide. The most notorious deaths in Poe's work are ghastly: characters killed by axes, buried alive, burned to death, or wasting away into corpses. "William Wilson" (1839) ends singularly and spectacularly with the possible suicide of its narrator. The story chronicles its narrator's descent into villainy. A law-less and willful boy, he comes of age at a British boarding school, achieving an "unqualified despotism" over his classmates.[6] Only William Wilson—his bodily and psychological double—rivals him. The narrator struggles against his feelings for Wilson, tormented by fear, respect, curiosity, irritation, attraction, repulsion, and finally, hate. Mortified by a nighttime confrontation with Wilson in his bedchamber, the narrator flees the school. Inexplicably, however, he cannot escape his double. Wilson follows him to Eton, Oxford, Paris, Egypt, Naples, and Rome. He uncannily interrupts the narrator's debauchery, card sharking, and sexual predation. Driven to a "frenzy of wrath" when Wilson obstructs his seduction of another man's wife, the narrator stabs him to death (447). After the narrator plunges his sword repeatedly into Wilson's chest, the dying double ominously says, "*In me didst thou exist—and, in my death, see by this image, which is thine own, how utterly thou hast murdered thyself*" (448). In killing Wilson, the narrator seemingly kills himself.

Whether they read psychic violence or physical violence in its ending, critics typically interpret the story as a chronicle of self-annihilation. Most scholars assume a single William Wilson, a protagonist haunted by his conscience, his alter-ego, or his doppelganger.[7] That said, the tale also suggests that Wilson and the narrator are two distinct men.[8] As Tracy Ware asserts, the story commits itself completely to "sustained ambiguity."[9] Lynn Langmade notes that "Poe himself wasn't sure whether the figure of his creation was an imaginary ghost or a real duplicate": He called Wilson a "phantom," a "reduplication," a "wraith," and a "duplication of the beholder."[10] Either the narrator kills himself, his co-twin, or a psychic specter. Whatever the reality, the tale deliberately confuses killing the other with killing the self. In "William Wilson," homicide is also suicide.

For my purposes, this confusion resonates beyond the extant scholarly emphasis on identity slippage in the story. The misapprehensions in "William Wilson"—the indeterminacy between self-murder and other-murder—cannot be understood apart from the story's interest in hate.

The story announces its investment in hate immediately. As we enter it, we learn the narrator hides his real name because it bears excesses of contempt: It "has been already too much an object for the scorn—for the horror—for the detestation of my race," he says (426). We learn, too, that the narrator himself is full of hate. The confessional tale details the evolution of his hatred for his classmate and rival, William Wilson (a pseudonym he assigns them both). Initially, he "could not bring myself to hate him altogether," he says (433). He struggles to discern his "real feelings towards him," detecting "some petulant animosity, which was not yet hatred, some esteem, more respect, with a world of uneasy curiosity" (433). In fact, he carefully records the moment when he feels a "positive hatred" for Wilson (436). In his last months at school, he "grew restive in the extreme under his distasteful supervision, and daily resented more and more openly what I considered his intolerable arrogance" (436). Here, the narrator commits to hate. From this moment forward, Wilson is "the hated" one (445). When he finally kills Wilson—and/or himself—he kills the object of this hate.

In this chapter, I read "William Wilson" as a study in self-hate, and more particularly, self-hate refracted through the prisms of historical gender and race. I argue first that the story reckons with the insecurities of status that often incite hate. The narrator hates his rival as an ego threat and a source of personal mortification. Hence, the story emphasizes the impact of *perceived* humiliations in the genesis of hate. Second, and drawing on Descartes and Freud, I analyze the actions—the movements—that hate compels. In hate, the narrator attempts to externalize, reject, or evade an enemy-other. But because Wilson is the *same*—the double, the co-twin, the self—the story exposes hate's struggle to expel its object.[11] As we shall see, hatred's expulsions are always incomplete. The narrator can never completely free himself from his own alterity.

Third, I examine the question of Wilson's alterity more closely, excavating the specific horrors that Wilson represents. I show that Wilson materializes the narrator's—and his culture's—masturbation panic. In the grips of his erotophobia, the narrator lives the self-contempt that the masturbation panic created for American men. More specifically, he personifies his culture's edicts against same-gender bodies; he represents the terror of "voluntary depravity" that stalked nineteenth-century boys and men; he personifies early America's conflicted relationship with the radical, often destructive autonomies of "self-willed" men; and he bears his culture's scorn for psychosomatic states of white male bondage. Ultimately, "William Wilson" reveals how the nineteenth century doubled, polarized, and fractured its men. Although it preached a dogma of masculine self-restraint, the culture simultaneously reveled in a manhood that expressed its constitutional freedom through an anarchic will to pleasure. As a result, it condemned its men to the suicidal self-hatred Poe's narrator personifies. In his autoerotic disgrace, Poe's narrator becomes untouchable, unknowable, and inviable.

FELT HUMILIATION

As we meet him, the narrator characterizes himself as an unapologetic dictator. In his first years at school, he enjoys a total autocracy. "If there is on earth a supreme and unqualified despotism," he admits, "it is the despotism of a master-mind in boyhood over the less energetic spirits of its companions" (431). Only Wilson tests his dominance. "My namesake alone . . . presumed

to compete with me," he recounts (431). The narrator experiences Wilson's
rivalry as insolence and revolt. Wilson challenges him "in the studies of the
class—in the sports and broils of the playground" (431). Wilson thwarts the
narrator's primacy in public arenas—the classroom, the playground—and
he resists his social dominance as well, defying the assertions of his "will"
among the boys of their "set" (431). For the narrator, this insurgency is "the
greatest embarrassment" (431). It bruises pride. It mortifies.[12]

More pointedly, Wilson destabilizes the narrator's *internal* perception of
his social ascendency. He admits he "could not help thinking the equality
which he maintained so easily with myself, a proof of his true superiority since not to be overcome cost me a perpetual struggle" (432). Wilson's
effortless resistance troubles the narrator's estimation of his own dominance.
Confronted with Wilson's equality, he feels inferior and inauthentic, as if
his supremacy has been exposed as artifice. In fact, the story places more
emphasis on *how the narrator sees* Wilson's preeminence, rather than how
others perceive it. The narrator alone recognizes Wilson's equality, "our
associates . . . seemed not even to suspect it" (432). Even Wilson remains
indifferent to the rivalry: "He appeared to be destitute alike of the ambition
which urged . . . me to excel" (432). The narrator speculates that for Wilson,
their contests are entirely playful, all impish jousting: he might have been
"actuated solely by a whimsical desire to thwart, astonish, or mortify myself"
(432). In his easy opposition, Wilson seems that much stronger and that much
more unsettling to the narrator's self-image.

A number of researchers illuminate the significance of *perceived* deficits of
sovereignty in the rise of hate. Leonard Berkowitz notes that "true haters" see
danger and menace in the world around them. They defend mightily against
affronts to pride, honor, and position. They are acutely sensitive to "felt
humiliation": the affective sense of betrayal, disgrace, or shame.[13] Willard
Gaylin reinforces the arbitrating influence of the hater's self-concept in "felt
humiliation." Gaylin observes, "Anything that diminishes self-confidence
or raises questions about one's strength, value, or worth" can fuel hatred. In
other words, hate can find its impetus in "psychological assault": the apparent threat of deprivation, inequality, infidelity, exploitation, or frustration. We
hate what seemingly diminishes the self. As Gaylin writes, "Anyone or anything that makes us feel less whole, less powerful, less useful, and less valued
will make us feel endangered."[14] In response, we hate the threatening agent.
This provocation to hate—the ego threat, the status threat—is perhaps easiest
to comprehend. But, more significantly for my purposes, this threat reinforces
the extent to which hate is an *intrapersonal* phenomenon. Hate emerges in the
relationship of self to self. Hate may find an external object, but it simultaneously churns claustrophobically within the subject. In hate, we see the object
of all our animosity, but our own insecurity or inferiority looks back.

SELF-SAME

"William Wilson" is especially invested in the intrapersonal effects of hatred. Indeed, Wilson's sameness makes the narrator's hatred intensely self-referential. Wilson twins the narrator in extraordinary ways. They share the same name and birth date; they enter the school on the same day; and they are physically identical. In addition, Wilson mirrors the narrator's dress, walk, gestures, and voice, becoming his "perfect" copy "in words and in actions" (434). The narrator's agitation increases with every appropriation. "The feeling of vexation . . . ," he explains, "grew stronger with every circumstance tending to show resemblance, moral or physical, between my rival and myself . . . " (434). Wilson both doubles and foils the narrator. Hence, in his hatred, the narrator shuns Wilson's opposition *as well his own likeness*.

In this section, I explore the significance of sameness in the hated one. Because Wilson is the same—equal and equivalent to the narrator—the story raises complex questions about hate's struggle to exteriorize its object. What happens when the enemy is both similar and proximate to the subject? How does hate work when the enemy is indistinguishable from the "I" that abhors him? What are the implications of a hatred that struggles to differentiate between self and other? A hatred that goes both outward and inward? A hatred that detests the self and its proxy?

To answer these questions, I track the philosophical and psychoanalytic resonances of the story. More specifically, I read the tale through Descartes's conception of hate as a passion of avoidance and Freud's understanding of the formative rejections of *aussotossung*. As previous scholarship illustrates, Poe was suspicious of Cartesian paradigms, and this suspicion informs "William Wilson."[15] Joan Dayan explains that Poe's "scene of consciousness" dismantles Cartesian distinctions between inside and outside, self and other.[16] At a psychic extreme, Poe recognized that the Cartesian ego may go rogue, operating independently from the body, will, or empirical reality. "William Wilson" suggests that Cartesian hate can likewise turn against the subject, leaving him in a perilous contradiction: polarized against himself. As I illustrate below, Freud's analysis of *aussotossung*—"pushing away, spitting, expelling"—helps us understand this polarization. Freud suggests that subjectification begins in a hateful movement, a spitting out of the otherness or ugliness within the self. But the exclusions of *aussotossung* are never complete. The self cannot fully or finally reject itself. Here, I show that "William Wilson" confirms the complexities of expelling self from self.

Much critical attention has gone to the narrator's hostility for the double in "William Wilson." This scholarship understands his vexation as an indictment of a democracy that stipulates that all men are equal, and that all men are therefore the same.[17] For my purposes, however, the narrator's antipathy for the same reverberates beyond political or legal terror. His fear is *personal*. It attaches to the person. Wilson has a body, a birthday, a disposition, a moral code. The substance of his character matters. In his embodiment, Wilson becomes a clear and present adversary. This is significant because hatred *must identify its enemy*.

A number of thinkers explicate the tactics of vilification essential to hate. Robert J. Sternberg defines hate by its penchant for character assassination. The hater sees "the target as barely human or even subhuman." In hate's judgments, the target might be debased, immoral, criminal, or malignant.[18] Likewise, Agneta Fischer et al. explains that the hater sees its object in stark, fixed terms: "The other *is* malicious, not just acts maliciously."[19] The attribution of immutable evil distinguishes hate from kindred emotions (anger, contempt, and disgust). Just as importantly, hate cannot survive without a combatant. As Gaylin elucidates, "the enemy becomes an essential ingredient in the life of the hate[r]." The enemy, moreover, answers an "inner anguish and rage," accounting for "our deprivations and misery." In other words, enemy-making relocates a personal guilt or defect. "We alleviate our internal conflicts and protect our self-esteem by placing the source of our misery outside our own area of culpability," Gaylin explains, "we find some other to blame."[20] Thus, the materialization of the enemy is crucial to the life of hate itself, and hatred thrives in projection—in the "symbolic displacements"—that assail the enemy.

We see this displacement—this blaming—in the narrator's aversion to Wilson. He attributes all his failures and disappointments to Wilson's interference. He identifies Wilson as "my admonisher at Eton . . . , the destroyer of my honor at Oxford . . . , him who thwarted my ambition at Rome, my revenge at Paris, my passionate love at Naples, . . . my avarice in Egypt" (445). The narrator finds his enemy-object in Wilson: the nefarious other that his hate needs to subsist. And yet Wilson's sameness means that this enemy remains coincident with the narrator's self. His hate is simultaneously an internal orientation, directed against himself, and external orientation, directed against an other. The narrator abhors Wilson as "the rival": the enemy opposition (445). And he abhors Wilson as the "companion": the coequal, the selfsame (445). For the narrator then, hate becomes an irreconcilable dilemma, always tangling him in the evil his enemy materializes. In other words, the narrator's hate catches him in impossible affective dictums: "I hate Wilson, therefore I hate myself"; "I hate myself, therefore I hate Wilson."

This predicament can be traced directly to Cartesian notions of hate. Descartes defines hate as a passion of dissociation. He repeatedly underscores hate's insistence on avoidance. According to Descartes, hate "incites the soul to . . . separate from objects that present themselves to it as harmful." We hate "what is bad" and we hate "what is ugly." For Descartes, hate is constructive and necessary because, in hate, the soul "employ[s] all its powers to avoid so immanent an evil." As a defense mechanism, hate propels revulsion and repulsion. In the process, hate carefully patrols the boundaries of the not-me. When we hate, we see the self as "entirely separate from the thing for which one feels aversion." But Descartes also allowed that one may "despise oneself." In other words, hate can recoil against the self, and it can manifest as self-aversion and self-avoidance. Descartes said it is "especially noteworthy when . . . it is our own worth that we . . . despise."[21] Noteworthy because when we hate "our own worth," the self becomes the enemy. Plausibly then, self-hate agitates a pressing need to break from the self.

"William Wilson" dramatizes the compulsions of avoidance in hatred as well as the difficulty of exiling the self from the self. In a state of hate, the narrator flees boarding school, and later, Eton, Oxford, Paris, or any place Wilson appears. He stays in almost constant flight: "From his inscrutable tyranny did I at length flee, panic-stricken, as from a pestilence; and to the very ends of the earth . . . " (444–45). The narrator turns fugitive, attempting to outdistance his double. But separation proves elusive and temporary. "*I fled in vain*," the narrator exclaims. The narrator cannot escape Wilson's "detestable interest" in his actions. Wherever the narrator goes, Wilson follows. The chase masters time and place. "Years, flew, while I experienced no relief. Villain!—at Rome, with how untimely, yet with how spectral an officiousness, stepped he in between me and my ambition! At Vienna, too—at Berlin—and at Moscow!" Wilson seemingly possesses a preternatural ability to arrive anywhere and thwart the narrator's objectives. He cannot outrun Wilson's surveillance. Hence, Poe disturbs Descartes's notion of the split self with an interrogation of the paradoxes of being that inevitably rupture it. In a Cartesian world, we can hate the self, but we cannot escape the self.

Freud elucidates the psychic implications of hate's futile yet furious momentum. Associated with the dynamics of *ausstossung*, hate is the act and action of ejection. As Massimo Recalcati explains, in this "movement of spitting, of expulsion," the ego rejects the malignancies inside itself. Because the "subject is traversed by an otherness that the psychic apparatus cannot metabolize," it tries to expel that otherness. Thus, hate coincides with "the subjective experience of the exteriority of the object." In other words, hate helps activate the psychic processes of differentiation and exclusion. Accordingly, Recalcati calls hate "a passion of separation." The ego tries to divest itself from its alterity.

More essentially, hate drives our earliest experience of personhood. Freud posits that subjectification begins in this hateful movement, this spitting out of an "internal, intimate" menace. In Freudian terms, we first know hate as "the subject's own experience of itself." Hence, the hated thing is simultaneously strange and familiar, far and near. As Recalcati puts it, "The expelled object, that which is spit out, is at once the closest thing to the subject and the thing that is the subject's most radical outside." This thinking understands hate as a formative, violent, and yet *incomplete* evacuation. That which is hated persists as an internal otherness, a terrible similarity. That which is hated remains inside the psyche, a refused but undeniable equivalence. Recalcati affirms, "Not everything that is unpleasurable can be expelled, evacuated, or separated from the subject."[22] Hatred's exorcisms are never finished or final. The subject can never empty itself of its otherness.

This psychic impasse accounts for the double's terrifying effects. The manifestation of the double "signals an intrusion of the other within the Same."[23] We are inhabited by an inescapable dissonance.[24] As Recalcati summarizes, the double owes its awful power to its ability to force a reckoning with the subject's "own alienated structure, its divided, split character," and the "impossibility of effecting any self-reunification." The double "exposes the radical non-identity, the non-coincidence of the subject with itself." In the act of spitting out, hatred tries to exorcise an intrinsic part of the subject. In this sense, hatred mobilizes "an exteriorization of the Same, of what is 'closest' to the subject." Hence, "it is not the alterity of the Other that is in play, but rather the identity of the Same."[25] In Wilson then, the narrator confronts the me that is not-me: everything he wants to refuse or unknow about himself. Although his hate finds its enemy in Wilson, the enemy is always *about* the self—its insufficiencies and vulnerabilities—or it *is* the self—its repudiated, hideous parts. Hate fixes the narrator in affective and subjective impossibilities: refuse the unrefusable, escape the inescapable.

SELF-POLLUTION

For my purposes, hatred's partial and incomplete expulsions generate more pointed questions about the alterity that Wilson represents. If the narrator is forever occupied by the hated one, what otherness persists inside him? What deviance or dissonance colonizes him? What *exactly* does he want to reject in Wilson and himself? What is he trying—and failing—to spit out?

These questions arise, in part, from critical discussions about the erotic connotations of the rivalry and the assumption that the narrator struggles against a nascent internalized homophobia. Leland Person situates "William Wilson" in a canon of Poe's fictions that depict "violent, homophobic repressions of erotic identification between men."[26] Nicholas Tyler Reich argues that the story reverberates with "bottom terror," a fear of bodily penetration by another man.[27] Gerald Kennedy sees a "perverse bonding" between the narrator and Wilson, a "mutuality of desire" in which two men develop "an obsessive awareness of the other" and "an intimate identification."[28] Certainly, the closeness between the narrator and his counterpart seems born of complex attractions.[29]

Yet previous scholarship perhaps overstates the story's investment in taboos against homosexuality. Our culture tends to assume that the narrator would be most threatened by his same-gender desires. Research maintains that homosexual attraction is especially prohibited for contemporary men. In his exploration of internalized homophobia, Donald Moss notes that when men discover their attraction to other men, they struggle with "extreme and unbearable states of mind," including "suicidal and homicidal despair." Any kind of erotic fulfillment only means a more profound damnation.[30] As Moss writes, "When the object is found . . . , the subject is defiled." Love curses "rather than redeems." Contempt turns inward: "One hates oneself for wanting what one wants, and therefore for being what one is."[31] In our time, same-gender desire crushes the masculine subject in self-punishment and self-loathing. The homosexual is the hated one.

In Poe's time, however, self-pollution—onanism and the onanist—were more noxious and terrifying. In this section, I examine Wilson as a locus of masturbatory desire. I show that the narrator admits to self-pollution and all its attendant evils. And, as I examine the implications of the narrator's masturbation panic, I show that his culture's stark prohibitions against self-pollution fuel his hatred for the self and the same.

Tellingly, the narrator confesses his sexual deviance immediately. He introduces himself as an "outcast of all outcasts most abandoned" (426). He admits to an "unpardonable crime," saying that "in an instant, all virtue dropped bodily as a mantle" (426). As Reich asks, "Apart from death, what single event has the power to so thoroughly deconstruct a person?"[32] With a pointed allusion, Poe answers this question: "From comparatively trivial wickedness I passed, with the stride of a giant, into more than the enormities of an Elah-Gabalus" (427). Elagabalus was one of Rome's most debauched emperors. In a four-year reign, he scandalized his empire with gender and sexual transgression. As Leonardo De Arrizabalaga Y Prado summarizes, his "ancient detractors accuse him, among much else of: ...throwing human genitals to beasts; polymorphous sexual perversity, active and passive, mutual and collective, with males and females; . . . wearing make-up and silk...; holding conventions for prostitutes of either gender...; appointing empires of state on the basis of phallic size."[33] His conduct so alienated his people that he was assassinated at eighteen. Through the ages, Elagabalus became an icon of the vilest depravity. For centuries, it was rumored that the emperor "'turned himself into a woman,'" surgically altering his genitals and commanding to be called "mistress" and "queen."[34] The nineteenth-century historian Barthold Georg Niebuhr declared, "The name Elagabalus is branded in history above all others" because of his "unspeakably disgusting life."[35] When the narrator associates his personal evil with the trespasses of Elagabalus, he admits to sexual and gender sins of the "worst" kind.

This disclosure certainly reverberates with the possibility that the narrator loves, desires, and hates another man. And yet, in nineteenth-century contexts, the narrator's "unpardonable crime" is more likely "self-pollution." Masturbation—loaded with the "horrors" of sodomy, homosexuality, nonprocreative sex, pre- and extramarital desire—was the era's most ubiquitous sexual sin.[36] Sylvester Graham's *A Lecture to Young Men on Chastity* (1834) effectively captures the masturbation terror in antebellum America. As Person notes, "If Poe had wanted to write a tale illustrating Graham's cautionary pronouncements about the slippery slope of self-abuse, he could hardly have done a better job than in 'William Wilson.'"[37] Graham ranked "self-pollution" as "the worst form of venereal indulgence." He repeatedly called it "evil": "one of the most alarming evils in our land" and "one of the most extensive and calamitous evils that afflict the human family." He saw direct correlations between masturbation and criminality, insisting that the majority of men in American jails "commenced their career of vice in the depraving and hardening practice of illicit sexual commerce."[38] Reportedly, one poor sufferer confided to his prison chaplain, "I am lost! I am lost! I have destroyed myself!—I have committed the unpardonable sin; and nothing but perdition awaits me." The narrator's confessions of wickedness and villainy echo Graham's hyperbole. Like Graham's self-polluter, the narrator assumes guilt for the most profane act, the most abhorrent crime.

"William Wilson" locates the narrator's masturbatory fall at its literal center, its middlemost point. Immediately after the narrator adopts a "positive hatred" for Wilson, he has "an altercation of violence with him" (436). A puzzling intimacy pervades the fight. Wilson speaks and acts "with an openness of demeanor rather foreign to his nature," and the narrator feels a palpable attraction to him, "something which first startled and, then deeply interested me" (436). Suddenly, he has "dim visions of [his] earliest infancy" and the uncanny awareness that he knew Wilson in a "past infinitely remote" (436). The violence initiates the men into a new affinity with each other. Remarkably, however, it only motivates the narrator to hurt Wilson more. He plans to accost Wilson in his bed at night, premeditating the "prank" as a potential hate crime, "resolved to make him feel the whole extent of the malice with which I was imbued" (437). His tunneling journey to Wilson's bedroom surges with forbidden, libidinal energy: "[I] stole through a wilderness of narrow passages from my own bedroom to that of my rival" (437). The eroticism of the scene escalates at the chamber's threshold. The narrator listens to the "sound of [Wilson's] tranquil breathing," and then he "slowly and quietly" withdraws the curtain around Wilson's bed. Inexplicably, the sight of Wilson's body arrests him. He is stunned by what he sees: "I looked;—and a numbness, an iciness of feeling instantly pervaded my frame." His reaction grows increasingly embodied: "My breast heaved, my knees tottered, my whole spirit became possessed with an objectless yet intolerable horror" (437). Although he names this sensation "horror," its physiology—heavy breathing, weak knees—is also sexualized. Enhancing his potential arousal, the narrator moves ever closer to Wilson. "Gasping for breath, I lowered the lamp in still nearer proximity to the face." Whatever his fear, the narrator pushes himself to a sensate extreme. He wants to see Wilson more clearly.

The bed closet episode hurls the narrator into an acute state of anxiety and apprehension. "Not thus he appeared," he exclaims, "—assuredly not *thus*— in the vivacity of his waking hours" (437). Reich insightfully connects this insistent "*thus*" to the narrator's opening confession: "man was never *thus* . . . tempted before—certainly, never *thus* fell" (427). With this repeated signifier, the story positions Wilson at the core of the narrator's deviant desires and subsequent disgrace. His plan to make Wilson "feel the whole extent of the malice" within him betrays other feelings, including his "desire to touch the body of his double . . . to understand how their bodies relate, how their bodies move through each other, or how they might further connect bodily."[39] Person argues that this event induces a "homo-panic" in the narrator: "a fear of homoerotic identification, a fear that deviant thoughts or sentiments will arise in the mind or heart if we stay too long identified with other men."[40] My contention is that the "homo" in the narrator's hysteria fixates more on its original Greek derivation *homos*, meaning "same."[41] While the narrator may want bodily contact with Wilson, the incident becomes a perplexing drama of bodily perception and *sameness*. "Were these,—*these* the lineaments of William Wilson?" the narrator questions. And again, "What *was* there about them to confound me in this manner?" He struggles to explain what is before his eyes. He enumerates the evidence of the doubling between them, as if sameness might explain his vision: "the same name! the same contour of person! the same day of arrival at the academy!" and his double's "imitation of my gait, my voice, my habits, my manner!" With more gravity, he asks is it "within the bounds of human possibility" that their twinning justifies "*what I now saw*" (437). Nearest to Wilson's face, the narrator can only express incredulity and confusion. No language or logic accounts for what he sees. The crisis of apprehension in the bedchamber becomes a crisis of comprehension. The narrator looks but cannot or will not understand the scene.[42]

To the nineteenth century, however, the narrator's "objectless horror" in Wilson's bedchamber has a clear, although unsayable, object.[43] Graham identified boarding schools and colleges as hotbeds of masturbation. According to Graham, schools were the most prolific "sources of instruction in this vice." He maintained that the extent of self-pollution in these settings is "beyond credulity" and "shocking beyond measure!" He also certified that, "I have known boys to leave these institutions at the age of twelve and thirteen, almost entirely ruined in health and constitution by" the act. Just as appallingly, such patients confided that "almost every boy in the school practiced the filthy vice." Apparently, boys taught each other how to masturbate and encouraged the behavior. Graham explained that the habit is "frequently communicated from on boy to another; and sometimes a single boy will corrupt many others." In addition, Graham declared that masturbation could be an individual pleasure, a shared activity, or even an erotic performance. The "youth [that] has made no small progress in the depravity of his moral feelings, who has so silenced the dictates of natural modesty," Graham wrote, "can, without the blush of shame, pollute himself in the presence of another—even his most intimate companion!" Graham understood self-pollution as a precursor to more pernicious sins. He made the connection between masturbation and sex between boys explicit. Many chronic masturbators at school "went to the still more loathsome and criminal extent of an unnatural commerce with each other!"[44] In Graham's mind, the self-polluter was an opportunistic evildoer, progressively advancing to more heinous transgressions.

Alone with Wilson's sleeping body then, the narrator plausibly feels the desire to masturbate, to see Wilson masturbate, to masturbate with him or for him, to move erotically and sexually into even closer intercourse. Some scholars suggest that the narrator gratifies this wanting in the murder scene, arguing that he masturbates there.[45] Certainly, the narrator's fate aligns with the future Graham forecasted for the incorrigible masturbator. Graham predicted a life of compounding evil for the self-polluter, and, eventually, suicidal self-loathing. He goes on to "advance in crime, till he terminates his career in ruin and infamy." Eventually, he "is regarded by mankind as a wretch too utterly depraved and destitute of virtue, to deserve the common sympathies of humanity." Over time, stigma and ostracism devastates his self-worth. He feels acute "self-contempt, and disgust, and reproach" until his self-hate turns nihilistic: "Self-destruction becomes the common theme of his thoughts. . . . He would give worlds to be annihilated. His life is intolerable. . . . " Graham's despondent masturbator cries out, "In the deep anguish and agony of his spirit—'Oh, wretched man that I am! who shall deliver me from this body of death?'"[46]

We meet Poe's narrator at this extremity: after a criminal career, in a state of "ruin and infamy," and on the edge of death. The narrator carefully details the vagaries of his immorality and criminality. He spends three years at Eton, on a course of "miserable profligacy." As a result, he develops "rooted habits of vice," including drinking, cards, and "more dangerous seductions" (438). Just before Wilson interrupts one debauch, for example, the narrator spends an entire week in "soulless dissipation," inviting a "small party of the most dissolute students to his room for a "secret carousal" (438). They have a night of "delirious extravagance" (438). Over the next two years at Oxford, the narrator turns gambler, becoming adept in the "despicable science." He "practice[s] it habitually" and rapaciously, "as a means of increasing [his] already enormous income at the expense of the weak-minded among my fellow collegians" (440). He calculates the financial ruin of a young aristocrat, Glendening, with ruthless precision. After Oxford, "years fly" in which he devotes himself to intemperance and greed (445). His wickedness seems absolute, confirming Graham's prophecies: His self-abuse leads inexorably to his villainy, self-loathing, and suicide.

VOLUNTARY DEPRAVITY

In Graham's exhortations, the mechanism that condemns the narrator to this abominable existence is the force of his own will. Graham attributed incurable self-pollution to the ravages of "voluntary depravity": an intentional decadence that becomes an immutable evil in men. Graham traced this possibility in his etiology of self-pollution. According to Graham, men could defy the "laws" of their own bodies. Graham maintained that men could rebel against essential physiological principles. In his words, a man could willfully "abus[e] his organs and deprav[e] his instinctive appetites." Because of this "voluntary depravity," men permanently and irreversibly degrade their nature. As a result, the "body of man has become a living volcano of unclean propensities and passions." Intriguingly, Graham articulates a politics of the body that reflects an early American politics of revolution and Jacksonian masculinity. By his logic, men "have the power and means to destroy the *government* of the *law* of instinct," to "violate the *laws* of his *constitution*, and injure his system" (my emphasis).[47] Exercising this preeminence, men could transgress any natural, moral, political, or social rule—even if that defiance meant permanent self-contempt, corruption, debility, or death.[48]

Through persistent "voluntary depravity," Graham argued, men could make lewdness a compulsion, a biology, and ultimately, an ontology. Graham imagined a formidable will to pleasure inherent to the penis' reproductive function.[49] When "the pleasures" of the "genital organs" become "the leading object of our pursuits," he said, men retard their reason and arrest their development. In effect, "The intellectual and moral nature of man becomes subordinate to his animal nature and gross sensuality becomes paramount to deliberate reason." Reduced to their "animal nature," men overindulge their carnal desires, and "man is thus debased, degraded, diseased, and destroyed!" Once corrupted, men can no longer resist libidinal impulses. As a result, they persist in a paradoxical state of self-induced slavery. According to Graham, the sexual appetite "acquires a power which irresistibly urges on the unhappy sufferer, in the voluntary course of self-destruction."[50] As one patient explained it, "he had become a slave to that vice…. 'I seem to have no power over myself.'" The logic here is specious: although the will to pleasure becomes irresistible, men still somehow choose their own degradation.

This thinking was pervasive. Intemperance, for example, was similarly diagnosed as a condition of self-willed enslavement. As Paul White explains, "Intemperance remained the most controversial of 'diseases' because of its relationship to the will." The renowned physician William Carpenter maintained that intemperance was caused by the excessive indulgence of base instincts and "a weakening of the controlling power of the will." Like masturbation, alcoholism "produced a progressive degradation" of mind, body, volition, and virtue, leaving men in 'a state of complete slavery.'"[51] Alcoholics, like Graham's self-polluters, were simultaneously free and enslaved, villains and victims. More provocatively for my purposes, such paradoxes of white masculine will made men more vulnerable to the delinquent desires and the self-hate that torments Poe's narrator. The agent—or the agency—that will destroy you is *in* you, it *is* you, and you cannot expel it.

Poe's narrator reinforces this notion of a voluntary but eventually fixed depravity with two tropes. First, he explains his surrender to vice with a logic of racial and familial degeneracy. "I am the descendant of a race whose imaginative and easily excitable temperament has at all times rendered them remarkable," he explains, "and, in my earliest infancy, I gave evidence of having fully inherited the family character" (427). This "remarkable" family disposition is exceptional for its instability. "As I advanced in years it was more strongly developed," the narrator continues, "becoming, for many reasons, a cause of serious disquietude to my friends, and of positive injury to myself" (427). He inherits a worrisome tendency to self-harm. His parents— "weak-minded and beset with constitutional infirmities akin to my own"— could do "little to check the evil propensities which distinguished me" (427). As he tells it, narrator's wickedness is a family trait, and he only gets more tempestuous as he comes of age.

The second rationale he offers for his gravitation to evil are the compulsions of a "self-willed" masculinity. "I grew self-willed," he asserts, "addicted to the wildest caprices, and prey to the most ungovernable passions" (427). In the narrator's account, his volition makes him more susceptible to the transgressions that will deliver him to abject self-contempt. The appellation "self-willed" actually names a complex tenet of Southern manhood. According to Lorri Glover, Southern white men were expected to embody a sweeping autonomy, an "independence of economic circumstance, conscience, and action." So much so, that parents boasted about their "self-willed" sons, supposing that their obstinance was evidence of an inherent sovereignty. "This intense—and racialized—zeal for independence was rooted in slaveholding," Glover explains. Only enslaved people were subject to force or command.[52] Southern boys and men "privilege[d] independence—the antithesis of enslavement—above all other attributes." The unruliness of the slave master's will, moreover, has a distinct history. Edward Ayers notes that "Thomas Jefferson observed that the unbridled authority wielded by slaveholders tended to breed impetuous behavior and shortness of temper, characteristics passed from one generation of masters to the next." Similarly, the wife of a Georgia planter observed: "Slaveholders' children, instead of being taught to govern their tempers, are encouraged to indulge their passions; and, thus educated, they become the slaves of passion."[53] Of course, Southern sons were still expected to internalize codes of honor, morality, success, and civic responsibility, but such prudence was an individual decision. The Southern devotion to "manly independence meant that parents chose to coax, rather than compel sons. And boys told so often to act independently actually listened to their elders."[54] Men and boys who own enslaved people must, even more fundamentally, own themselves—for better or for worse.

Thus, as "William Wilson" reinforces, self-willed does not necessarily mean self-controlled or self-subdued. Instead, it means a radically autonomous will. It means a will that can revolt against the precepts of virtue and reason. It means a will that can exceed familial, social, and personal holds; a will that can alienate body from mind; a will that can make an enemy of opposing wills or contrary impulses. The self-willed man is a dangerously fragmented subject.[55] He experiences an intensity of volition that he finds difficult to resist.

Essentially, Poe's narrator argues that—despite his immense privilege and power—he cannot subdue his illicit desires. He cannot master his rogue appetites and save himself from ruin. He is helpless before his own will. Indeed, the narrator offers cryptic assertions of his innocence, or at least mitigated guilt. He claims to "have been, in some measure, the slave of circumstances beyond human control" (427). He believes that other men might discern "some little oasis of *fatality* amid a wilderness of error." And he asserts that he is "now dying victim to the horror and the mystery of all sublunary visions" (427). Read through a logic of masculine volition, the narrator constitutes an intricate problem of will. Quizzically, "William Wilson" posits a masculinity that willfully—but not intentionally—comes to hate itself and destroy itself.

A number of critics confirm the significance of a disordered masculine will in "William Wilson," deconstructing the story's title—and the narrator's pseudonym—as an anagram for this investment (e.g., Will I am Will's Son). Most saliently for my argument, Theron Britt argues that the narrator personifies a sociopathic will: "an avatar of self-reliance run amok." Britt sees narrator as a manifestation of the "unbridled will" of Jacksonian America: its appetite for liberty, laissez-faire capitalism, Indian removal, slavery, and westward expansion.[56] As Michael Paul Rogin notes, Andrew Jackson himself was heralded as a "self-willed" man.[57] Jackson was renowned for his violence, as well as drinking, wagering, and pranking. A man who knew Jackson when he was reading law in North Carolina said that "Andrew Jackson was the most roaring, rollicking, game-cocking, horse-racing, card-playing, mischievous fellow that ever lived." He also "had moods of manic omnipotence, paranoid rage, and occasional deep depression." Jackson believed that white men had an inherent, natural "right to violence." And he acknowledged that many people "conceive me to be a most ferocious animal, insensitive to moral duty, and regardless of the laws both of God and man." In principle and practice, Jackson seemed ever ready to foment revolution. As Rogin remarks, "Jackson symbolized, in the years of his ascendency the free American, dependent on and subservient to no one."[58] His defiant masculinity became synonymous with American freedom and autonomy. In social and political terms, liberty was such a sacred principle that early America was reluctant to "govern" its men into moral order.[59] In 1849, Henry David Thoreau affirmed, "All men recognize the right of revolution: that is, the right to refuse allegiance to and resist the government when its tyranny or its inefficiency are great and unendurable." More personally, he proclaimed: "I was not born to be forced. I will breathe after my own fashion."[60] In this historical context, masculine self-rule had a powerful political salience. The lawlessness of white men demonstrated a *constitutional* freedom, in both a national and gendered sense. Poe's narrator is an apotheosis of Jacksonian masculinity.[61] Although his own volition is pathological, he indulges its promptings. He cannot be coerced into a more temperate conformity with sociomoral codes.

Indeed, the nineteenth century fixed men in paradigms that naturalized their violence and profligacy. As Richard Stott notes, the culture assumed "many men simply could not restrain themselves from drinking, fighting, gambling, and playing pranks, even if they wanted to." Such behavior was considered a "natural force," a manifestation of the "animal man"—the precivilized essence—of all men.[62] Some men literally acted like animals at pivotal or ritualized moments. Soldiers on their way to war roared and hissed like beasts; Christmas was often a time when men howled; the winner of a brawl might imitate the cock of the walk, crowing and flapping his arms.[63] Even when the culture complicated biological explanations of male wilding, it sanctioned manly trespasses with other excuses. Some pundits argued that certain men retained a boyish, youthful essence and were, therefore, morally immature. Whatever the justifications, masculine impropriety "was accepted as inevitable and unchangeable: it was men's nature."[64] Curiously, this logic did not challenge patriarchal primacy. Because this "nature" often expressed itself through domination—violence, intimidation, and humiliation—masculinity retained its power. And because this nature was proof of an irrepressible autonomy, masculinity retained its freedom.

In "William Wilson," Poe pushes us to grapple with a masculinity riddled with the paradoxes of a "self-willed" and "voluntary" depravity. At the same time, he refuses to reduce his narrator—and the masculinity he represents—to an uncomplicated social pariah.[65] For most of his life, the narrator's rascality are matters of both power and pride. At boarding school, his exuberance gives him preeminence. "In truth, the ardor, the enthusiasm, and the imperiousness of my disposition, soon rendered me a marked character among my schoolmates," he recalls, "and by slow, but natural gradations, gave me an ascendancy over all not greatly older than myself . . . " (431). At Eton, he grows taller and stronger as his corruption deepens; these years "added, in a somewhat unusual degree, to my bodily stature." At university, his malfeasance is openly admired. His chums regale him as "the gay, the frank, the generous William Wilson—the noblest and most liberal commoner at Oxford" (440). His friends also excuse his delinquency as "follies of youth and unbridled fancy." For the men around him, his "errors [are] but inimitable whim," his "darkest vice but a careless and dashing extravagance" (440). His profligacy is pardoned and praised.

"William Wilson" strategically reinforces the charisma of white masculine transgression. Poe gives his first-person narrative over to the degenerate, not his more virtuous counterpart. Wilson, the voice of scrupulous restraint, cannot speak above a whisper. We only *see* Wilson in relation to the narrator's wickedness, and he comes and goes like a specter. Apart from the narrator's licentiousness, Wilson's life is invisible and, implicitly, less interesting.

Thus, Poe catches his narrator in irreconcilable conflicts. He is a self-proclaimed and self-willed "evil." But his story fascinates and enthralls. He mercilessly catalogues his venality. But his drinking, gambling, and violence attest to a robust manliness. He embodies a manhood acculturated to transgression and revered for its raucous autonomy. But this masculinity comes to hate itself for exercising its immense appetites and prerogatives. As David Leverenz observes, Poe's narratives exaggerate masculine contradictions, "especially the double imperatives of cool reasoning and impulsive bravado."[66] In "William Wilson," we meet a masculinity fractured by the tensions between liberty and lawlessness. In "William Wilson," we meet a masculinity that is split—and *doubled*—by polarizing psychosocial realities.

The duality itself is the central tragedy of the tale. Critics have assumed that the narrator might have somehow lived and thrived if he could have reconciled himself to Wilson's sameness.[67] But the terminal truth of the tale is that reconciliation is impossible and masculine survival is a dubious proposition. As the narrator himself puts it, "Oh, gigantic paradox, too utterly monstrous for solution!" (429). In "William Wilson," the individual man is mired in contradictions, endowed with equivalent capacities for virtue and vice, anarchy and order. This paradox makes potential monsters of all men.

Poe never resolves this inconsistency because his culture subscribes to it. Indeed, pundits like Graham detail the miseries of permanently wretched men.[68] Astonishingly, Graham argued that some men were so captive to masturbation that shackles were their only hope for a cure. "[N]othing but constant watching, and pinions, and manacles, can prevent the continuance of this shocking practice," he declared. To validate this remedy, he presented the case study of a man who "declared that he had not the power to refrain from the loathsome act." When Graham suggested manacles, he "received the proposal with joy, and submitted to the confinement of his hands for several months." The chains liberated him from the practice, but he remained a slave to the temptation. When the fetters were removed, "he returned to the destructive practice . . . and filled his body with the most distressing and loathsome disease, and his soul with anguish, and remorse, and despair;— and finally fell victim to the transgression."[69] This testimony is appalling by nineteenth-century standards, evoking the horrors of white masculine enslavement. The image of a shackled white man awakens the terrors of racial reversals: white men "blackened" by their own iniquity; white men helpless before their own impulses and instincts.

Significantly, the prospect of white male slavery returns us to hate and to hate's negotiations with power. Recall that hate organizes against the ego threat, the wound to pride, and felt humiliation; hate organizes against anything—real or perceived—that "makes us feel less whole, less powerful, less useful, and less valued."[70] Helplessness both distinguishes and intensifies hate. Edward Royzman et al.. summarize an extensive body of research that documents the imbrication between hate and powerlessness. More than anger or other adjacent emotions, hate is defined by a subjective sense of "weakness, inefficacy, and insurmountable obstacles."[71] As Fischer et al. puts it, "feelings of powerlessness" are a "characteristic condition in the development of hate."[72] In other words, hate emerges at a site of impotence. And it thrives in a collision between diminishing power and worsening frustration. More pointedly, Gaylin designates certain violations—particularly exploitation and manipulation—as prime movers of hatred. We hate whatever "assaults" our agency. When the subject becomes object or instrument— when we feel *used*—hate mobilizes against the abuse. According to Gaylin, enslavement constitutes the "ultimate, rawest, and most outrageous use of people."[73] Psychic and physical conditions of slavery then—states of bondage, servitude, and captivity—this is the helplessness that hate cannot stand.

Thus, the narrator hates that which holds him in the detention of his own desires, that which subjugates him to his own volition. The fatality that victimizes him is the agency within all white men. The circumstance beyond his control is the force of his pathological will. And his volitional depravity makes him the most abominable object of all: the "object for the scorn—for the horror—for the detestation of my race" (426). In the end, he embodies the twin horrors of white male helplessness and enslavement.

KNOWING

In his final moments, the narrator sees—and knows—the terrible truth of his own existence: the truth of his diseased volition, the truth of his voluntary depravity. Graham argued that masturbation produces a crisis of apprehension and comprehension for nineteenth-century men, a crisis that recalls the narrator's bedchamber horror. "[A]ll who give themselves up to the excesses of this debasing indulgence, carry about with them, continually, a consciousness of their defilement," Graham explained. The self-polluter carries the knowledge of his own evil. In addition, he has a "secret suspicion that others look upon them as debased beings. So much so, that he "cannot meet the look of others. . . . "[74] In "William Wilson," the narrator cannot face himself, at least for a time. After the last fateful night at Bransby's, Wilson hides "the features of his face" from the narrator whenever they meet (445). The narrator sees Wilson's face again only at the point of death. In death, the narrator recognizes every element of Wilson's face as *"mine own"* (448). With the italics, the narrator answers to the "not *thus*"—"not thus he appeared"—that came before: the confused, stupefied misidentification in the bedchamber. *"Mine own"* establishes the relations of time, place, and circumstance that connect the narrator to Wilson. Wilson's face is "mine own." Wilson is "mine." Wilson is my "own." The narrator sees, knows, and avows Wilson and himself. Wilson's dying words are equally revelatory, *"In me didst thou exist—and in my death, see by this image, which is thine own, how utterly thou hast murdered thyself"* (448). Wilson commands the narrator to look and understand. *"See by this image,"* he counsels: See your self, see your life, see your death. Whether we read the ending as suicide, murder, or masturbation, the story culminates in a climax of recognition.

As I close this chapter, I want to excavate this tangled relationship between seeing, knowing, and hating. As we shall see, hate often propels a consuming need to know its object, or more pointedly, to *comprehend the otherness* that the object represents. Hate seeks this knowledge in the service of possession, dominance, and destruction. In other words, hate wants to know the object in order to more completely kill the object. Acts of affective violence—murdering a loved one—evince this intersection between hate, death, and knowledge. Affective killers murder a parent or a partner to fix them in memory and language. They realize an ecstatic climax of knowing as they exact the death of the other. In "William Wilson"—when the other is the self or the same—self-murder constitutes another form of affective violence and an equivalent catalyst of awareness.

Hate's cognitions are as much a consummation as sex or death. C. Fred Alford explains that hate propels a libidinal need to know. "Hate reflects a perverted desire to know otherness, fusing with it to become what otherness knows—or is," he writes. "In this regard, hatred comes frighteningly close to love, and love intriguingly close to the pursuit of knowledge, an affinity with which the West is long familiar." Knowledge animates an erotic coalescence with the self or the hated object. Alford posits that hate's epistemological goal is "to know the answer to the question that cannot be uttered." The human "inability to formulate the question of their suffering, their desire, and their wonder" produces a vicious frustration. That obstruction is not simply a metaphysical dilemma. We want to know the other—and the otherness within the self—because we want to colonize it. With M. Chadwick, Alford reminds us that "'the desire to know and the desire to possess are one.'"[75] Alford suggests that this desire—to cling, consume, and control—propels hate's insistence on knowledge. With his questions about Wilson's composition and his own, Poe's narrator seeks to own the hated one, to subdue the other inside himself and out.

Indeed, after he leaves boarding school, the narrator's need to know intensifies, and his questions about Wilson multiply. He repeatedly cross-examines Wilson's nature, his origin, and his intentions. When Wilson interrupts his debauch at Eton, he asks, "But who and what was this Wilson?—and whence came he?—and what were his purposes?" (439). When Wilson follows him all over the globe, he wails, "And again, and again, in secret communion with my own spirit, would I demand the questions 'Who is he?—whence came he?—and what are his objects?'" (445). He also wonders what he can articulate about his own feelings. When Wilson exposes him as a grifter at the card table, he demands, "Can I—shall I describe my sensations? Must I say that I felt all the horrors of the damned?" (443). When he sees the image of his "dying antagonist" in a mirror after he stabs him, he challenges, "But what human language can adequately portray *that* astonishment, *that* horror which possessed me at the spectacle then presented to view?" (447). Again, the narrator only expresses incredulity and the limits of the expressible. The narrator struggles to understand the object of his hatred, and he struggles to name the affects of his animus.

In Alford's research, affective violence—violence against a relative or a lover, particularly violence that necessitates close physical contact with the victim—answers this need to know. Offering a case study of a man who committed parricide, Alford notes that the killer murdered his parents in order to know them: "He just wanted to know." His questions were ineffable ("why was he born to them? Why was he himself, and not someone else? Why was he even born?"), but "he could not, evidently, even begin to formulate these questions, much less the answers, until after had killed his parents." Effecting the death of the hated object enables symbolization, language, and understanding. Thus, Alford postulates, "We must mourn to know."[76] We must lose the object—or the self—to possess it more completely it in memorialization. Significantly then, Poe's narrator tells his story in the aftermath of Wilson's death and as his own approaches. In a moment of grief, he captures himself and Wilson in language. More provocatively, the narrator's access to forbidden, foreclosed knowledge peaks in the murder-suicide. In the story's conclusion, the narrator and Wilson have more explicit bodily consciousness than ever before. He sees Wilson's face and his own. He learns that their existence is symbiotic.[77]

There is powerful clarity and continuity in "Wilson's" denouement. *"You have conquered, and I yield,"* Wilson says. In this desistance, the narrator achieves the obliteration that affective violence promised him. We come to understand that affective violence "is a destructiveness of a certain type": Hate propels a "rage to obliteration: of self, of other, of tension with the other, of tension in the self."[78] The more fractured and fragmented the existence, the more seductive this rage—this annihilation—becomes. In killing Wilson and his self, the narrator masters the hated one. He answers the questions of his desire and his identity. He sees his own face plainly as well as the other's. All tensions are gone, and only his own death remains: *"Henceforward art though also dead,"* Wilson continues, *"dead to the World, to Heaven and to Hope"* (448). For Poe's narrator, self-hatred makes self-knowledge unlivable. Once he sees himself clearly—in all his aberrance and impotence—he moves beyond self-regard and, more fundamentally, he moves beyond self-saving. In essence, he cannot live down the truth of his personhood.

In this violent renunciation, Poe's narrator becomes a historical specter: a shade of the "masturbating child" and the "perverse adult" that Michel Foucault credits with the emergence of a modern sexual regime. The masturbating child and the perverse adult, Foucault writes, became "privileged objects of knowledge" in the eighteenth and nineteenth centuries. In the process, power took hold of bodies and subjects: "Sex was a means of access to both the life of the body and the life of the species."[79] Through the mechanisms of sex and sexuality, power infiltrated psyches, families, and nations. Eve Kosofsky Sedgwick reenters this history to argue that "the status of the masturbator . . . was uniquely formative" in the rise of distinct, and deviant, sexual identities.[80] Foucault and Sedgwick prioritize the genealogy of homosexuality, and the crisis it incited, in this archive. Poe reminds us that onanism was also a gendered, racialized, and political pathology.

The masturbation panic presupposed a diseased white American manhood. It presupposed a sickness of white masculine volition. Just as importantly, the masturbation panic did not simply prohibit men from knowing—seeing, wanting, touching, and loving—other men. It prohibited them from that intimacy with themselves.

NOTES

1. Howard L. Kushner, "Suicide, Gender, and the Fear of Modernity in Nineteenth-Century Medical and Social Thought," *Journal of Social History* 26, no. 3 (Spring 1993), 467, 469, 468.

2. In the summer of 1835, Poe left Baltimore for Richmond on the tentative hope that Thomas Willis White would hire him at the newly launched *Southern Literary Messenger*. White gave him a job at sixty dollars a month. But, in Poe's absence, his cousin, Nielson Poe, offered sanctuary to his pubescent fiancée, Virginia. Nielson's intervention meant rescue for Virginia from poverty, poor health, and the prospect of a too-early marriage to Poe. Poe became despondent at the potential loss of Virginia, home, and family. He drank recklessly and thought about killing himself. He wrote his aunt and Virginia's mother, Muddy, "I have no wish to live another hour.... My last my last my only hold on life is cruelly torn away—I have no desire to live and *will not*" (Edgar Allan Poe, "The Letters of Edgar Allan Poe," Ltr 048, Edgar Allan Poe Society of Baltimore, www.eapoe.org/people/clemmmp.htm#letters). He wrote his friend, John Pendleton Kennedy with even more desperation: "I am suffering under a depression of spirits such as I have never felt before. I have struggled in vain against the influence of this melancholy. . . . I am wretched, and know not why. Console me—for you can. But let it be quickly—or it will be too late. Write me immediately. Convince me that it is worth one's while—that it is at all necessary to live, and you will prove yourself indeed my friend" (Edgar Allan Poe, "The Letters of Edgar Allan Poe," Ltr 050, Edgar Allan Poe Society of Baltimore, www.eapoe.org/people/kennedjp.htm#letters). When he left the *Messenger* and Richmond to marry Virginia after only a few months, White described him as a "victim of melancholy," saying, "I should not be at all astonished to hear that he had been guilty of suicide" (Kenneth Silverman, *Edgar A. Poe: A Mournful and Never-ending Remembrance* [New York: Harper Perennial, 2008], 107).

3. Ibid., 374.

4. Edgar Allan Poe, "The Letters of Edgar Allan Poe," Ltr 323, Edgar Allan Poe Society of Baltimore, www.eapoe.org/people/clemmmp.htm#letters.

5. Charles Baudelaire, "Edgar Allan Poe: His Life and Works," trans. H. Curwen, in *The Works of Edgar Allan Poe* (London: John Camden Hotten, 1873), 1–21, www.eapoe.org/papers/misc1851/1873000m.htm.

6. Edgar Allan Poe, "William Wilson," in *Edgar Allan Poe, Tales & Sketches, Volume 1: 1831–1842*, ed. Thomas Olive Mabbot (Urbana: University of Illinois Press, 1978), 431. Hereafter cited parenthetically in the text.

7. As D.J. Moores summarizes, "To be sure, the story is deeply concerned with conscience, but it is more than a simple allegory, for Poe demonstrates a rich understanding of the psyche.... Critics have read the story as exhibiting the Freudian tension between id and superego, as well as the opposition between the Lacanian self and the specular other." Moores reads the doppelganger as synonymous with the Jungian shadow ("'Oh Gigantic Paradox': Poe's 'William Wilson' and the Jungian Self," *The Edgar Allan Poe Review* 7, no 1 [2006]: 32).

8. The narrator opens the tale with the assertion that he survived the murder and that Wilson's body lies before him (426). At school, other boys seemingly confirm Wilson's presence: A rumor circulates "among the senior classes" that the two boys are brothers, and later, an opaque "rumor touching a relationship" between them gains currency "in the upper forms" (432, 434). And finally, when Wilson interrupts the narrator's seduction of the duchess in Rome, he wears the same blue velvet cloak that the narrator has as well as a black silk mask. The mask and cloak are materially, persistently there—on the floor where Wilson threw them—after Wilson's death (448).

9. Tracy Ware, "The Two Stories of 'William Wilson,'" *Studies in Short Fiction* 26, no. 1 (1989): 44.

10. Lynn Langmade, "The Wilson Duplex: Corporatism and the Problem of Singleton Reading in Poe's 'William Wilson' (or, Why Can't You See Twins?)," *Poe Studies* 45, no. 1 (2012): 18.

11. Clive Bloom reinforces the connections between Poe's fiction and Freudian ideas: "Poe's texts themselves embody certain concepts that question and then change those in applied psychoanalysis and the newer critical practices based upon Freudian ideas" (*Reading Poe Reading Freud: The Romantic Imagination in Crisis* [Houndsmills: MacMillan Press, 1988], 4).

12. E. Anthony Rotundo testifies to the volatility of boyhood friendships in nineteenth-century America, specifically New England: "Friendships among boys were volatile affairs—intense, short-lived, and constantly shifting. To a great extent, then, boys' realm was—like the grown-up world of their fathers—based on the isolated individual. Although it was a little culture based on constant play and full of exuberance and high spirits, it was also a cruel, competitive, uncertain, and even violent world" (*American Manhood*, 40).

13. Leonard Berkowitz, "On Hate and Its Determinants: Some Affective and Cognitive Influences," in *The Psychology of Hate*, ed. Robert J. Sternberg (Washington, D.C.: American Psychological Association, 2005), 176, 168.

14. Willard Gaylin, *Hatred: The Psychological Descent into Violence* (New York: Public Affairs, 2003), 46, 55.

15. Stanley Cavell reads "William Wilson" as a parody of Cartesian philosophy in "Being Odd, Getting Even (Descartes, Emerson, Poe)," in *The American Face of Edgar Allan Poe*, eds. Shawn Rosenheim and Stephen Rachman (Baltimore: Johns Hopkins University Press, 1995), 3–36. Nancy Berkowitz Bate contends that the story topples the validity of Descartes's assumption that thinking is being: "William Wilson thinks, but is not" ("I Think, But Am Not: The Nightmare of William Wilson," *Poe Studies/Dark Romanticism: History, Theory, Interpretation* 30, no.1–2 [1998]: 27). Joan Dayan argues that Poe's alliance with John Locke inspired a comprehensive

repudiation of Descartes's understanding of personhood. With Locke, "Poe felt the need to annihilate a sure notion of identity" and difference (*Fables of Mind: An Inquiry into Poe's Fiction* [Oxford: Oxford University Press, 1987], 181). Jeffrey Folks maintains that unlike Descartes, Poe could not believe in the transcendent power of human reason; instead, he saw a human mind riddled with "selfishness, disorder, and criminality" ("Poe and the *Cogito*," *Southern Literary Journal* 42, no. 1 [Fall 2009]: 58).

16. Dayan, *Fables of Mind*, 134.

17. Theron Britt argues that the story takes us inside the "central problem of the subject" in American democracy: If all men are equal, then all men are the same. For Brit, the story dramatizes the "psychological death" of the individual in democracy's devotion to the "mob" ("The Common Property of the Mob: Democracy and Identity in Poe's 'William Wilson,'" *Mississippi Quarterly* 48, no. 2 [Spring 1995]: 203, 209). Likewise, Thomas Peyser contends that the narrator is caught in a "nightmare of equality," tormented by the "enforced uniformity" his double represents ("Poe's William Wilson and the Nightmare of Equality," *Explicator* 68.2 [2010]: 102). Peter Jaros suggests that Poe's depiction of the "protagonist's two bodies as simultaneously identical and distinct" inscribes the horror of "the [American] law of corporations," the legal mechanism that swallowed diverse persons into the corporate body ("A Double Life: Personifying the Corporation from Dartmouth College to Poe," *Poe Studies* 47 [2014]: 22).

18. Robert J. Sternberg, "Understanding and Combating Hate," in *The Psychology of Hate*, ed. Robert J. Sternberg (Washington, D.C.: American Psychological Association, 2005), 39, 43.

19. Agneta Fischer, Eran Halperin, Daphna Canetti, and Alba Jasini, "Why We Hate," *Emotion Review* 10, no. 4 (October 2018): 310.

20. Gaylin, *Hatred*, 175, 179, 176.

21. Rene Descartes, *Passions of the Soul and Other Late Philosophical Writings*, trans. Michael Moriarty (Oxford: Oxford University Press, 2015), 226, 229, 231, 227, 257.

22. Massimo Recalcati, "Hate as a Passion of Being," trans. Ramsey McGlazer, *Qui Parle* 20, no. 2 (Spring/Summer 2012): 153, 154, 156, 154, 155, 152.

23. Ibid., 164.

24. Freud associates this occupation with the dreadful materializations of the uncanny. Freud describes an encounter with his own double in his essay on the uncanny, a moment when he does not recognize his image reflected in the window. Freud feels a palpable aversion: "I can still recollect that I thoroughly disliked his appearance," he writes. In other words, Freud acknowledges that we can experience the self as the stranger—unfamiliar and unwelcome ("The Uncanny," in *The Standard Edition of the Complete Works of Sigmund Freud*, vol. 17, trans. James Strachey [London: Hogarth Press and the Institute of Psychoanalysis, 1958], 248).

25. Recalcati, "Passion of Being," 164, 154, 165.

26. Leland S. Person, "Queer Poe: The Tell-Tale Heart of His Fiction," *Poe Studies* 41, no. 1 (2008): 8.

27. Reich maintains that the narrator's homophobia resonates with a fear of his own attraction to Wilson: "The closer same-sex desire comes to being part of a coherent identity, the more terrifying it can be." Thus, the story registers the nineteenth-century constitution of "what we now call homophobia," how it evolved "from a disgust toward unspeakable acts to a genuine terror about how that unspeakability manifests in the very essence of a person's selfhood" ("Bottom Terror in Poe's William Wilson," *The Edgar Allan Poe Review* 21, no. 1 [2020]: 103).

28. J. Gerald Kennedy, *Poe, Death, and the Life of Writing* (New Haven: Yale University Press, 1987), 131.

29. The narrator's relationship with Wilson teems with admiration, understanding, fondness, and desire. The narrator admits that "it is difficult, indeed, to define or even to describe, my real feelings towards him" (433). More than "petulant animosity," he feels "esteem," "respect," and "curiosity" for his schoolmate (433). Similarly, Wilson relates to him with a "most inappropriate, and assuredly most unwelcome affectionateness of manner" (432). The narrator reads this tenderness as "patronage and protection" (432). Such terminology suggests a connection of interest, regard, and caretaking. Moreover, Wilson knows the narrator well enough to offer wise "advice" and "counsel" (435). An intuitive understanding circulates between them. So much so, that the narrator has precognitive, prelingual knowledge of Wilson: "I discovered . . . [in him] something which first startled, and then deeply interested me, by bringing to mind dim visions of my earliest infancy—wild, confused and thronging memories of a time when memory herself was yet unborn" (436). Wilson and the narrator seem soul-mated, bonded by mutual affinities.

30. Tellingly for my purposes, Moss defines internalized homophobia as an excruciating disruption in "self-concept": One feels deformed, deficient, and immoral. The subject feels "inadequacy in his very being." Moss specifies that homosexual shame goes underground—it "must be kept a secret"—and it often alienates the subject from community ("Internalized Homophobia in Men," in *Hating in the First-Person Plural*, ed. Donald Moss [New York: Other Press, 2003], 201, 202).

31. Ibid., 205.

32. Reich, "Bottom Terror," 89.

33. Leonardo De Arrizabalaga Y Prado, *The Emperor Elagabalus: Fact or Fiction?* (Cambridge: Cambridge University Press, 2010), 1.

34. Martin Icks, *The Crimes of Elagabalus* (Cambridge: Harvard University Press, 2012), 117. Icks concludes, "In all likelihood, many, if not most of the stories about Elagabalus's effeminate, luxurious, and licentious behaviour have sprouted from the imaginations of ancient authors, or are based on the gossip and jokes of contemporaries. More than any facts, though, they have defined the reputation of the emperor. Real or imaginary, Elagabalus's excesses have never ceased to haunt his memory" (122).

35. G. B. Niebuhr, *The History of Rome*, vol. 3, trans. William Smith and Leonhard Schmitz (Philadelphia: Lea & Blanchard, 1844), 144.

36. For more on the masturbation panic in America and Europe, see G. J. Barker-Benfield, *The Horrors of the Half-Known Life: Male Attitudes Toward Women and Sexuality in Nineteenth-Century America* (New York: Harper Colophon Books,

1976), and Michel Foucault, *The History of Sexuality: An Introduction, Volume 1* (New York: Vintage Books, 1978).

37. Person, "Queer Poe," 17.

38. Sylvester Graham, *Lectures to Young Men on Chastity*, 2nd edition (Boston: Light & Stearns, Cocker & Brewster, 1834), 87, 95–96, 160, 77, 206, collections.nlm.nih.gov/catalog/nlm:nlmuid-7704062-bk.

39. Reich, "Bottom Terror," 93.

40. Person, "Queer Poe," 20.

41. "homo- comb. form," Etymology, *Oxford English Dictionary*, www-oed-com.ezproxy.otterbein.edu/view/Entry/87990?.

42. With this self-referential encounter, Poe again challenges Cartesian ideologies. Descartes imagined romantic love as the discovery of an eroticized double, saying "the most powerful attraction comes from the perfections we imagine in a person we think may become another self." In love, Descartes believed we find an idealized twin self, a spiritual and bodily match. Descartes argued that we are otherwise incomplete, "merely half of the whole." While Descartes stipulated that "a person of the opposite sex should be the other half," Poe exposes the perilous instability of that prerequisite. His narrator finds his "other half" in a long-lost twin and a same-sex complement (Descartes, *Passions*, 231).

43. One of Graham's sufferers said he "did not dare speak" about his habit, even to a doctor, although "he had become a slave to the vice" (Graham, *Lectures*, 202).

44. Ibid., 92, 93, 94, 92, 98, 94.

45. Julia Stern argues that "what began as a symbolic rape has degenerated even further into a scene of self-abuse" ("Double Talk: The Rhetoric of the Whisper in Poe's 'William Wilson,'" *ESQ* 40.3 [1994], 200). Likewise, Reich contends that the ending depicts a "sadomasochistic masturbatory penetration," and that the narrator "shatter[s] his sense of self by performing the act so laden with cultural taboo" ("Bottom Terror," 91, 99.) In the end, the narrator satiates desire and sentences himself to a physical and metaphysical death. Indeed, Graham claimed that chronic masturbation could be fatal. Essentially, Poe weaponizes this prognosis in "William Wilson's" outcome. Self-abuse becomes self-murder.

46. Graham, *Lectures*, 132, 127, 127–28, 131.

47. Ibid., 33, 32.

48. Graham was not alone in his conception of an almighty masculine reason. Descartes believed that men could be "masters of ourselves" and that their ability to "master" volition gave men an infinite potential for virtue. "Only one thing . . . gives us a good reason to esteem ourselves," he declares: self-mastery. "Baseness," in contrast, comes from weakness, as if "one cannot help doing things that one knows one will subsequently regret" (Descartes, *Passions*, 257, 258, 260).

49. Graham believed that, "Constituted as man is, two grand FUNCTIONS of his system are necessary for his existence as an individual and as a species. The first is NUTRITION and the second is REPRODUCTION." The "sexual appetites" were connected to reproduction as a "law" of instinct and life itself (Graham, *Lectures*, 1, 2).

50. Ibid., 70, 71, 96, 202.

51. Paul White, "Acquired Character: The Hereditary Material of the 'Self-Made Man,'" in *Hereditary Produced: At the Crossroads of Biology, Politics, and Culture, 1500–1870*, eds. Staffan Müller-Willie and Hans-Jörg Rheinberger (Cambridge: MIT Press, 2007), 385.

52. Lorri Glover, *Southern Sons: Becoming Men in the New Nation* (Baltimore: John Hopkins University Press, 2010), 23, 24. As Timothy R. Buckner and Peter Caster write, "Enslavement proved the most significant cultural force shaping black masculinity in the first century of the United States, particularly in obviating self-ownership, challenging the fundamental integrities of male and female kinship bonds, divorcing labor from production, transforming the body into a machine, and limiting both native language use and English literacy" ("Introduction," in *Fathers, Preachers, Rebels, Men: Black Masculinity in U.S. History and Literature, 1820– 1945* [Columbus: The Ohio State University Press, 2011], 5).

53. Edward L. Ayers, *Vengeance and Justice: Crime and Punishment in the 19th-Century American South* (Oxford: Oxford University Press, 1984), 10, 11.

54. Lorri Glover, *Southern Sons*, 27.

55. Poe's interrogation of self-willed white manhood participates in his deconstruction of "gentry fictions of mastery." As David Leverenz explains, "Typically, he displays cultivated narrators unable to master themselves" ("Poe and Gentry Virginia," in *The American Face of Edgar Allan Poe*, eds. Shawn Resenheim and Stephen Rachman [Baltimore: Johns Hopkins University Press, 1995], 212).

56. Britt, "Common Property," 206, 201. Peter Goodwin further attests to Poe's interest in deconstructing Jacksonian manhood, particularly in his contributions to *Burton's Gentleman's Magazine*. Goodwin writes that "Poe seems to be searching in vain for the robust, integral, wholesome gentleman that was supposed to grace the pages of the magazine. In the place of this idealized but elusive figure, Poe posits a fractured masculine subject whose potency derives not from self-sufficiency, but from desire" ("The Man in the Text: Desire, Masculinity, and the Development of Poe's Detective Fiction," in *Edgar Allan Poe: Beyond Gothicism*, ed. James M. Hutchisson [Newark: University of Delaware Press, 2011], 50).

57. A nineteenth-century biographer described Jackson as "self-willed, somewhat overbearing, easily offended, very irascible, and upon the whole 'difficult to get along with'" (Michael Paul Rogin, *Fathers and Children: Andrew Jackson and the Subjugation of the American Indian* [New York: Routledge, 1991], 43).

58. Ibid., 52, 45, 42, 44, 40.

59. As Richard Stott notes, the early American government did not have—nor did most people want them to have—the sort of authority it would have taken to suppress white masculine mayhem. The new republic insisted that men had to govern themselves (*Jolly Fellows: Male Milieus in Nineteenth-Century America* [Baltimore: Johns Hopkins University Press, 2009], 69).

60. Henry David Thoreau, "Civil Disobedience," in *The Norton Anthology of American Literature*, 7th edition, Volume B: 1820–1865, ed. Nina Baym (New York: W.W. Norton & Co, 2007), 1859, 1867.

61. The narrator also personifies the torments of the tensions between equality and individualism in Jacksonian American. David G. Pugh explains that Jacksonian

egalitarianism stipulated "that each man had the right to be like all other men, while at the same time it tormented him with the implication that to be only a part of the masses and nothing more—to be 'common'—was a sure sign of weakness" (*Sons of Liberty: The Masculine Mind in the Nineteenth-Century* [Westport, CN: Greenwood Press, 1983], 25). Theron Britt shows that Wilson threatens the narrator with the "common," motley identity of an egalitarianism that "submerge[es] all into the mob" ("Common Property," 202). Thomas Peyser similarly argues that the narrator revolts "against the threat of mere equality . . . that his double represents" ("Nightmare," 102).

62. E. Anthony Rotundo argues that an idealization of the "animal man" peaks in the latter half of the nineteenth century, when men increasingly believed their "animal instincts" and "animal energy" was "their male birthright and that it demanded expression" (*American Manhood*, 229).

63. Poe himself complicated the distinctions between the human and animal in "Instinct vs Reason." He writes, "The line which demarcates the instinct of brute creation from the boasted reason of man is, beyond doubt, the most shadowy and unsatisfactory character." Ultimately, he concludes that instinct is "the most exalted intellect of all" (*Alexander's Weekly Messenger* 4, no. 5 [January 29, 1840], www .eapoe.org/works/essays/ivrbcata.htm).

64. Stott, *Jolly Fellows*, 49, 53, 54, 55, 40.

65. As Michael Kimmel explains, nineteenth-century men were indoctrinated with dogmas of self-regulation, strictures against any excess of passion or pleasure. In postrevolutionary America—a freer, more economically volatile, more socially mobile world—"identity was no longer fixed." In response, masculinity stabilized itself with a credo of "self-control and unremitting effort" (*Manhood in America*, 33). Stott confirms that precepts of nineteenth-century masculinity often valorized "mastery" and "restraint." But it is more difficult to discern how good fellows understood masculinity. Unruly men had few defenders; no one argued that men "should" make mayhem. "Jolly fellowship lacked a vocabulary," Stott explains; it could not readily justify its actions (*Jolly Fellows*, 56).

66. Leverenz, "Gentry Virginia," 212.

67. As Jones contends, the narrator fails to recognize Wilson as an "essential, internal" facet of himself, an alterity that he must integrate in order to survive ("Counterparts," 239). And Valentine C. Hubbs concludes that "He simply cannot comprehend how two contrary personalities can function harmoniously within one being, or that it is the nature of the individual to incorporate into his complex personality many inconsistencies and ambiguities which, when considered separately, seem incompatible, even mutually exclusive" ("The Struggle of Wills in Poe's 'William Wilson,' *Studies in American Fiction* 11, no. 1 [Spring 1983]: 73).

68. In these fatalities, lust becomes "the tyrant of the ruined soul." It drives the self-polluter "with maniac instinct . . . to the continual perpetration of the destructive and horridly abominable vice!" In other words, Graham's sufferer masturbates against his will, powerless to resist the thrall of self-pleasure. The man lost to licentiousness cannot regulate the borders of his mind: "Unclean thoughts and lascivious images will frequently . . . force themselves, like the ghosts of the murdered, even

into his most consecrated moments." He cannot restrain the actions of his body: "At unguarded moments," he will find himself "hurried into the performance of those acts which his better feelings abhor." Graham explained that the inveterate masturbator "feels himself the subject of circumstances and influences which he cannot control" (Graham, *Lectures*, 129, 131, 133). Saliently, we can discern echoes of the narrator's self-characterization here. Like the habitual masturbator, the narrator insists that the temptations that ruined him were extraordinary. In addition, like the sufferer tormented by obscene images, he is "dying a victim to . . . sublunary visions." And, like Graham's most compulsive patients, he calls himself "the slave of circumstances beyond human control."

69. Ibid., 128, 209, 201.

70. Gaylin, *Hatred*, 55.

71. Edward B. Royzman, Clark McCauley, and Paul Rozin, "From Plato to Putnam: Four Ways to Think about Hate," in *The Psychology of Hate*, ed. Robert J. Sternberg (Washington, D.C.: American Psychological Association, 2005), 17.

72. Fischer et al., "Why We Hate," 301.

73. Gaylin, *Hatred*, 54.

74. Graham, *Lectures*, 98, 99.

75. C. Fred Alford, "Hate Is the Imitation of Love," in *The Psychology of Hate*, ed. Robert J. Sternberg (Washington, D.C.: American Psychological Association, 2005), 237, 242, 243.

76. Alford, "Hate Is the Imitation," 244, 245.

77. Analogously, Alford describes the logic of a woman who kills her lover instead of killing herself. She attached a note to his body that read: "In killing [him], I killed myself." The interdependencies of love can turn murder into a kind of suicide. "Those who inflict violence are almost always attached to their victims," Alford confirms, and "Most people murder a part of themselves rather than another." It is a substantive "ethical difference," Alford observes, "but perhaps not such a momentous psychological distinction." Some facet of the self dies in the other's death ("Hate Is the Imitation, 245, 237, 239).

78. Ibid., 238.

79. Foucault, *History of Sexuality*, 105, 146.

80. Eve Kosofsky Sedgwick, "Jane Austen and the Masturbating Girl," *Critical Inquiry* 17, no. 4 (Summer 1991): 826.

Chapter Two

Melancholia

In 1823, *The American Medical Recorder* outlined its century's understanding of melancholy, a disease with a potentially fatal progression. Its physician-writer explained that the disorder begins with a "great depression of the animal spirits," a bodily low, and "there is usually added grief, fear, irresolution, anxiety, or jealousy." As the illness advances, the sufferer becomes withdrawn and "misanthropic." Paranoia sets in: "He believes there is some secret enemy bent on his destruction." He cannot be comforted or reasoned back into a sense of safety. His symptoms extend to "perpetual taciturnity, excessive weeping, watchfulness, and extreme timidity." Without a cure, life becomes a "heavy burden," and "in a state of despair, he either terminates his afflictions by suicide or sinks into idiotism." The *Medical Recorder* stipulated that men were exponentially more vulnerable to melancholy, accounting for more than 85 percent of cases. Current medical wisdom also held that depression was a disorder of the professional, wealthy, and educated classes—rare among laborers, and rarer still among enslaved and indigenous populations: "I have not seen or heard of a solitary case of this disease among negroes," the writer testifies, and he believes "the savages of this country" were likely also immune. Indeed, by the nineteenth century, even "fixed melancholy"—a disease that historically plagued enslaved people during the Middle Passage—was redefined as a somatic rather than a psychic disorder, a malady caused by slave-ship epidemics of dysentery and scurvy.[1] Affective melancholy seemed to be a white man's scourge.[2]

Described as "melancholic" for most of his life, Poe struggled with a depression he did not fully understand. He wrote that he circled a "psychal want, or necessity," that his soul tried "to regain the lost" or "assume the position which, under other circumstances, would have been its due." He turned to alcohol in a "desperate attempt to escape from torturing memories, from a sense of insupportable loneliness, and a dread of some strange impending doom."[3] At his death, Charles Baudelaire commented that Poe drank "as if he had within himself something that must be killed."[4] Perhaps unsurprisingly, given this personal and cultural context, Poe populated his fictions with melancholic men.

Poe's "Tale of the Ragged Mountains" (1844) centers on the melancholy of its protagonist, Augustus Bedloe. Bedloe suffers from chronic depression and neuralgic attacks. He cannot survive without regular doses of morphine and the steady ministrations of his personal physician and mesmerist, Dr. Templeton. After his habitual breakfast hit of opium, Bedloe walks the mountains outside Charlottesville, Virginia, every day. One afternoon, he time-travels, finding himself in eighteenth-century British India. There, he becomes a British soldier, subduing a violent Indian insurgency. Although he dies in battle, Bedloe somehow makes it home to tell the story. He immediately learns he has just relived an episode in Templeton's military past: Templeton fought with Warren Hastings's troops in a notorious Indian uprising.[5] Apparently, Bedloe died the death of Templeton's "dearest friend," Oldeb.[6] Increasing the story's weirdness, Templeton admits that he was writing his own account of the mêlée when Bedloe experienced it. Sharing Oldeb's portrait, Templeton further reveals an eerie, twin-like similarity between Bedloe and his fallen comrade. The tale ends with Bedloe's actual death. Because Templeton mistakenly treats him with a venomous leech, he dies a week after this incident.

To understand "Ragged Mountains," we must understand the history that Poe summons in the story. In 1778, Warren Hastings—the first governor-general of British India—began a three-year shakedown of Chait Singh, the raja of Benares. Desperate to subsidize British military operations, Hastings pressed Singh for more money and more soldiers. When Singh finally resisted in 1781, Hastings decided the raja must be punished. He ordered Singh's arrest, sending two companies of soldiers to take him into custody. A brawl broke out. The fight turned to carnage; Hastings troops were massacred; and Chait Singh rappelled down the palace walls on a rope made of turbans. Benares exploded into a bloody revolt that took the British almost three months to quell. In the end, Hastings's army expelled Singh from the city and pillaged his palace. (Hastings appropriated Singh's Sanskrit manuscripts.) Singh never recovered from the decimation, spending the remainder of his life in exile. Five years after the revolt, Hastings was impeached: charged with "a series of the most wanton oppressions and cruelties" against Chait Singh and the Indian people.[7]

Poe was intrigued by this history. Scottish soldier and military writer, G. R. Gleig, published a multivolume biography of Hastings in 1841. British historian and politician Thomas Babington Macaulay reviewed it that same year. Macaulay's assessment of Hastings ranks as one of his most celebrated essays. Poe read both texts, and he turned Hastings, Singh, and Benares into historical specters in "Ragged Mountains."

Although Poe coveted "Ragged Mountains" as one of "his favorite compositions," it ranks as a dubious fiction in Poe's canon.[8] A generation of scholars reckoned it dimwitted and poorly written.[9] G. R. Thompson judged it "one of the least satisfying and most gimmiky of Poe's Gothic works."[10] Even worse, the story contains blatant instances of plagiarism, lifting passages from Macaulay's and Gleig's writing.[11] More recently, however, critics have begun to re-examine the story's relevance to histories of nationalism, colonialism, and trauma. Andrew Horn argues that Poe's retelling of the Benares insurrection operates as a political allegory for American racism and imperialism.[12] Michael Williams contends that "Ragged Mountains" stages crises of racial difference and historical authority to reveal the despotism already present in the American national project.[13] Daniel Philippon tracks the text's parallels between violence against American Indians and the tyrannies of colonial India.[14] Christina Zwarg illuminates the story's interest in the traumatic legacies of colonial wounds.[15] This critical trajectory solidifies "Ragged Mountains" relevance to the abuses of empire.

My study extends this inquiry into a more comprehensive investigation of the story's invocation of Hastings's impeachment as governor-general and masculine melancholia. When Poe enters this history, he opens a crypt of manly affects: attraction, sorrow, fear, regret, and depression. In the process, "Ragged Mountains" complicates the affective distinctions between history's victors and the vanquished.[16] Poe's white men—fat with the spoils of dominance—must unfeel and unknow facets of their experience. As we shall see, the Hastings trial persisted as a symbol of imperial plundering, national denials, and unresolved losses. In response, my questions become: How does "Ragged Mountains" (re)imagine this history? What do British India and Hastings signify in this text? What can we see when we decode this cipher? And how might this reading revise our understanding of white, imperial masculinity, the affects of supremacy, and the psychosocial significance of Poe's melancholy men?

To answer these questions, I draw on the sources that Poe consulted, including Macaulay's essay, Gleig's biography, and Richard Sheridan's speeches. This material helps me reconstruct the realities of the massacre and the trial. It enables me to analyze how Hastings functions as a historical symbol in Poe's fiction. But it does not make sense of the connections between Bedloe's melancholy and the imperial trauma he re-enters. For that, I turn to historical conceptions of depression. My study draws on the most ubiquitous and influential ideas about melancholia in early America, especially those of Philippe Pinel and Jean-Etienne-Dominique Esquirol, as well as scholarly histories of the disease.[17] In addition, I follow this history forward, reading Poe's melancholy men into Freud's understanding of mourning and melancholia. Freud's notions of pathological grief drew on nineteenth-century ideas about diseased despondency. His theory offers a generative framework for illuminating the perverse desires and attachments that disfigure Poe's men. Just as pertinently, contemporary queer and critical race theory has repurposed Freudian melancholia to contend with the traumas of normative identity formation. This thinking becomes pivotal to my analysis of the ambiguity and ambivalence that Poe's men leave behind.

The men of "Ragged Mountains" present us with problems of sadness, sickness, longing, and violence. But that problem actually originates in the imperial genealogy that frames the story. To the nineteenth century, Warren Hastings was a paradoxical forefather, a progenitor of villainy and ruin as well as triumph and redemption. His impeachment resurrected issues of empire and revolt that addled American nationalism. The trial was also a hothouse of masculine affects, including lost fraternity, humiliation, and depression. Poe cathects these feelings onto Bedloe's character. In this way, his illness and his psychosomatic connection to Templeton function as an affective metonym for the legacies of white masculine colonialisms. "Ragged Mountains" dramatizes predicaments of desire and grief that hold its white men in networks of reoccurring trauma across time, place, and bodies. We will see that Poe's men mourn a history of imperialist violence. They mourn the failures of tyranny. They mourn relationships formed in the trenches of colonial warfare. Thus, their melancholia becomes the clear and present danger in the story. Ultimately, I read "Ragged Mountains" as an affective cautionary tale, a warning against a selective retrieval of melancholic attachments to lost objects.

HISTORY

The British reckoning with Hastings's leadership became a foundational text of empire. Hastings's impeachment fomented a renegotiation of Britain's identity as an intentional superpower as well as its respect for the autonomy of a colonized people.[18] More crucially, as Nicholas Dirks writes, "The trial produced conditions not just for the empire's success but also for its transformation into a patriotic enterprise."[19] In addition, the impeachment revived the still unsettled implications of the American Revolution.[20] Macaulay's essay–the text that Poe borrows from in his retelling—registers all of these repercussions, crediting Hastings with protecting British power in Asia after its "fatal" loss in America.[21] Thus, Poe's allusions—to Hastings, the Benares uprising, and the impeachment—resound with the ideologies of both British and American nation formation.

They also evoke vivid recollections of an indignant and fallen white masculinity. Hastings was tried on twenty-two counts of "injustice, cruelty, and treachery against the faith of nations." The allegations included abuse of power, taking bribes, deceit, and torture. The indictment spanned more than one hundred pages in the court transcript.[22] Evidence was heard on four principal charges, including financial corruption, the exploitation of Chait Singh, and the extortion and torture of begums of Oude.[23] Edmund Burke and Richard Sheridan presented the case against Hastings.[24] Scores of people came to watch the trial. As Macaulay describes, "There were gathered together, from all parts of a great, free, and prosperous empire, grace and female loveliness, wit and learning, the representatives of every science and every art."[25] Burke spoke first, igniting the crowd. "[W]e have brought before you," Burke thundered, "one in whom all the frauds, all the peculations, all the violence, all the tyranny in India are embodied, disciplined, and arrayed."[26] Burke's words sent his audience into hysterics. In Macaulay's record, "The ladies in the galleries . . . were in a state of uncontrollable emotion. Handkerchiefs were pulled out; smelling bottles were handed round; hysterical sobs and screams were heard; and Mrs. Sheridan was carried out in a fit." When Sheridan made his opening statement, he likewise castigated Hastings: "In his mind all is shuffling, ambiguous, dark insidious, and little."[27] Sheridan's tirade again agitated the crowd. Macaulay writes, "He sat down, not merely admist cheering, but amidst the loud clapping of hands, in which the Lords below the bar and the strangers in the gallery joined. The excitement of the House was such that no other speaker could obtain a hearing; and the debate was adjourned." The prosecution turned the trial into theater.

A few months later, Sheridan pilloried the events that culminated in the Benares massacre. His speech lasted four days, and, Macaulay states, at its conclusion he sank "back, as if exhausted, into the arms of Burke, who hugged him with the energy of generous admiration." Burke's final summation went nine days, a torrent of invective. "He is a captain general of iniquity—thief—tyrant—robber—cheat—sharper—swindler," Burke harangued. "We call him all of these names, and are sorry the English language does not afford more terms adequate to the enormity of his offenses."[28] This was a drama of iniquity.

Despite diatribe and evidence, Hastings was acquitted of all charges. During the impeachment, a nation struggled with what to feel about Hastings's disgrace. After his exoneration, it struggled to integrate his absolution. The East India Company awarded Hastings a substantial annual pension and an advance to cover his legal costs. But that was not enough to settle Hastings's debts. He lived in infamy, unable to secure employment and denied reparations from the House of Commons. "Though acquitted," Hastings lamented, "I yet stand branded . . . as a traitor to my country and false to my trust."[29] Gleig enumerates, "His worldly prospects were blighted" and the "doors of public life were . . . shut against him . . . for ever [sic]."[30] And Macaulay confirms, "He was a ruined man." At least for a time.

Eventually, Hastings's ethos was rehabilitated. In 1813, he returned to the House of Commons to testify for the Company's charter renewal. When he entered the chamber, the Members of Parliament "'rose with their heads uncovered, and stood in silence.'"[31] As Macaulay punctuates, "The reappearance . . . of a man who . . . who seemed to have risen from the dead, could not but produce a solemn and pathetic effect." Oxford awarded Hastings an honorary doctorate in civil law. He was favored by the prince regent and the king. After his death, historians and biographers sanctified him as a victim of political persecution and a savior of empire. Gleig's memoir applauds his "genius," "absolute unselfishness," "the self-possession that never deserted him," and the "dignity which threw its halo over all his proceedings."[32] The Company erected a statue of him in India House and his portrait hangs in the India Office Record room of the British Library. Such memorialization, however, happened only through a willful repression of Hastings's crimes. It was part of a collective "national amnesia" that forgot its own imperial trespasses. Through disavowal, Britain made global sovereignty a "sacred responsibility" and a sacred mission.[33] Thus, Hastings left a legacy of denial and dubious re-canonization.[34]

The tensions around Hastings's bios infiltrate Macaulay's essay on the governor-general. Macaulay depicts Hastings as "a ruler of great talents and few scruples." He commends Hastings's "fertile genius and serene courage," and yet he acknowledges Hastings's willingness to resort to "extreme exercise[s] of power." More explicitly, Macaulay offers a reproachful catalog of Hastings's brutality. For Macaulay, the Benares insurrection was an event of "indiscreet violence," and Hastings only became "more violent" in its wake. At times, Macaulay impugns Gleig's defense of Hastings.[35] Still, Macaulay maintains that no governor-general "ever surpassed Hastings." And he cannot resist encomium: "Even now, after the lapse of more than fifty years, the natives of India still talk of him as the greatest of the English." Macaulay's Hastings is obstinate ambiguity. He judges Hastings "deficient" in ethics, in his "respect for the rights of others" and in "sympathy for the suffering of others." And yet he extols Hastings's intellect, fearlessness, and command. In the end, Macaulay leaves us with a Hastings fixed in contradiction.

Holistically then, the Hastings allusion functions as an enigmatic signpost. With it, Poe returns us to a troubled past of colonial ascendency: the rise and fall and rise of a criminal patriarch; Hastings's greed and violence; and a history of white masculine ruthlessness, indictment, and rehabilitation. This history connects most immediately to Templeton's character. Templeton was a member of the forces under Hastings's command. With comrade soldiers, he was ordered to Benares to suppress the insurrection. And yet, as we shall, see the history of Hastings's tyranny and infamy also courses through Bedloe's illness and his strange experience in the Ragged Mountains.

ATTACHMENT

Scholarly interpretations of Poe's recuperation of the Hastings's history are vexed and varied. It has been read as plagiarism; as a reasonable use of extant material; as a hoax; and as a deliberate challenge to the coercive authority of imperial history.[36] Yet critics have neglected the gender and sexual affects of the story, particularly its attention to white masculine attachment and grief. The men in "Ragged Mountains" are sick, sad, and strangely interdependent. I begin my investigation with this attachment. Here, I explore the connotations of homosocial intimacy in both the Hastings affair and the story. Like the men on "Ragged Mountains," Hastings knew close and complex homosocial bonds. Poe translates that history into the preternatural connection between Templeton and Bedloe. Indeed, Templeton is named for Nathaniel Middleton, a witness judged Hastings's proxy at trial, his "second self."[37] Poe turns the Hastings-Middleton legal alliance into a metaphysical metaphor, making it the basis for the telekinetic link between Templeton and Bedloe. As Templeton's "second self," Bedloe suffers with his sorrow and longing.

As the story opens, its unnamed narrator vividly describes Bedloe's affinity with Templeton (940). Templeton "devote[s] his time and medical experience exclusively to the care of the invalid," relieving the "acute pains of his patient" through magnetic remedies. Bedloe believes he receives a "great benefit" from the attentions of his physician. Over time, "a very distinct and strongly marked *rapport*, or magnetic relation" emerged between Templeton and Bedloe, a bond of "great intensity." Ultimately, Templeton achieves a total mesmeric "triumph" over Bedloe (941). He can mesmerize Bedloe at will and without Bedloe's conscious detection. Their interconnection grows so profound that Bedloe telekinetically relives Templeton's military past (an event I analyze more fully below). Thus, "Ragged Mountains" exaggerates its embodied intimacies between men.

In addition, the story triangulates its male-male ties. In one triangle, the narrator ruminates on the Bedloe-Templeton puzzle. In another, Templeton, Bedloe, and Oldeb connect in a nexus of affection and affliction. (Recall that Bedloe becomes Oldeb, the fallen soldier in the Benares massacre, when he time-travels to British India.) Initially, these are relationships of "curiosity." Templeton says he feels "an uneasy, and not altogether horrorless, curiosity" about Bedloe (948). The narrator likewise admits to a "profound interest and curiosity" in Bedloe, as well as an "uneasiness" in his presence (939, 940). "Curiosity" is a state of desire—a desire to know, to understand, to realize, to grasp. At its most fevered pitch, curiosity compels a total immersion in its object. And yet, even as it pushes for active pursuit or investigation, curiosity registers insufficiency, that which is incomplete or ungratified. As Barbara Benedict writes, "Curiosity is the mark of discontent, the sign of a pursuit of something beyond what you have."[38] In their curiosity about Bedloe, the narrator and Templeton betray a desire for a complete knowing of another man. Their interest surges with homoerotic interest. The story's relationship triangles then, capture men in labyrinths of attraction, longing, and confusion.

Templeton confesses that he "became much attached to" Oldeb in Calcutta when he was twenty years old. Decades later in Saratoga, as a seventy-year-old man, Templeton gravitates to Bedloe because of his "miraculous similarity" to Oldeb. Templeton's memory of his dead friend drives his attraction to Bedloe. Because Bedloe looks so much like Oldeb, Templeton "accost[s]" him and seeks his friendship. He orchestrates "those arrangements that resulted in [his] becoming [Bedloe's] constant companion" (948). Templeton's actions are deliberate and purposeful: He desires nearness to Bedloe and the shade of Oldeb that he sees in him.

Intriguingly, Bedloe's bodily response to Oldeb's death further sentimentalizes and sexualizes the story's masculine attachments. Oldeb is killed by an arrow "made to imitate the body of a . . . serpent . . . long and black, with a poisoned barb" (947). This obviously phallic dagger strikes him in the right temple. On the mountain, Bedloe will die Oldeb's death. Provocatively, however, Bedloe has felt Oldeb's pain for years, long before he relives Oldeb's experience at Benares. Bedloe suffers from chronic "neuralgic attacks": acute, episodic nerve pain typically in the head or the face (940). The attacks are so severe they often threaten to kill him. Bedloe's almost-fatal neuralgia is a metonym for Oldeb's lethal head wound. It reenacts the pain Oldeb endured before he died. This suffering disfigures Bedloe: The episodes "had reduced him from a condition of more than usual personal beauty" (940–41). However, despite this metamorphosis, Templeton recognizes Bedloe as Oldeb's double in Saratoga. Presumably, Templeton sees Oldeb *both* in Bedloe's past beauty and present debility. In Bedloe, he sees Oldeb's youthful attractiveness and his last agony. He also discerns the object of his grief, the absence at the core of his sadness and longing. Thus, Bedloe's body localizes multiple forms of masculine anguish: Oldeb's wound, Oldeb's death, and Templeton's mourning. In addition, Bedloe's distress is all *past* pain and the pain of *other men*. His body is occupied by historical relationships and historical losses.

The story's investment in bygone manly allegiances is literally written into Templeton's name. Templeton is understood as a fictional double for Nathaniel Middleton, a figure of fidelity and attachment at the impeachment.[39] Middleton served as Hastings's appointed representative at Oudh. As such, he administered the imprisonment, torture, and extortion of the Oudh nobility. At trial, Sheridan called Middleton Hastings's "second self," castigating him for the crimes he committed as Hastings's "agent." In the prosecution's reasoning, Hastings and Middleton represented an indivisible alliance. "*Quid facit per alium, facit per se,*" Sheridan pontificated, summoning the legal maxim that makes a senior officer liable for whatever he commands of a subordinate.[40] In the witness box, however, Middleton refused to offer any testimony that would incriminate Hastings, responding to virtually every question Sheridan asked with the claim that "he did not recollect." Consequently, Middleton was pejoratively christened "Memory Middleton" in popular discourse. The insult mocked Middleton's alleged perjury, but it also underscored his devotion to Hastings. In Sheridan's estimation, Middleton tried to take the blame for Hastings's misdeeds, to "claim the whole infamy in those transactions, and to monopolize the guilt! He dared even to aver that he had been condemned by Mr. Hastings for the ignominious part he had acted." Middleton proved a formidable witness for Hastings's defense, withstanding the pressure to sacrifice Hastings to the wolves that circled him. All told, Middleton represents a stalwart masculine loyalty, a faithfulness so strong it creates a symbiotic doubling, a "second self."[41]

The closeness between Hastings and Middleton mirrors the bond Bedloe shares with Templeton. In their mesmeric link, Bedloe becomes Templeton's agent, his proxy. Once Templeton achieves mesmeric rapport with his patient, Bedloe's will "succumb[s] rapidly" to the physician's exertions. Templeton can induce the trance "almost instantaneously" through a simple act of "volition . . . , even when the invalid was unaware of his presence" (941). Under the force of Templeton's magnetism, Bedloe becomes his surrogate self. Templeton assures Bedloe that he experienced "with the minutest accuracy" the "events of the insurrection of Cheyte Sing" at the precise time when Templeton was "detailing them upon paper here at home" (949). Hence, the story converts the legal principle that condemned the Hastings-Middleton confederacy—*quid facit per alium, facit per se*—into a metaphysical partnership. This tenet of law made Hastings vicariously liable for whatever Middleton did as his emissary. Similarly, Templeton acts through Bedloe; his will carries Bedloe back to Benares; and his grief and longing animate Bedloe's re-experience of the battle.

Across nations and generations, "Ragged Mountains" puts men into strange contact with one another. They feel curious about other men. They scrutinize the male body. They carry portraits of dead friends. They live the other's memories. They experience the other's pain. They get sick and sad with an ineffable sorrow. In these odd affinities, "Ragged Mountains" considers the emotional imprint of forfeited fraternity, especially when villainy or catastrophe complicate the loss. David Grevon argues that Poe's fictive disaster narratives conceive "opportunities for the disorganization of normative manhood." In *Pym*, for example, shipwreck and mutiny enable "lonely, outcast men to share in a common grief," to mourn a lost Other, to retake that Other into the body through slippages of identity.[42] In "Ragged Mountains," illness, debility, and death likewise facilitate masculine ties and affective expression. Templeton finally speaks of Oldeb, finally confesses his pain, after Bedloe has relived his death. Templeton, Bedloe, the narrator, and Oldeb are tangled up in one another—in body, mind, space, and time. With these couplings, Poe substantiates the masculine solidarities of the Hastings prosecution and depicts men working *through* each other. Men inside each other; men assimilated in body and mind; men acting in concert; men inextricably caught in a white, imperial past.

SICK, SAD MEN

Despite Middleton's fealty, Hastings's impeachment was fueled by the treachery of other men.[43] Most poignantly, Macaulay concluded that the trial came to represent the "lamentable instability of friendship." The trial saw the death of past fraternity between men who led a nation: "The great chiefs were still living, and still in the full vigour of their genius. But their friendship was at an end. It had been violently and publicly dissolved, with tears and stormy reproaches. If those men, once so dear to each other, were now compelled to meet for the purpose of managing the impeachment, they met as strangers . . . and behaved to each other with cold and distant civility." Hastings lived the turbulence of masculine affairs.

Similarly, for all its emphasis on masculine attachments, "Ragged Mountains" obscures the relationships between its men with disquiet, mystery, and illness. As I note above, both Templeton and the narrator feel an inexplicable trepidation around Bedloe. While Bedloe's memory of the Benares devastation inspires Templeton's truth-telling, Templeton remains reticent and selective in his confession. We learn only that Oldeb was his "dearest friend"; that they became "much attached" in Calcutta; that Templeton "did all he could to prevent" Oldeb's "fatal sally"; and that Templeton has a "regretful memory of the deceased" (949). More sinisterly, "Ragged Mountain" tallies multiple masculine deaths and debilitating illnesses. Bedloe is an addict and a perpetual patient; Oldeb does not survive the charge he spearheads; and Bedloe dies twice before the story ends. The men in "Ragged Mountains" live in states of anxiety and nihilism.

Here, I turn to Bedloe's body and his illness. Bedloe's melancholia indexes a masculinity in crisis, and its expression is entirely somatic. His body speaks this gendered anguish. Tellingly, the nineteenth century articulated certain emotions through the body. Dana Luciano underscores the primacy of the body in nineteenth-century grief, for example. With its pain, the body testified to "the importance of interpersonal attachment."[44] But how might we make sense of a body aggrieved with another person's sorrow? And with a transnational, intergenerational imperial loss? What does Bedloe's pathological sadness signify? How did the nineteenth century understand its sad, sick patriarchs? What does Bedloe's illness express about the impact of white masculine imperialism on individual men? What does it reveal about the white masculine body? And about the connections *between* men's bodies, the body and politics, and the body politic?

In its first passages, the story delineates Bedloe's sickly alterity. The narrator observes: "He was singularly tall and thin. He stooped much. His limbs were exceedingly long and emaciated. His forehead was broad and low. His complexion absolutely bloodless. His mouth was large and flexible, and his teeth were more and wildly uneven . . . than I had ever before seen in a human head" (940). Bedloe's long, lanky body registers an Ichabod Crane–like association with lechery, conquest, and capitalism.[45] Bedloe is so "wealthy" he keeps Templeton as his personal physician with a "liberal annual allowance" (941). But his wasting—and his "stoop"—betray the bodily costs of economic dominion and the exhaustion of his "spermatic economy."[46] So much so that he embodies living death: His gaze recalls "the eyes of a long-interred corpse." He is also visibly sad: His smile can only express "profound melancholy . . . a phaseless and unceasing gloom" (940). We meet Bedloe as a shade of enfeebled privilege, an ailing masculinity.

Bedloe's condition reflects his century's conception of "melancholy" as a psychosomatic illness. As Stanley Jackson notes, the terms "melancholy" and "melancholia" historically named a diseased despondency.[47] With the phrase "profound melancholy" then, Poe describes Bedloe's disposition and diagnosis. Historical readers would have readily detected the symptoms of melancholia in Bedloe's persona. His deadened eyes, waxy pallor, and emaciation are prominent signs of melancholia.[48] In addition, Bedloe's primary physical complaint—neuralgic attacks—somatized melancholia in nineteenth-century discourses.[49] In sum, Bedloe's physical state confirms a serious and chronic illness.

Nineteenth-century alienists saw melancholia as a blood malady, an affective disorder, and particularly pertinent to my purpose, a nervous disease—a dysfunction of the body's nervous system. Defined as a sickness of feeling, rather than intellect, melancholia slowed the blood and depleted a patient's "nerve force."[50] For the nineteenth century, the body's nerve circuitry served a crucial function, accounting for the vitality that determined if a body was alive or dead.[51] The nerves, moreover, had both psychological and physiological import. As Janet Oppenheim elucidates, "Every term used to describe and

explain the operations of the nervous system—tension, sympathy, excit-
ability, irritability, sensibility, and depression—reached into the mind and
body."[52] Nervous characteristics—like "sympathy" or "depression"—were
simultaneously biological and emotional states. Invoking this lexicon, the
narrator explains that Bedloe "was, in the highest degree, sensitive, excitable, enthusiastic" (942). Each of these traits—like his melancholy—are also
nervous conditions.

According to his epoch's logic, Bedloe's nervous circuitry relied on the
existence of invisible connections *within* his body and *between* bodies. The
nineteenth century believed that "nerves possessed . . . an agency . . . and
a consciousness of their own." The nerves could work without cognitive
detection or decision. They could animate human breathing, for example,
without any act of will or noticeable sensation. As Laura Salisbury and
Andrew Shali explain, the nerves could be "powered independently of the
brain," and they communicated with one another automatically. By the
1830s, nineteenth-century neurologists theorized the existence of "reflex
arcs"—channels of nervous communication—that instinctively responded to
internal and external influences. This breakthrough posited the existence of
a bodily consciousness distributed "throughout the nervous system." At this
juncture, nineteenth-century neurology made formative distinctions between
the body's nerve structure and individual intent or awareness. More specifically, it extended a decisive power to the stimulus. Stimuli were essential to
survival: "The entire nervous system, including the brain, required the 'interference'" of proximate forces to operate. Just as importantly, the body could
not detach from its location: The body was "*functionally* connected to its
environment," tied to a world that could alternately sustain or irritate it (my
emphasis).[53] In other words, the nervous body could not discern or regulate
its own borders. Entangled with place, people, and event, the body was determined by whatever coursed through its nerve network. But no body could
fully know or speak its nervous truths. Controlled by the intercourse between
stimuli and the nerve circuitry, a body might behave agitatedly, passionately,
or dejectedly without detectable explanation. Thus, Templeton and Bedloe
are nervous provocations to one another, rousing psychosomatic drives that
they cannot see or sense. As a stimulus, Bedloe revives Templeton's prior
trauma and grief. And, aroused by the force of Templeton's pain, as well as
his mesmeric direction, Bedloe reexperiences Oldeb's death.

In addition, the gendered significance of Bedloe's melancholia resonates
beyond his nervous union with Templeton. He is also sick with the trials and
tribulations of a generation of men. The nervous body's interstates meant
that nineteenth-century men were relentlessly susceptible to the caprices of
capitalism and politics. Clark Lawlor illustrates that "the dominant metaphor"
for any nervous break was "economic." Sufferers bankrupted their nervous

energies with timeworn excesses: too much drink, sex, masturbation, work, study, grief, unrequited love, disappointment, deviance, and so on. More evocatively, physicians held that excessive sociopolitical change—or strain—could also sink men into depression. As Lawlor explains, rapid transformation had debilitating impacts: "Men were most prone to these 'shocks' because they were 'more exposed to numerous sources of cerebral excitement in the worry and turmoil of the world.'" In addition, frustrated ambition, financial failure, and political revolutions were all instigators of melancholia.[54]

Many of the case studies that premised the medical understanding of melancholia featured insecure tyrants and bankrupt everymen. Philippe Pinel[55] cites Tiberius Caesar and Louis IX as examples of a "brooding" melancholia caused by ineptitude: "Each of them a prey to dark suspicions . . . and terrors ever new and imaginary, which increased with their advancing lives." In Pinel's taxonomy, Tiberius and Louis IX exemplified an illness caused by ineffectual leadership. In essence, Pinel saw melancholia as a pathology of masculine failure. Pinel also emphasized that for broken patriarchs, melancholia could be "distinguished by an exalted sentiment of self-importance, associated with pretensions to unbounded power and inexhaustible riches." In men flattened by sociopolitical downturns, melancholia brought on delusions of grandeur. More revealingly, Pinel's illustrations directly implicate the reversals of revolution in masculine melancholy. One man "lost his property by the revolution" and was imprisoned for his alliance with the old regime. He went "insane" and "soon complimented himself with the title and prerogatives of the king of France." Another man, "ruined by the revolution," imagined himself "the sovereign of the world."[56] Men in this catalog were vulnerable to a melancholia triggered by shattered privilege and political retaliation. Their delusions seemingly compensated for intolerable emasculations.

Jean-Étienne-Dominique Esquirol[57] accentuates these formative connections between masculine shame and delusional melancholia. Esquirol records the descent of M. W., who took "an active part during the reign of terror." Demoted to an inferior embassy post, "He soon persuades himself that he is king, and abandons himself to all the pretensions with which such a conviction inspires him." Indeed, "He requires that every one should prostrate himself before him, is constantly making and unmaking ministers, and prodigal of favors, honors and wealth."[58] For M. W., political turnabouts compel the assertion of kingly majesty. Esquirol also confirms the power of "the event" to precipitate delusional depression. He recounts the case of a merchant, dangerously close to bankruptcy, who subsequently confronts "political events . . . which oppose his views, [and] plunge him into a melancholy delirium from which nothing relieves him."[59] The events in these medical histories—financial disaster, professional mortification, and political punishment—presage a compromised masculinity, a manhood crushed by worldly volatility.

Are such reversals implicated in the etiology of Bedloe's depression then? Given his obvious wealth, what betrayals or degradations has he experienced? Whose failures does his body encipher? Does he suffer with Templeton's moral or political bankruptcy? Is he plagued with Hastings's shame?

Fascinatingly, these case studies recall the spectacle of disgrace that the Hastings's trial laid bare. Hastings was a marvel of mortification during the impeachment. When the trial began, Francis Burney commented: "'What an awful moment for such a man!—a man fallen from such height of power to a situation so humiliating—from the almost unlimited command of so large a part of the Eastern World to be cast at the feet of his enemies . . . '" To people that knew his prowess, Hastings seemed a conquered Goliath. William Windham, Whig representative, observed: "'What a sight is that! To see that man, that small portion of human clay, that poor feeble machine of earth, enclosed now in that little space, brought to that Bar, a prisoner in a spot six foot square—and to reflect on his late power! Nations at his command! Princes prostrate at his feet!—What a change! How he must feel it!'"[60] Confined to the dock, Hastings's vulnerability became a visual feast. Macaulay's description of Hastings in court amplifies the contrast between Hastings's past command and present fragility: "Hastings advanced to the bar, and bent his knee. . . . He had ruled an extensive and populous country, had made laws and treaties, and sent forth armies, and set up and pulled down princes. And in his high place he had so borne himself, that all had feared him. . . . He looked like a great man, and not like a bad man. A person small and emaciated, yet deriving dignity from a carriage . . . [of] habitual self-possession and self-respect. . . . " The trial brought a debased overlord center stage. It reduced Hastings to a political and gender wreckage. As a result, he implicitly became a historical progenitor of masculine melancholy.

Melancholia was a disease of manly fiasco, a sickness experienced by men who lost fortune and prestige. For Hastings, the Benares massacre was that fiasco. The Benares charge was the first to be judged grounds for impeachment, ensuring that Hastings would stand trial. In Macaulay's assessment, Hastings's arrest of Chait Singh was a fatal miscalculation: "In taking these strong measures, Hastings scarcely showed his usual judgment." Macaulay believed that Hastings underestimated the rajah's popularity and the grit of his people.[61] The showdown with Singh opened a Pandora's box of Indian resistance. Although British troops eventually subdued the revolt, it made Hastings irrationally vindictive when he moved to extort more money from the Oude aristocracy. To strong-arm the begums of Oude out of their fortune, Hastings confined them to their apartments, providing only a starvation's ration of food. Macaulay was especially appalled by this protracted coercion: "Month after month this cruelty continued, till at length, after twelve hundred thousand pounds had been wrung out of the Princesses, Hastings began to think he had really got to the bottom of their coffers, arid that no rigour could extort more." In addition, Hastings imprisoned two senior councilors, held them in irons, and tortured them. Macaulay writes, "It was resolved by an English government that these two infirm old men should be delivered to the tormentors. . . . What horrors their dungeon there witnessed can only be guessed." Burke further accused Hastings of ordering public whippings to obtain the payouts, including lashing Indian magistrates with bamboo canes until "blood ran out of their mouths, eyes, and noses" and hammering "wedges of wood and iron" between the fingers of Indian laborers.[62] The trial depicted Hastings as a leader capable of horrific atrocities. These tortures evidenced his inability to responsibly govern a colonized people.

This is the affective history—and the affective complexity—that Poe conjures with the Benares plotline and Bedloe's physicality. Bedloe's melancholy materializes the trespasses and the humiliations that haunted white imperial masculinity. In other words, Bedloe's lives a depression of converging emotional and historical forces. Nineteenth-century melancholia was a nervous disorder, a disease driven by potent interdependencies between the body and external stimuli, including other bodies, environmental factors, and sociopolitical events. Hence, Bedloe's physical "peculiarities" attest to (dis)figurements of feeling that go beyond the pain of Templeton's heartache and war memory. Bedloe is a bellwether of multiplying affective currents, including white masculine dishonor and failure. And, ultimately, Bedloe's body itself is an artifact of degeneration. Unaccountably, he projects a bizarre agedness: "He certainly *seemed* young—and he made a point of speaking about his youth—yet there were moments when I should have had little trouble in imagining a hundred years of age." The narrator also observes that "physically, he had not always been what he was" (940). His chronic debility has "reduced him from a condition of more than usual personal beauty, to that which I saw" (940–41). Like Hastings at trial, Bedloe endures a tragic alteration. He is sick and sad with the white man's debacles. He suffers the pain of conquerors. His melancholy functions as a cryptogram for white masculinity's neuroses: for its vulnerability to political and economic collapse; for its tendency to blunder, trespass, and fall from grace; and for its predisposition to reparative fantasy.

DELUSION

Bedloe's illness, therefore, troubles one of the organizing claims of the American political body: As Luciano writes, America defined itself through its distance and difference from "the English tyrant."[63] But on Ragged Mountains, the English tyrant lives in memory and dis-ease. The tyrant—the criminal, Governor-General Hastings—haunts Templeton's despondency and Bedloe's illness. The tyrant also lives in the story's geography: at the sites of ethnic carnage in America and India. Daniel Philippon documents Poe's unprecedented focus on place in "Ragged Mountains." Unlike most of Poe's fictions, "Ragged Mountains" tarries with the material dimensions of season and setting. For example, Bedloe takes his preternatural walk during "Indian Summer" (942). The reference to Indian summer foreshadows Bedloe's return to the Benares revolt, and it simultaneously connotes especially embattled cycles of American colonialism.[64] The trial, too, was a portal into time travel. Macaulay ruminates, "Every step in the proceedings carried the mind either backward, through many troubled centuries, to the days when the foundations of our constitution were laid; or far away, over boundless seas and deserts, to dusky nations living under strange stars, worshipping strange gods, and writing strange characters from right to left." Bedloe is similarly transported across "troubled centuries" and "strange stars." With the reference to the Indian summer, Poe situates Bedloe in two imperial masculinities, two imperial times, and two imperial places.

The associations between setting and the discourses of a colonizing masculinity escalate as Bedloe goes further into the mountain haze. Bedloe connects the intensified "impressions" that the mist creates to his belief that he is the "very first and sole adventurer" to "penetrate" the "recesses" of the gorge and its "virgin" solitude (942). Williams detects the reiteration of a foundational "colonizing claim" in Bedloe's language here: "The figure of the penetration of the virgin zone is a familiar one in narratives of exploration" and "the repeated term 'adventurer' . . . alludes to a long history of mercantile and colonizing endeavors dating back at least to Henry VII's Society of Merchant Adventurers."[65] Thus, geographical cues connect Bedloe to generations of white masculine invaders, turning him into the iconic explorer.[66]

Still, much of this analysis presupposes that we can discern the truths of Bedloe's experience. But truth stays phantasmic on Ragged Mountains. Bedloe's perception remains constitutionally unreliable, compromised by opiates and illness. As Bedloe "adventures," he gets high and lost. My attention turns to this daze now and Bedloe's experience on the mountain itself. As previously explained, the nervous body could not reliably determine or regulate itself. Its systems could operate apart from awareness and volition.

In addition, we saw that masculine melancholy was vulnerable to delusions of greatness. Thus, Bedloe's perplexity as he adventures through the gorge, then, is vitally important to the story's representation of the colonial project. I wonder how Bedloe's melancholy contributes his confusion. Is Hastings's history present here as well? What happens to the living legacies of white imperial masculinity as Bedloe goes deeper into this past?

Intriguingly, Bedloe loses his way on the twisted path of white conquest. He admits: "So dense was this pleasant fog, that I could at no time see more than a dozen yards of the path before me. This path was excessively sinuous, and as the sun could not be seen, I soon lost all idea of the direction in which I journeyed." Just as he becomes directionless, the morphine kicks in:

> [T]he morphine had its customary effect—that of enduring all the external world with an intensity of interest. In the quivering leaf—in the hue of a blade of grass—in the shape of a trefoil—in the humming of a bee—in the gleaming of a dew-drop—in the breathing of the wind—in the faint odors that came from the forest—there came a whole universe of suggestion—a gay and motley train of rhapsodical and immethodical thought.

Bedloe's drug haze turns leaf, grass, and bee into objects of rapture. He revels in the Virginia terrain, and his thoughts become erratic. Captivated by his euphoric communion with the landscape, Bedloe walks on for "several hours," getting more and more lost: "'The mist deepened around me to so great an extent, that at length I was reduced to an absolute groping of the way'" (943). Bedloe's adventuring devolves into confused bewilderment.

In the process, Bedloe personifies two additional tropes of colonization: the fantasization of the new world as well as the literal misplacement of it. Columbus's eyewitness description of the Americas presented a similar dreamscape: "plenty of rivers so good and great it is a marvel" and the "most lofty mountains incomparably beyond the Island . . . ; all most beautiful in a thousand shapes, and all accessible, and full of trees of a thousand kinds, so lofty that they seem to reach the sky."[67] Columbus rhapsodized about the American topography. Just as infamously, he was lost. He believed he had landed off the coast of East Asia when he was actually anchored in the Bahamas. Similarly, generations of conquistadors quested to find incredible cities of white gold that lay hidden in the North American interior.[68] Stories of colonization, like Bedloe's memory, were the product of chimera and mistaken compass points.

Just as pertinently, Bedloe's opioid addiction is also a product of imperial enterprising, directly linked to Hastings's governorship. Hastings established the East India Company's trade in opium. He trumpeted this accomplishment at trial, listing it as one of many reasons that the "Government over which I presided . . . increased in population, wealth, agriculture, and commerce."[69] Opium ranked as the East India Company's chief export to China, where it was exchanged for tea. (In fact, the tea that American revolutionaries dumped into the Boston Harbor had shipped from China on Company boats.) Bedloe owes his morphine to Hastings's India, and it exacerbates his lostness.

At trial, too, Hastings seemed a delusional imperialist. He struggled to grasp the gravity of the accusations against him. As Macaulay recounts, he "was not sensible of the danger of his position." Tragically, "that sagacity, that judgment, that readiness in devising expedients, which had distinguished him in the East, seemed now to have forsaken him." Despite a voluminous indictment, the prosecution's protracted orations, and the scandal-loving audience in the galleries, Hastings underestimated his own precarity. He could not trust his own judgment, and he could not see his own errata.

Both Hastings and Bedloe prove unreliable observers then. Like Hastings, Bedloe insists on the soundness of his vision. As he inexplicably becomes Odleb (or, in his words, a "new man"), he asserts his equilibrium, saying he went "steadily and complacently" on his way. When he discovers he has time traveled to eighteenth-century India, he attests to his lucidity: "I felt that I had perfect command of my senses" (944). He even plays scientific empiricist, "enter[ing] into a series of tests" to confirm that the phenomenon is not a dream (946). Bedloe and Hastings assert the infallibility of their perspectives at the precise moment when empirical evidence suggests that they cannot be seeing clearly.

Such optical failures are not simply a comment on white, imperial masculinity's disordered gaze. Although they certainly perpetuate an image of a clueless empire-builder, these lapses in vision are also characteristic of clinical despondency. Esquirol confirmed that melancholia could generate a perceptual fog. Adopting the voice of his patients, Esquirol wrote: *"Objects do not come to me, do not identify themselves with my being; a thick cloud, a veil, changes the hue and aspect of bodies."* Melancholia produced its own ocular field, a sightline of brooding murkiness. Bedloe's vision then, is further impaired by his illness. In addition, his location exacerbates his debility. Esquirol noted that "seasons and climates" were a principal cause of melancholia; hence, the "foggery and humid atmosphere" that envelops Bedloe in the Ragged Mountains could magnify a depressive's symptoms.[70] Indeed, depression could disrupt Bedloe's ability to know where and even who he is. Johann Christian Heinroth posited that "in melancholia the disposition has lost its world, and becomes an empty, hollow Ego. . . . " Heinroth further noted that a melancholic has a "tendency to lose oneself . . . and thus gradually fade out into nothing."[71] In melancholia, borders cannot hold. Self and locus disappear. Bedloe's subjective absorption into the landscape and imperial masculinity reify this nothingness, this evaporation of stable personhood.

The story literalizes Bedloe's self-dissolution with his easy assimilation to the colonial scene. As he walks into Benares, Bedloe "f[alls] in with an immense populace," moving fluidly with the crowd. This immersion changes him: "Very suddenly, and by some inconceivable impulse, I became intensely imbued with personal interest in what was going on. I seemed to feel that I had an important part to play, without exactly understanding what it was." Although he does not comprehend the battle or his role in it, Bedloe stakes the political turmoil with individual significance. He feels an abrupt and decidedly British "animosity" toward the throng and takes up arms against the natives (946). Animated by white masculine identifications, Bedloe fights the colonizer's battle.

Bedloe's tendency to lose his self climaxes in his re-occupation of Oldeb's death. As he dies, Bedloe demonstrates a remarkable openness to self-obliteration. "'For many minutes,'" Bedloe states, "'my sole sentiment—my sole feeling—was that of darkness and nonentity, with the consciousness of death'" (947). Bedloe becomes obscurity, a "nonentity." Then he seemingly leaves his body. "I had no bodily, no visible, audible, or palpable presence," he recounts (948). Bedloe loses materiality. He cannot be seen, heard, or touched. He knows his corpse lies fatally wounded beneath him, "but all these things I felt—not saw. I took interest in nothing. . . . Volition I had not, but appeared to be impelled into motion, and flitted buoyantly out of the city . . . " (948). Bedloe can sense but not see. He has no will or agency. He unbecomes as effortlessly as he becomes. He vacates the imperial body and the colonial city as if he has no definite self, no fixed location.

Entranced and occupied by Templeton's memory, Bedloe cannot be trusted. Although he is not intentionally manipulative, his body is not his own. Intriguingly, the name "Bedloe" enters the historical record as a persona of deceit. Chronicling an earlier political conspiracy against Hastings in India, and the men that turned against him, Macaulay notes that "in that part of the world, a very little encouragement from power will call forth, in a week, more Oatses, and Bedloes, and Dangerfields, than Westminster Hall sees in a century."[72] In Macaulay's text, a "Bedloe" is a turncoat, forsaking integrity when power knocks. In Poe's text, a Bedloe forsakes the self, surrendering individuality to become the colonial marauder. Thus, Bedloe's story illuminates the generational reach of white imperial masculinity. Its gendered compulsions take possession of a man across generations, nations, time, and place. Subject to its dominion, Bedloe loses his very name, and not just in the slippage into Oldeb's personhood. Bedloe's obituary calls him "Bedlo," dropping the final 'e' in his surname. The missing 'e' renders Bedloe a missing person, absented from the public record of his life and death.

"Ragged Mountains" methodically erodes the bearing, perception, and reliability of its colonial adventurer. Inebriation obscures his navigation.

Colonizing identifications interrupt his relationship to place and people. Bedloe sees and feels through a melancholic shade. He loses his way and his self. Bedloe's disorientation reinforces imperial masculinity's tendency to romanticize new worlds and to mistake its own whereabouts. It also reflects Hastings's obtuseness, his inability to see the severity of the impeachment proceedings. Put simply, Bedloe's character empties imperial masculinity of credibility.

FEAR

Holistically then, the Bedloe-Templeton relationship enacts the multiple threats that lurk beneath the story's masculine allegiances: the threat of loss, sadness, and getting sick with sadness; the threat of washout and calamity; and the threat of disorientation and self-obliteration. Such menaces help explain the trepidation that men feel about each other in "Ragged Mountains." Indeterminate anxieties haunt their interactions. In a pivotal exchange, Templeton shows Bedloe a watercolor drawing of Oldeb dated 1780. It reveals the physical twinning between Bedloe and Templeton's fallen friend. The narrator confirms that the miniature is a "miraculously accurate" likeness of Bedloe's "own very remarkable features." Templeton admits that he should have shown Bedloe the portrait before, but "an unaccountable sentiment of horror" kept it back. The picture stuns Bedloe: "Its effect upon Bedloe was prodigious. He nearly fainted as he gazed" (948). Quizzically, Templeton's response to the drawing is categorized—he feels "horror"—but Bedloe's feeling goes unspecified. Bedloe almost collapses when he sees the picture, but we do not know why. What awfulness does Bedloe confront in the portrait? And what horror prevents Templeton from revealing it sooner?

The story takes a fateful turn here, and, I believe, a lethal one. In its ultimate identity slippage, "Ragged Mountains" takes Bedloe inside Templeton's affective truth, feelings he concealed with the portrait. It exposes Templeton's loss. It enables us to resee Bedloe's depression as a vector of both Templeton's sadness and Oldeb's wounding. With this revelation, we recognize Templeton as the melancholic behind Bedloe's melancholy. The doctor might be as sick—or sicker—than his patient. It was Templeton all along. Templeton caught in a traumatic imperial past; Templeton the delusional adventurer; Templeton channeling the fiascos and failures of Hastings's India and encrypting them in Bedloe's body.

In nineteenth-century medical discourses, the portrait reveals the axis of Templeton's delusion, or his idée fixe. Both Pinel and Esquirol emphasized melancholia's liability to derange its sufferers with a single-minded focus. Pinel claimed that "Melancholics are frequently absorbed by one exclusive idea . . . which appears to engage their whole attention . . . ," although they might seem rational "in all other faculties of the understanding."[73] Similarly, Esquirol postulated that the melancholic object absorbs his patients "with a degree of intenseness that is almost insurmountable," yet he also defined melancholy as "a partial delirium," allowing that the sick might seem sensible apart from the mania.[74] Once engaged, however, a melancholic could not be moved from his infatuation. Melancholia could have such an obsessive pull that Johann Christian Heinroth described it as a "[p]aralysis of the disposition" and emphasized its tyranny: The patient "is seized by some depressing passion, and then has to follow it."[75] Melancholia teemed with obsessive predilections.

With the revelation of the portrait then, the story exposes the crux of Templeton's myopia: Oldeb, his loss, his yearning. Yet Templeton's fixation is also a locus of "horror." He fears his own idée fixe. Given its homoerotic bent—and his century's sexual panics—Templeton's fear seems logical enough. Templeton fears his attraction to other men. Less obviously perhaps, Templeton may also fear his compulsion to revive his lost desire through Bedloe. And, just as importantly, he may fear the *disclosure* of his compulsion. When Bedloe sees the drawing, he sees into Templeton's longing and deviance. Templeton's horror and Bedloe's almost-collapse reinforce the shock of revelation: Something awful has been *uncovered*; something terrifying has been *unhidden*.

Tellingly, fear was believed to an integral component of melancholia. Nineteenth-century medical wisdom held that depressives were often tormented by paranoia and dread. Pinel named "gloomy suspicions" as a definitive symptom of the disease. More concretely, Pinel cited the case of "two Austrian prisoners" so petrified of the guillotine that they fell "victims to their apprehensions" and died of fright.[76] Esquirol likewise listed fear as a primary symptom of melancholia: "Fear, with all its shadows, whether the cause of it be real or imaginary, exercises the most general influence over melancholics."[77] In its construction of melancholia, the nineteenth century made no distinction between pathological sadness and pathological fear. Depression could manifest as chronic sorrow or chronic anxiety.

Accordingly, fear is a primary affect in "Ragged Mountains." Dread streams through Bedloe just before he becomes Oldeb. In this instant, Bedloe has a terrorizing encounter with the mountain: "And now an indescribable uneasiness possessed me—a species of nervous hesitation and tremor. I feared to tread, lest I should be precipitated into some abyss" (943). Bedloe may literally fear he might fall into gully or gulch, but he also fears a more indefinite void: what Freud will later call "the uncanny"—a terror animated by that which is strange yet familiar, closeted yet threatening to come out.[78] In the grip of the uncanny, we are afraid because some part of us senses the submerged. We are afraid because something in the present recalls a past "which should have been locked away or buried but which has emerged to haunt the current scene."[79] Bedloe feels this uncanny fear as he enters the realities hidden in Templeton's troubled memory. And the portrait intensifies his aphasiac disturbance.

With appalling consequences, Bedloe learns the source of Templeton's guilt. Recall that Templeton has a *"regretful* memory" of Oldeb (my emphasis). Regretful means full up with remorse, apology, and penitence. But what exactly does Templeton regret? The text suggests that Templeton may lament his inability to save Oldeb. Templeton says he "did all he could to prevent . . . [Oldeb's] rash and fatal sally" (949). We could conclude then, that Oldeb's death stalks Templeton with his soldierly failure. But Bedloe's re-experience of the skirmish that kills Oldeb does nothing to confirm Templeton's testimony. Recounting the charge from a kiosk where he and small band of soldiers took cover, Bedloe says only that "a new object took possession of my soul," and he persuades a few members of the company to his "purpose" (947). In Bedloe's retelling, no comrade presses him to remain in the pavilion. Why this discrepancy? How do we account for it? Particularly given that Templeton says Bedloe has "described, with the minutest accuracy . . . the actual events of the insurrection of Cheyte Sing" (949). Why certify the "accuracy" of Bedloe's account when Templeton's confession contradicts it? Why claim consistency and then destabilize it?

The answers to these questions emerge in the manipulations of melancholic fear. Pinel understood that melancholic fright could manifest in hostility, cunning, and violence. A "certain sourness of disposition, and a sturdy misanthropy of character" made the melancholic abusive, devious, or worse. Pinel knew patients that were "remarkably skillful in tormenting themselves and their neighbors, by imagining offences which were never intended and indulging in groundless suspicions." Melancholic paranoia could even incite murder. "Those deluded or dangerous beings can commit [the] most barbarous homicides in cold blood," Pinel warns.[80] Amplifying the workings of melancholic fear, Esquirol cataloged patients tormented by specific phobias: the wrath of God, an unjust death sentence, the toxic effects of electricity, etc. He also noted that melancholics could be racked with more nebulous apprehensions: "*I fear*, say these patients, *I fear*; but wherefore! I know not, *yet I fear.*" Although none of the patients in Esquirol's study become homicidal, many are cruel and vicious. For instance, Esquirol profiled a thirty-year-old woman, Manceau, whose "fury is almost continual": She "provokes all by her abuse," and she "strikes with the intention of doing much injury." Manceau's rage is "uncontrollable," defying forcible restraints. Another patient, Barbe, exhibited both dread and malice: "She appeared to tremble with fear, so soon as anyone approached her. . . . She drove persons from her, threatened them, called them villains, rascals, and poisoners. She seemed to recognize in us the object of her hatred, her fears and her fury."[81] The nineteenth-century melancholic could seethe with a fearful gall. Just as importantly, the idée fixe was not simply a lost object. A depressive's delusion could fixate on *menace*, a person or event that threatens ruin or death. And melancholia could incite a vindictive, retaliatory violence.

Templeton's "regretful memory" of Oldeb, then, kindles darker affects than attraction and sorrow. His obsession plausibly churns with rage, hate, and fear. Templeton's fixation—that is, the melancholic's idée fixe—is inscribed in the drawing. The picture evidences his sorrowful, paranoid, angry obsession with Oldeb. It materializes his attraction to Oldeb's double. And it exposes his desire to punish or even kill Bedloe in order to re-entomb that secret. Indeed, with a sinister ambiguity, Templeton becomes an elusive yet malicious truth in the story. We never know if Templeton orchestrates Bedloe's traumatic experience on the mountain or if it is a paranormal accident. We never know if Bedloe dies by Templeton's error or intention. The narrative explains that Templeton attempts to treat a cold and fever in Bedloe with the application of leeches to the temples. But a venomous leech gets confused with the medicinal species in the apothecary jar. The "creature fastened itself upon a small artery in the right temple," and Bedloe died quickly. The poisonous leech which Templeton purportedly (and mistakenly) uses to treat Bedloe does not actually exist. But even if the leech were real, the narrative assails the integrity of its explanation of Templeton's blunder. The story stipulates that "the poisonous sangsue of Charlottesville may always be distinguished from the medicinal leech by its blackness, and especially by its writhing or vermicular motions, which . . . resemble those of a snake" (950). Templeton fails to differentiate between two species of parasites that can "always be distinguished" by color and motility. More incriminatingly, Templeton delivers a death to Bedloe that simulates the malignant arrow that pierced Oldeb's head. Gripped by trauma, Templeton may be as compelled to re-enact Oldeb's death as he was to revive their closeness. He may be the resentful, murderous melancholic in the nineteenth-century's medical lore, punishing his lost or indifferent love object.

The unnameable horror between men in "Ragged Mountains" is their terrible vulnerability to one another. These men register the paranoia and homicidal urges that can lurk beneath fraternity, love, and grief. They fear that their desires, delusions, or failures will be exposed. They fear that comrades will turn traitor or enemy combatant. They fear that their losses will go unmourned. And they remind us that imperial masculinity closets tyrants, deviants, and melancholics alike.

FREUDIAN MELANCHOLIA

Poe's depiction of melancholic masculinity anticipates Freud's understanding of mourning and melancholia. As Mary Bradbury attests, "In many ways Freud's conception of the mental states of depression and grief was quintessentially nineteenth-century."[82] Like Poe's historical moment, Freud saw melancholia as a malady caused by loss and an obstruction of inherent energies. He believed that melancholia worked subconsciously on mind and body, and that it plagued its sufferers with obsession and delusion. Just as importantly, Freud wrestled with the intricate relationships between grief, fear, rage, and injury. He knew that some losses could be paralyzing. Freud described melancholia as "a profoundly painful dejection, cessation of interest in the outside world, loss of the capacity to love, inhibition of all activity, and a lowering of the self-regarding feelings to a degree that finds utterance in self-reproaches and self-revilings, and culminates in a delusional expectation of punishment."[83] For Freud, melancholia was a disease of the libido, a disordered form of identification and attachment. Freud maintained that the melancholic relentlessly grieves a lost object: a "loved person" or a metonymic "abstraction" that is equally dear, "such as one's country, liberty, [or an] ideal."[84] Mourning for dead comrades and former hegemonies—sick and anxious with sadness—Poe's melancholy men readily fit this criterion.

In Freud's paradigm, debilitating melancholia contrasts with healthy mourning. Loss hurls the ego into both an identity and survival struggle. In mourning, the bereaved must reclaim the parts of the self that were erotically invested in the other. Without this reclamation, the self cannot retain any sense of psychic wholeness or integrity. When the ego mourns productively, it does not identify with the dead. Instead, the survivor confronts the reality of loss and detaches the libido from what is gone. Absence "is met by the verdict of reality that the object no longer exists; and the ego . . . is persuaded by the sum of the narcissistic satisfaction it derives from being alive to sever its attachment to the object that has been abolished."[85] In uncomplicated grief, the ego confirms that the dead are dead and separates from the lost object. Intriguingly, this separation happens through a testing of reality, through trials of memory.[86] Constructive mourning relies on excessive remembering. As Tammy Clewell explains, in "obsessive recollection . . . the survivor resuscitates the existence of the lost other in the space of the psyche, replacing an actual absence with an imaginary presence." Through memory, the mourner reckons with loss. Absence gains dimension, weight, and actuality. A Freudian grief process converts remembrance into "a futureless memory."[87] Certainly, "Ragged Mountains" underscores the primacy of memory in mourning, dramatizing a recollection so intense it transports Bedloe into a re-experience of Templeton's loss. In Freud's trajectory, this memory work must be wrenching. It must compel a final fracture. Grief-stricken recollection must return the subject to a life-giving egoism so that the ego is "free and uninhibited again," ready to attach to a new object.[88]

More pathologically and in contrast, the melancholic identifies with the missing. The melancholic internalizes absence. "Thus the shadow of the object falls upon the ego," Freud writes, and "an object loss [is] transformed into an ego-loss." In melancholia, the ego holds on to the lost object, brings emptiness into itself, and makes loss the locus of libidinal investment. The length and intensity of Templeton's grief—evidenced in his concealment of Oldeb's portrait, his preoccupation with an idee fixee, his attraction to Bedloe as Oldeb's double, and so on—reflect the melancholic's ego-deficiency. Freud said that "The complex of melancholia behaves like an open wound, drawing itself to cathetic energies . . . from all directions, and emptying the ego until it is totally impoverished." Recalling the nineteenth century's belief in nervous bankruptcies, Freud described melancholia as an emotional insolvency. Indeed, he noted that "the fear of becoming poor" was a "striking feature of melancholia." Thus, Freudian melancholia turns the nineteenth-century dread of economic failure into a metaphysical chasm: "In mourning it is the world which has become poor and empty; in melancholia it is the ego itself."[89] Templeton is this poor and empty self. And Bedloe is his sickly proxy.

Contemporary race and queer theorists have reconsidered Freudian melancholia, using it to grapple with the inconsolable losses and sorrows that attend normative identity formation. Judith Butler argues that the heterosexual subject must renounce its queer desires and the possibility of queer intimacy, but it cannot openly grieve this loss. Instead, the loss disappears into a melancholic underground, permanently exiled from heterosexual consciousness. As a result, homosexuality becomes an "ungrievable loss" inside the heterosexual subject.[90] Homosexuality subsists in the heterosexual ego as a refused but obstinate specter, continuing to haunt the subject in its melancholic identification with the ghosted. David Eng and Shinee Han reconsider this melancholic attachment, reviving melancholia as a "depathologized 'structure of feeling'" and a "collective psychic condition" generated through assimilation, racialization, sexualization, and other modes of cultural becoming.[91] Immigrants and people of color, for instance, persist in a melancholic relation with whiteness and Americanness. They achieve cultural viability through a ceaseless effort to approximate an identity they can never fully attain. Because they also disown facets of their own being in that effort, they lose—and grieve—fragments of self as well. As Eng and Han write, "The effacing of a particular racial, sexual, or gender identity marks the emergence of a precarious social and psychic life."[92] Hence, melancholia infiltrates the psychic lives of both the marginalized and the dominant. The ego forms through disavowal and detachment. Freud presumed a self that could break with ex-love objects and move on—weightless and free—to new devotions. But the ruptures are inevitable, and the mourning is unavoidable. We are all forged in bereavement.

Templeton is the paradigmatic melancholic in "Ragged Mountains." He refuses to let go of lost objects. Yet his losses are multiple and contradictory. Templeton holds on to Oldeb and Bedloe, to queer love and queer death. But he also holds on to imperialist failures, thwarted privilege, and past sovereignties. Heather Love rightfully recognizes that we cannot always know the effects of dark affects. "It is difficult to distinguish between 'good' and 'bad' melancholy; melancholia itself cannot be sealed off from more problematic feelings and attitudes such as nostalgia, depression, and despair."[93] Melancholia also cannot be reserved for forms of political grief that protest the wrongful deaths of systemic oppression. Melancholia is not exclusively the province of the marginalized. Anger, sorrow, and despair are produced by the pain of oppression, but they are also produced by the "pain" of destabilized entitlements. Templeton feels such pain. He grieves from a position of supremacy, although certain griefs could destroy him.

More contentiously, Templeton reminds us that narcissism subsists at the core of melancholia. Freud's theory restricts grief to a closed economy of the self. For Freud, an essential "ego-libido" prioritizes self-love and self-survival. As it moves out of the wholeness of infancy, the ego invests in itself, cathects to itself. This ego-libido emerges as a "primary narcissism." Eventually, the subject also develops a more mature "object-libido" that cathects to objects and others outside the self. In the process, the subject constructs an ego mediated by external entities. Love is the ultimate expression of the object-libido: "It is only when a person is completely in love that the main quota of libido is transferred on to the object and the object to some extent takes the place of the ego." But the ego-libido is still nurtured by this exchange. An intense and prior self-love is reallocated to an other. As Tammy Clewell explains it, "We love others less for their uniqueness and separateness, and more for their ability to contract our own abundance, that is, to embody and reflect back that part of ourselves we have invested in them."[94] In Freud's terms, the love we feel for an other remains self-referential. The other mirrors whatever dimensions of the self that the ego-libido eroticized. We never perceive the other's otherness, and the other we love is intrinsically replaceable. Melancholia exacerbates this libidinal self-absorption. Freud saw melancholic fixation as a *"regression . . . to* original narcissism."[95] The melancholic ego quests for its own completeness. The slippage between Bedloe and Oldeb reflects the misrecognition of the love object as well as its substitutability. Templeton mistakes Bedloe for Oldeb because the ego does not see beyond its own wants and interests. Templeton substitutes Bedloe for Oldeb because his ego

quests to be whole and alive in object-love. The subject's fundamental obligation is to its own desire, its own unity, its own vitality. In this epistemology,
"the subject acquires legitimacy at the expense of the other's separateness and
well-being."[96] The melancholic always refuses the other's separateness. He
refuses to be abandoned and broken by mourning.[97]

Some thinkers maintain that this refusal is a more ethical response to loss.
Because mourning demands estrangement and eradication, melancholia is
extolled for its commitment to the dead. As Eng and Kazanjian write, melancholia "is an enduring devotion on the part of the ego to the lost object."[98]
It keeps the dead alive. Judith Butler asserts that grief itself can give life: A
"grievable life" gets seen and valued; a grievable life "counts as human."[99]
Sara Ahmed contends that this thinking "points to an ethical duty to keep the
dead other alive. The question of how to respond to loss requires us to rethink
what it means to live with death."[100] Reassessments of Freudian melancholia
affirm its intimacy with the other and its inability to forget the dead.

But it is important to remember the aggressions that melancholia autho-
rizes. The melancholic's devotion is voracious: "The ego wants to incorporate
this object into itself," Freud states, "and . . . it wants to do so by devouring
it."[101] Freud theorizes melancholia as a consumptive energy, allied with the
"oral or cannibalistic phase of libidinal development."[102] It is a hunger, an
appetite. Moreover, the melancholic encrypts the lost object in the ego so
that he can reject its absence *and* punish it. Freud argued that the depressive's self-condemnations are actually "internalized-object criticisms."[103]
As Freud writes, "everything derogatory that they say about themselves is
at bottom said about someone else." The Freudian depressive smolders with
nineteenth-century melancholic bile. Like the patients in an earlier century's
case studies, Freud's clients churn with anger and scorn. If the original object
of loss—the neglectful parent, the former lover—remains nearby, the woe-
ful melancholic takes revenge for his anguish, "tormenting" the source of
his injury. Because melancholia is a "narcissistic identification," it releases
a profound "ambivalence" in the mourner, the opposing forces of "love and
hate." Indeed, ambivalence (not simply unyielding attachment) distinguishes
melancholia from mourning. Mourning grieves one loss—one death—melancholia grieves a death and "all those situations of being slighted, neglected
or disappointed" which complicate a relationship or "reinforce an already
existing ambivalence." Freud claims that melancholic ambivalence catches
the ego in a love-hate relationship with the lost object. When "hate comes
into operation," the melancholic abuses and debases the "substitutive object
. . . making it suffer and deriving sadistic satisfaction from its suffering." Even when sadism turns inward, punishing the subject's own ego, it is
actually aggression against the other. The "self-reproaches are against a love

object" which endures in the "patient's own ego."[104] Melancholia is bound up with both ardor and abuse.

Templeton's hold on Bedloe reinforces the perils of melancholic intimacy. For years, Templeton keeps Bedloe dangerously near him, giving "his time and medical experience exclusively to the care of the invalid" (941). Bedloe's condition does not improve under Templeton's care. Indeed, he is a "reduced" relic of his former self. His closeness with Templeton sends him into war and death. The trauma Bedloe experiences inside Templeton's memory is starkly visible as he speaks. When the narrator questions the veracity of Bedloe's death on the mountain, Bedloe "hesitated, trembled, became fearfully pallid, and remained silent" (947). A week later, Bedloe dies as a result of Templeton's malpractice or malfeasance.

Freud worried about the relationship between melancholia and death. He struggled to understand the melancholic's risk for suicide. Given the herculean strength of narcissistic libido, Freud could not conceive how the "ego can consent to its own destruction." He could only conclude that "the ego can kill itself only if . . . it can treat itself as an object," only if object-cathexis proves so potent the ego will get rid of the lost object with its own death. Freud observed, too, that no "neurotic" thinks of suicide without first nursing "murderous impulses against others." Templeton does not kill himself, but death is all around him.[105] In the end, Templeton lives and Bedloe dies. The older patriarch and the patriarchy endures. Templeton memorializes his memory of the massacre in his notebook. While Bedloe is erased from official history, misnamed "Bedlo" in the newspaper notice of his death. And although Templeton may still grieve for Oldeb, who grieves for Bedloe? Sick, sad Bedloe. Colonized by Templeton's volition and pain. Possessed by an imperial masculinity he never fully understands. Dying another man's death before he dies his own.

Judith Butler, Zeynep Gambetti, and Leticia Sabsay note that assertions of pain operate at the scene of power.[106] "Ragged Mountains" reminds us that testimonies of hurt come from the victors and the vanquished. But obstruction is not always oppression. Despair is not always proof of victimization. Pain can be "real." Without necessarily being realistic in the history or the politics it creates. We should be wary of the broken patriarchs that waylay succeeding generations. We should be mindful that their "pain" has convoluted origins. We should understand that their melancholia may be as nostalgic for lost sovereignties as it is for queer intimacies. We should know that their ambivalence could kill us again—keep killing us—with the forces of sadism and hate, and with a narcissistic stake in their own persistence. We should be wary of our own melancholic identification with a bereaved white masculinity. Like Bedloe, like the narrator, we may gravitate to the relics of a dying ascendency. But mourning certain deaths—letting go of the ex-love objects that implicate us in enduring traumas and oppressions—can make us all freer. And it can open us to world of new commitments.

NOTES

1. As Ramesh Mallipeddi documents, "While eighteenth-century nautical medicine explained melancholy as a psychosomatic affliction, modern epidemiology somaticized the disorder, locating it squarely in the body. The symptoms of melancholy are produced by gastroenteritis, not by the dejection occasioned by displacement." Intriguingly, however, enslaved men seemed to be disproportionately stricken by fixed melancholy: "It was thought to wear off with young slaves and women, but the men continued 'dejected, and appeared unhappy in the extreme' throughout their forced migration" ("'A Fixed Melancholy': Migration, Memory, and the Middle Passage," *Eighteenth Century 55*, no. 2/3 [Summer/Fall 2014]: 246, 241).

2. Geo. R. Pitts, "Hints on Melancholy," *American Medical Recorder* (Oct. 1823): 596, American Periodicals.

3. Quoted in Jeffrey Meyers, *Edgar Allan Poe: His Life & Legacy* (New York: Charles Scribner's Sons, 1992), 89.

4. Charles Baudelaire, "Edgar Allan Poe: His Life and Works," in *The Works of Edgar Allan Poe* (London: John Camden Hotten, 1873), 1–21, www.eapoe.org/papers /misc1851/1873000m.htm.

5. Contemporary Varanasi.

6. Edgar Allan Poe, "A Tale of the Ragged Mountains," in *Edgar Allan Poe Tales & Sketches, Volume 2: 1843–1849*, ed. Thomas Mabbott (Urbana: University of Illinois Press, 2000), 950. Hereafter cited parenthetically in the text.

7. Jeremy Bernstein, *Dawning of the Raj: The Life and Trials of Warren Hastings* (Chicago: Ivan R. Dee, 2000), 140, 211. Plagued by delays and interruptions—including the madness of King George—the trial lasted seven years (1788–1795)—convening a little more than one hundred days in that entire span and bankrupting Hastings in the process.

8. Daniel J. Philippon, "Poe in the Ragged Mountains: Environmental History and Romantic Aesthetics," *Southern Literary Journal* 30, no. 2 (1998): 1. Michael J. S. Williams, "Poe's Ugly American: 'A Tale of the Ragged Mountains,'" *Poe Studies* 34, no. 1–2 (2001): 51.

9. Williams, "Poe's Ugly American," 51.

10. G. R. Thompson, "Is Poe's 'A Tale of the Ragged Mountains' a Hoax?" *Studies in Short Fiction* 6 (1968–1969): 454–55.

11. As Mukhtar Ali Isani explains, "Poe went back to Macaulay's essay of 1841 primarily for the description of Benares and for a review of historical information clearly in the public domain. . . . Macaulay's Indian experience (1834–1837) and the immediate availability of his description made him a logical source, of which Poe made liberal yet legitimate use" ("Some Sources for Poe's 'Tale of the Ragged Mountains,'" *Poe Studies* 5, no. 2 [1972]: 38).

12. Andrew Horn, "Poe and the Tory Tradition: The Fear of Jacquerie in 'A Tale of the Ragged Mountains,'" *ESQ* 29, no. 1 (1983): 25–30.

13. Williams, "Poe's Ugly American," 52.

14. Philippon, "Poe in the Ragged Mountains," 1–16.

15. Christina Zwarg, "Vigorous Currents, Painful Archives: The Production of Affect and History in Poe's 'Tale of the Ragged Mountains,'" *Poe Studies* 43, no. 1 (2010): 7–33.

16. Walter Benjamin theorizes these differences in his conception of dominant history. According to Benjamin, the conventional historian "re-experience[s] an epoch" through purposeful denial. He "remove[s] everything he knows about the later course of history from his head" and carries "the heaviness at heart, the acedia, which despairs of mastering the genuine historical picture." The essence of "this melancholy becomes clearer, once one asks the question, with whom does the historical writer of historicism actually empathize. The answer is irrefutably with the victor." For Benjamin, this empathy is actually atrocity. "There has never been a document of culture, which is not simultaneously one of barbarism." Benjamin holds that the erasures of history create their own violence and grief. They leave a culture mourning the bodies, counter truths, and subversive feelings buried in its silences. With Benjamin, this essay posits that "Ragged Mountains" explores the anguish that persists for the hegemon ("Theses on the Philosophy of History," in *Illuminations*, ed. Hannah Arendt, trans. Harry Zohn [New York: Schockden Books, 1968], 256).

17. Janet Oppenheim and Clark Lawlor confirm the connections between American, British, and European discourses on melancholia. Practitioners attended to the developments and insights of physicians across borders and shared a conception of melancholia as an affective disorder, a brain disease, an inherited predisposition, and liable to mania.

18. For more on imperial ideologies inherent in the trial, see Lida Maxwell, *Public Trials: Burke, Zola, Arendt and the Politics of Lost Causes* (Oxford: Oxford University Press, 2014), 37–81; Mithi Mukherjee, *India in the Shadows of Empire* (Oxford: Oxford University Press, 2010), 1–44; Jennifer Pitts, *A Turn to Empire: The Rise of Imperial Liberalism in Britain and France* (Princeton: Princeton University Press, 2005), 63–85.

19. Nicholas B. Dirks, *The Scandal of Empire: India and the Creation of Imperial Britain* (Cambridge, Mass: Belknap Press, 2006), 125.

20. In another direct parallel to the American past, Hastings's defense team argued that his actions saved the British empire at a time when America's independence had eroded its global dominion. As Macaulay writes, "The only quarter of the world in which Britain had lost nothing was the quarter in which her interests had been committed to the care of Hastings" (Thomas Babbington Macaulay, "Warren Hastings," in *Critical, Historical, and Miscellaneous Essays* [New York: Sheldon and Company, 1860], www.gutenberg.org/files/55905/55905-h/55905-, hereafter cited by author in the text).

21. Macaulay writes, "It is not too much to say that if he had been taken from head of affairs, the years 1780 and 1781 would have been as fatal to our power in Asia as to our power in America."

22. Bernstein, *Dawning of the Raj*, 224.

23. Now the northeastern region of Uttar Pradesh.

24. British philosopher, Edmund Burke (1729–1797) warred against the abuses of the East India Company in Parliament for two decades and retired after Hastings's impeachment. Scholars have long seen his writing on the trial as pivotal to the tenets and ethics of empire (Maxwell, *Public Trials*, 38). Irish playwright and impresario Richard Brinsley Sheridan (1751–1816) was elected to Parliament in 1780, launching a political career that would compass three decades. His speeches at the Hastings trial made him one of the most lionized orators of his generation (Jack E. DeRochi and Daniel J. Ennis, "Introduction," in *Richard Brinsley Sheridan: The Impresario in Political and Cultural Context* [Lewisburg, PA: Bucknell University Press, 2013], 13).

25. Thomas Babbington Macaulay, "Warren Hastings," in *Critical, Historical, and Miscellaneous Essays* (New York: Sheldon and Company, 1860), www.gutenberg.org /files/55905/55905-h/55905-h.htm. No fixed page numbers available. Hereafter cited by author in the text.

26. Quoted in Dirks, *Scandal of Empire*, 89.

27. Quoted in Glynis Ridley, "Sheridan's Courtroom Dramas: The Impeachment of Warren Hastings and the Trial of the Bounty Mutineers," in *Richard Brinsley Sheridan: The Impresario in Political and Cultural Context*, eds. Jack E. DeRochi and Daniel J. Ennis (Lewisburg: Bucknell University Press, 2013), 178. As Ridley further documents, Sheridan repeatedly likened Hastings to "the fallen angel turned tempter of mankind, that 'trickster,' 'tyrant,' and serpentine 'tempter,' Satan himself" (187).

28. Quoted in Bernstein, *Dawning of the Raj*, 257.

29. Ibid., 281.

30. G. R. Gleig, *Memoirs of the Life of the Right Hon. Warren Hastings*, Volume 3 (London: Richard Bentley, 1841), 341, play.google.com/books/ reader?id=7IIUAAAAcAAJ&pg=GBS.PP4&hl=en.

31. Quoted in Dirks, *Scandal of Empire*, 130.

32. Gleig, *Memoirs*, 531, 535, 538.

33. Ibid., 126, 125.

34. Burke never forgot Hastings's evils. During the last years of his life, Burke was still battling to convict Hastings in the popular mind. And Macaulay explains: "He saw that Hastings had been guilty of some most unjustifiable acts. . . . His reason, powerful as it was, became the slave of feelings which it should have controlled." For Burke, the Hastings decision abided as a "cruel, daring, unexampled act of public corruption." He brooded so much about Hastings's exoneration that he wanted his only memorial to be the Hastings tribunal: "Let my endeavors to save the nation from that Shame and guilt, be my monument; the only one I will ever have. Let everything I have done, said, or written be forgotten but this." Burke hoped his death would reignite the Hastings prosecution in the British consciousness. He hoped the recognition of "this barbarous and inhuman" verdict would be his estate. "Above all make out the cruelty of this pretended acquittal," he wrote (Dirks, *Scandal of Empire*, 128).

35. Declaring that Hastings allied with a tyrant, Macaulay challenged Gleig's assertion that Hastings had no power to stop a genocide: "Will Mr. Gleig seriously maintain this opinion? Is any rule more plain than this, that whoever voluntarily gives

another irresistible power over human beings is bound to take order that such power shall not be barbarously abused?"

36. See the previously cited work by Isani, Thompson, and Williams; as well as Sidney E. Lind, "Poe and Mesmerism," *PMLA*, 62 (1947):1078–85.

37. Richard Brinsley Sheridan, "At the Trial of Warren Hastings," in *World Famous Oration, Volume VI Ireland*, ed. William Jennings Bryan (New York: Funk and Wagnalls, 1906), 93, ia800705.us.archive.org/28/items/worldsfamousorat19067brya/worldsfamousorat19067brya.pdf.

38. Barbara M. Benedict, *Curiosity: A Cultural History of Early Modern Inquiry* (Chicago: University of Chicago Press, 2001), 2–3.

39. See Isani, "Source," 38–39.

40. Sheridan, "At the Trial," 93.

41. Ibid., 93.

42. David Greven, "'The Whole Numerous Race of the Melancholy among Men': Mourning, Hypocrisy, and Same-Sex Desire in Poe's *Narrative of Arthur Gordon Pym*," *Poe Studies* 41, no. 1 (2008): 31.

43. As Macaulay recounts, Prime Minister William Pitt praised Hastings's financial exploitation of Chait Singh and praised his "ability and presence of mind" during the insurrection, but "to the astonishment of all parties," he voted to impeach. In India, Hastings's leadership was notoriously besieged by his arch rival, Philip Francis. They pistol-dueled in 1780 (Francis was wounded but not killed). Francis turned public opinion against Hastings with a series of anonymous pamphlets excoriating his malfeasance, and he colluded with Sheridan and Burke in his prosecution. Macaulay corroborates the "inveterate hatred" Francis felt for Hastings.

44. Dana Luciano, *Arranging Grief: Sacred Time and the Body in Nineteenth-Century America* (New York: New York University Press, 2007), 2.

45. See David Anthony, "'Gone Distracted': 'Sleepy Hollow,' Gothic Masculinity, and the Panic of 1819," *Early American Literature* 41, no. 1 (2005): 111–44.

46. As G.J. Barker-Benfield writes, nineteenth-century "men believed their expenditure of sperm had to be governed according to an economical principle." The indiscriminate "discharge of sperm obliterated, prostrated, and blotted out the energies of the system altogether" (*The Horrors of the Half-Known Life: Male Attitudes Toward Women and Sexuality in Nineteeth-Century America* [New York: Harper & Row, 1976], 181, 180).

47. By the seventeenth century, "melancholia" increasingly denoted psychological disorder, and melancholy referenced more transient bouts of "sorrow, dejection, or despair," but "melancholy" consistently circulated as a synonym for the medical malady (Stanley W. Jackson, *Melancholia and Depression: From Hippocratic Times to Modern Times* [New Haven: Yale University Press, 1986], 5).

48. Esquirol attributed a "pale and sallow complexion" to melancholia as well as "motionless" eyes (*Mental Maladies: A Treatise on Insanity*, Classics of Medicine Library, trans. E.K. Hunt [Philadelphia: Lea and Blanchard, 1845], 203). *Mental Maladies* was first published in 1838.

49. Medical wisdom held that a depressive's diminished nervous energy could result in "'headache, backache, neuralgia, dyspeptic troubles, muscular weakness,

insomnia, chronic gout,' and even graver afflictions, such as tuberculosis" (Janet Oppenheim, *Shattered Nerves: Doctors, Patients, and Depression in Victorian England* [Oxford: Oxford University Press, 1991], 86).

50. Clark Lawlor, *From Melancholia to Prozac: A History of Depression* (Oxford: Oxford University Press, 2012), 105.

51. Jackson, *Melancholia and Depression*, 126.

52. Oppenheim, *Shattered Nerves*, 86.

53. Laura Salisbury and Andrew Shail, "Introduction" in *Neurology and Modernity: A Cultural History of Nervous Systems, 1800–1950* (New York: Palgrave MacMillan, 2010), 21, 23, 24.

54. Lawlor, *Melancholia to Prozac*, 108, 111.

55. Pinel (1745–1826) was one of the most innovative and influential physicians of the eighteenth century. He rejected the enduring association between mental illness and demonic possession, arguing that psychological disorders were caused by cultural or personal trauma, heredity factors, or physiological disease. The architect of the "moral treatment" movement, Pinel refused to treat patients with bleeding, purging, and blistering. Instead, he advocated for a therapeutic connection between doctor and patient and purposeful activity. A generation of alienists, led by Jean-Etienne-Dominique Esquirol (1772–1840), disseminated Pinel's ideas throughout Europe. Benjamin Rush, considered the first American psychiatrist, visited Pinel in Paris, cited Pinel in his work, and fueled the moral treatment movement in the United States.

56. Phillipe Pinel, *A Treatise on Insanity*, Classics of Medicine Library, trans. D. D. Davis (London, 1806), 137, 143.

57. A student of Pinel, Esquirol continued to advocate for the humane treatment of the mentally ill. He was the first physician to distinguish between cognitive ability and madness, arguing that a person's mind could be diseased and yet they could still reason and rationalize. The term "monomania" diagnosed this partial insanity. His *Mental Maladies* (1838) is considered one of the first treatises of clinical psychiatry and remained a foundational text for fifty years.

58. Esquirol, *Mental Maladies*, 213.

59. Ibid., 215.

60. Quoted in Bernstein, *Dawning of the Raj*, 204, 225.

61. Macaulay writes that as the rebellion gained momentum, "For hundreds of miles round, the whole country was in commotion. The entire population of the district of Benares took arms. . . . The infection spread to Oude. The oppressed people of that province rose up . . . refused to pay their imposts, and put the revenue officers to flight. Even Bahar was ripe for revolt."

62. Maxwell, *Public Trials*, 67, 66.

63. Luciano, *Arranging Grief*, 9.

64. In colonial Virginia, Indian summer was understood as the "smoky time," a season when Indians attacked white settlements under the cover of "smoke," including the fog that blankets the Virginia mountains and the smolder of combat fires (Philipon, "Poe in the Ragged Mountains," 7). Bedloe underlines the materiality of this environmental "smoke" when he says that the "thick and peculiar mist, or

smoke, which distinguishes the Indian Summer . . . hung heavily over all objects" and "deepen[ed] the vague impressions which these objects created" (943).

65. Williams, "Poe's Ugly American," 54.

66. This simultaneity gets more pronounced when Bedloe arrives in Benares. He sees the city from the vantage point of white masculine mastery, literally elevated above the scene. As Williams elucidates, this bearing denotes a familiar masculine command and surveillance ("Poe's Ugly American," 55). Bedloe visually penetrates Benares before he physically enters it.

67. Christopher Columbus, *The Spanish Letter of Columbus to Luis de Sant Angel* (London: G. Norman and Sons, 1893), 11.

68. Spanish conquistadors, including Juan Ponce de Leon, Hernan Cortes, Cabeza de Vaca, and others, quested to find the precious gems and metals rumored to saturate the lands north of Mexico. The most seductive stories detailed the wealth of the Seven Cities of Cibola, a "golden realm" that rivaled the riches housed by the Aztecs and Incas (Peter O. Koch, *Imaginary Cities of Gold: The Spanish Quest for Treasure in North America* [Jefferson, NC: McFarland and Company, Inc., 2009], 2).

69. Quoted in Dirks, *Scandals of Empire*, 123.

70. Esquirol, *Mental Maladies*, 206, 209.

71. Quoted in Jackson, *Melancholia and Depression*, 158.

72. Bedloe Macaulay was an English informer against the Papists in the seventeenth century.

73. Pinel, *Treatise on Insanity*, 141, 149.

74. Esquirol, *Mental Maladies*, 208, 201.

75. Quoted in Jackson, *Melancholia and Depression*, 156.

76. Pinel, *Treatise on Insanity*, 136, 142.

77. Esquirol, *Mental Maladies*, 206.

78. As Freud writes, the uncanny "is the name for everything that ought to have remained . . . secret and hidden but has come to light" ("The Uncanny," *The Standard Edition of the Complete Psychological Works of Sigmund Freud*, Volume XVII, trans. James Strachey [London: Hogarth Press, 1955], 225, uncanny.la.utexas.edu/wp-content/uploads/2016/04/freud-uncanny_001.pdf). The uncanny distinguishes itself from more pedestrian fears because it presses against a pivotal boundary: "If we have a sense of the uncanny it is because the barriers between the known and the unknown are teetering on the brink of collapse" (David Punter, "The Uncanny," in *The Routledge Companion to the Gothic*, eds. Catherine Spooner and Emma McEvoy [New York: Routledge, 2007], 130).

79. Punter, "The Uncanny," 130.

80. Pinel, *Treatise on Insanity*, 142, 138, 142.

81. Esquirol, *Mental Maladies*, 207, 222, 221.

82. Mary Bradbury, "Freud's Mourning and Melancholia," *Mortality* 6, no. 2 (2001): 214.

83. Sigmund Freud, "Mourning and Melancholia," *The Standard Edition of the Complete Psychological Works of Sigmund Freud*, Volume XIV, trans. James Strachey (London: Hogarth Press, 1964), 244, www.sas.upenn.edu/~cavitch/pdf-library/Freud_MourningAndMelancholia.pdf.

84. Ibid., 243.

85. Ibid., "Mourning," 253.

86. Freud writes, "Each single one of the memories and expectations in which the libido is bound to the object is brought up and hypercathected, and the detachment of libido is accomplished in respect of it . . . " (ibid., 245).

87. Tammy Clewell, "Mourning Beyond Melancholia: Freud's Psychoanalysis of Loss," *Journal of the American Psychoanalytic Association* 52, no. 1 (March 2004): 44.

88. Freud, "Mourning," 245.

89. Ibid., 249, 253, 252, 246.

90. Butler writes, "The foreclosure of homosexuality appears to be foundational to a certain heterosexual version of the subject. The formula 'I have never loved' someone of similar gender and 'I have never lost' any such person predicates the 'I' on the 'never-never' of that love and loss. Indeed, the ontological accomplishment of heterosexual 'being' is traced to this double negation, which forms its constitutive melancholia, an emphatic and irreversible loss that forms the tenuous basis of that 'being'" (*The Psychic Life of Power* [Stanford: Stanford University Press, 1997], 23).

91. Sara Ahmed, *Cultural Politics*, 158.

92. David L. Eng and Shinee Han, *Racial Melancholia, Racial Dissociation: On the Social and Psychic Lives of Asian Americans* (Durham: Duke University Press, 2019), 35.

93. Ibid., 38.

94. Love, *Feeling Backwards*, 150.

95. Clewell, "Mourning Beyond," 46.

96. Freud, "Mourning," 249.

97. Clewell, "Mourning Beyond," 48.

98. Freud, "Mourning," 249.

99. David L. Eng and David Kazanjian, "Introduction: Mourning Remains," *Loss: The Politics of Mourning* (University of California Press, 2002), 3.

100. Judith Butler, "Violence, Mourning, Politics," in *Precarious Life* (London: Verso, 2004), 20.

101. Ahmed, *Cultural Politics*, 158.

102. Freud, "Mourning," 249–50.

103. Ibid., 249.

104. Bradbury, "Freud's Mourning," 216.

105. Freud, "Mourning," 248, 251.

106. Ibid., 252, 257.

107. "For instance, when nations advertise their hypervulnerability to new immigrants, or men openly fear that they are now the victims of feminism, the recourse to vulnerability in such instances can become the basis for a policy that seeks to exclude or contain women and minorities, as when the vulnerability of white people constructs black people as a threat to their existence" (Judith Butler, Zeynap Gambetti, and Leticia Sabsay, "Introduction," in *Vulnerability in Resistance* [Durham: Duke University Press, 2016], 4).

Chapter Three

Disgust

In February 1806, *The Philadelphia Medical Museum* published a vivid "Account of the Dissection of a Young Man."[1] The article graphically details the man's postmortem appearance, describing "ten or eleven pints" of light brown fluid and "one pint of pus" in his abdomen; his liver "thickly coated with yellow matter"; his "inflamed" rectum; and the "blackish red colour[sic]" of his penis.[2] Nineteenth-century medical journals published scores of articles like this one, presenting the dissected innards of animals, infants, and afflicted bodies.[3] Mesmerism[4] likewise laid the nineteenth-century body bare. In *Facts in Mesmerism* (1840), Chauncey Hare Townshend prophesied that mesmerism would reveal "the exact and peculiar state of every organ and function of the human body" and that "By mesmerism we best dissect man."[5] Adam Crabtree notes that medical clairvoyance—"the somnambulist's apparent ability to diagnose disease, predict its course, and prescribe effective remedies"—ranked as "the most frequently reported" magnetic phenomenon.[6] Somnambulist Cynthia Gleason, for instance, could purportedly describe disorders of the human heart, blood, lungs, liver, and stomach.[7] Medical and mesmeric discourses represent a mass cultural interest in exposed, dead, and disgusting bodies. The corpse was integral to the rise of dissection, anatomy illustration, the rural cemetery movement, consolation literature, postmortem photography, mourning mementos, and funerary practices.

Edgar Allan Poe's "The Facts in the Case of M. Valdemar" (1845) reflects its culture's fixation on the dying and dead body. Presented as an experiment in mesmerism,[8] the story details M. Valdemar's eighteen-month surrender to tuberculosis, the magnetic suspension of his death, and the dissolution of his body when the trance ends. "Valdemar" testifies to Poe's fascination with liminal ontologies: living death, ostensible death, and mistaken death.[9] Yet "Valdemar" remains most distinct for its unchecked investment in disgust. The story painstakingly catalogues gross elements of Valdemar's physical death: his "swollen and blackened tongue"; his "distended and motionless jaws"; his "gelatinous" voice; the foul-smelling, yellow discharge from his eyes; and the "detestable putrescence" of his rotten frame.[10] Kenneth Silverman deems "Valdemar" Poe's "most gruesome tale." Jonathan Elmer applauds its evocation of "shock and disgust and uneasiness." And Thomas Mabbott calls it a "repulsive masterpiece."[11] "Valdemar" is a story of ooze, decay, and repugnance.

Valdemar's body and the disgust it elicits center my inquiry here. "Valdemar" stages nineteenth-century medicine's intercourse with the cadaver, historical anxieties about corpse contact, and the unsettling of medical detachment through revulsion. Valdemar's body disturbs P (his mesmerist) with a persistent and excessive force. Excavating that disturbance, this chapter makes two inter-related arguments. First, I contend that P's reaction reifies disgust's primary instigators: a helter-skelter mess of life and death, the perils of stickiness, and a treacherous proximity to the other. With his disgust, P rejects the odium that could penetrate his body and self as he attends Valdemar's death. And second, I hold that P's revulsion underscores a procreant relationship between disgust and desire. Valdemar's corpse activates queer, homoerotic, and necroerotic yearnings. The interworkings of mesmerism, moreover, intensify the dying body's seductive clutches. In effect, P's disgust betrays the awfulness of his own sexual hungers.

We cannot understand P's attraction to Valdemar's body—and the force of Valdemar's queerness—without an analysis of P's disgust. Saliently, the elements of disgust that "Valdemar" sensationalizes[12]—rot, degradation, proximity, and otherness—can be illuminated through the recent theorization of disgust as "affect." Gregory J. Seigworth and Melissa Gregg explain that affect studies investigate "a body's *capacity* to affect and to be affected."[13] Affect theory sees emotion as a cultural discourse, a historical construct, a subjective experience, a bodily phenomenon, and a negotiation of extant sociopolitical realities. My understanding of disgust is informed by the work of William Miller, Colin McGinn, and others. While this is a contemporary lexicon, historical studies of nineteenth-century death culture, mesmerism, and dissection ground my analysis in early American contexts.[14]

This chapter also contributes to a body of scholarship that queers Poe's canon. Gustavus Stadler reads "Valdemar" as a queer narrative, arguing that it depicts "homoerotic friction" and "the erotic sensations and substances produced in encounters between male interest and male bodies."[15] Leland S. Person examines the force of homoeroticism and homophobia across a number of Poe's tales, tracking "identificatory" experiences "so potent that a telepathic communication of thoughts and feelings occurs between two men." According to Person, these experiences are answered by violent refusals, denial, and repression. Thus, Poe's fiction registers "the inception of a powerful homophobia in the middle of the nineteenth century."[16]

To queer "Valdemar," I draw on queer history and queer theory, including the work of Sarah Ahmed, Judith Butler, Tim Dean, and Martha Nussbaum. Queer theory has generated innovative paradigms for thinking about past and present conceptions of the body, desire, and subjectivity. The history of sexuality is, of course, a robust interest of the field.[17] This work suggests that encounters with historical queer subjects reverberate with alterity, grief, and grievance. As Heather Love puts it: "The history of Western representation is littered with the corpses of gender and sexual deviants. Those who are directly identified with same-sex desire most often end up dead; if they manage to survive, it is on such compromised terms that it makes death seem attractive." "Valdemar" adds another body to this representational graveyard, dramatizing the half-life of queer survival and the tantalizing pull of death. In that sense, it contributes to what Love calls a queer "history of injury"—a history of "social damage," a history of "failure, impossibility, and loss."[18]

My study enters into this history, analyzing the intercourse between disgust, desire, and the body in "Valdemar." In the process, it explores the cultural and literary significance of the corpse; it contributes to histories and theories of disgust; it deciphers the textual allusions that queer Valdemar's character; and it interrogates historically distressed connections between sexual deviance, physical death, and social death.

DECOMPOSITION

"Valdemar" centers on the quintessential object of disgust: the decomposing body. The story ends with a stark depiction of a disintegrating cadaver: "[Valdemar's] whole frame at once—within the space of a single minute or even less, shrunk—crumbled—absolutely *rotted* away beneath my hands. Upon the bed, before that whole company, there lay a nearly liquid mass of loathsome—of detestable putrescence" (414). Colin McGinn concludes that "the rotting corpse"—the "corpse as it undergoes the process of putrefaction or decay"—is the "paradigm of the disgusting object." Winnifred Menninghaus likewise calls the decaying corpse "*the* emblem" of disgust. And Aurel Kolnai maintains that "the prototypical object of disgust is . . . the range of phenomenon associated with putrefaction. This includes corruption of living bodies, decomposition, dissolution, the odor of corpses, in general the transition of the living into the state of death."[19] McGinn notes that the corpse is at its most repulsive in the weeks immediately after death, when it liquefies, fragments, and falls apart. Thus, the depiction of Valdemar's body as a gooey mass of "putrescence" closes the story at the apex of revulsion (rather than the last stages of bodily decay).

This section focuses on that apex, considering its theoretical and historical import. I argue that Valdemar's putrid corpse leverages a pivotal engine of the disgust response: a terrible confusion of life and death. In addition, historically specific jeopardies permeate Poe's depiction of Valdemar's body. The nineteenth-century corpse agitated physical and metaphysical anxieties: fears of transition, contagion, and death itself. At the same time, antebellum American culture, and medicine in particular, quested to penetrate the corpse, bare its entrails, and comprehend its significance. Similarly, "Valdemar" immerses itself in the corpse; it represents the medicalization of nineteenth-century death watches, and yet provocatively, disgust rattles the cool detachment of the medical gaze in the story, reinforcing the hazards of the dead body.

The final scene in "Valdemar" works through the disgust that death-in-life situations provoke. McGinn declares that disgust happens in a messy, uncomfortable simultaneity of life and death. The putrid corpse represents "a riot of posthumous life" and a dead human subject. "Not pure life or pure death," the rotting corpse is an entity of "incongruity," "uncertainty," and "ambivalence." In response, McGinn concludes that a singular kind of flux—a transition—is the core of disgust: "It is the *process* of putrefaction that excites our disgust, as it shifts on object from prior life to manifest death."[20] As we shall see, "Valdemar" methodically chronicles the physical fluctuations that mark its protagonist's declension, noting a number of "fearful alteration[s]" that usher Valdemar into death (409). In historical terms, however, the process of putrefaction—Valdemar's change state—aggravated profound conundrums of identity. As Gary Laderman's work reinforces, the nineteenth-century corpse was a proxy for the lost subject: "[T]he corpse had a sacred quality greatly determined by its liminality: the former living being who had inhabited the body continued to be associated with the remains . . . and these remains were seen as unstable, indeterminate, and ambiguous." The dead body was a mediating entity, redolent with an individual's life and death. Laderman continues: "Indeed, the feelings of horror and danger provoked by the lifeless corpse combined with a sense of obligation and fidelity to the deceased. . . . "[21] Immediately after death, moreover, the fact of death itself hung in the balance; the prospect of live burial was a very real nineteenth-century fear.[22] That anxiety made the corpse seem potentially sentient and alive. Ontological, theological, and philosophical questions about the cadaver's afterlife perplexed nineteenth-century culture: Does the body have any identity-based utility after burial? Will it be raised and reunited with its wandering soul? In this epoch, the corpse had personhood and purpose; it remained vital to a dead person's subjectivity and to earthly relationships. And yet, the corpse also represented a metastasis of identity. Thus, Valdemar's awfulness invokes this indeterminacy.

Intriguingly, "Valdemar" directly engages the corpse's unknowability, chronicling a scientific quest to discover something about the terminal body. P presents Valdemar's story as a case study in death and mesmerism, framing it with three organizing queries:

> [N]o person had as yet been mesmerized in articulo mortis [in the grasp of death]. It remained to be seen, first, whether, in such condition, there existed in the patient any susceptibility to the magnetic influence; secondly, whether, if any existed it was impaired or increased by the condition; thirdly, to what extent, or for how long a period, the encroachments of Death might be arrested by the process. (408)

Driven by scientific interests, P wants to know if the dying body can be mesmerized and if mesmerism can slow death. Answering P's implicit hypothesis, Valdemar abides in a medically assisted state of deferred death for seven months.

P's investigation evidences a medical fascination with ebbing life forms and a concurrent attempt to comprehend death.[23] As Megan Stern contends, "Valdemar" reflects nineteenth-century medicine's eagerness to "understand dying, to pinpoint the moment of death, to isolate the dying and dead from the living and to demystify the status of the corpse." Medicine increasingly "scrutinized the dying process" and asserted "the need for medical expertise in diagnosing death."[24] Through dissection, autopsy, experimentation, diagnosis, prognosis, and deathbed care, nineteenth-century medicine courted death. In the process, it became that much more intimate with dying bodies, decaying bodies, and the disgust that both inspire. "Valdemar" reifies these intimacies. P, two doctors (Doctors D and F), a medical student, and an unspecified number of nurses attend Valdemar's protracted death. The story conscientiously recounts the physicians' projected time of death, their assessments of Valdemar's status, and the clinical determination that "death (or what is usually termed death) had been arrested by the mesmeric process" (413). P, Dr. D, and Dr. F make "daily calls" at Valdemar's house, examine him, take his pulse, attempt to draw his blood, check his breathing; P's hands make regular mesmeric passes over Valdemar's body; and so on (414). Holistically, the narrative methodically emphasizes the visual, spatial, and tactile familiarities of medical supervision. Death's immanence governs medical time, medical observation, and medical action in the story, and it insists on regular contact between the doctors, the magnetist, and the terminal subject.

Conspicuously, medical witnessing consistently collides with the repulsive force of Valdemar's body. In two prominent instances, the tale underscores the assembly's disgust and retreat from Valdemar's corporeality. First, when Valdemar's jaws fall open and his distended, discolored tongue appears, "so hideous beyond conception was the appearance of M. Valdemar at this moment, that there was a general shrinking back from the region of the bed" (412). And second, when he speaks at one point, "No person present even affected to deny, or attempted to repress, the unutterable, shuddering horror which these few words, thus uttered, were so well calculated to convey. Mr. L---l (the student) swooned. The nurses immediately left the chamber, and could not be induced to return" (413). Valdemar's body assumes such gross potency that it activates fainting and flight in his treatment team. Just as conspicuously, references to seeing and touching Valdemar's frame punctuate the story's ultimate image of total dissolution: P makes frenzied "mesmeric passes" as his body rots "beneath [his] hands" and a viscous pile of corporeality lies "before that whole company" (414). The "company" observes and recoils, but P stays, attends, and touches. Significantly, Poe's narrative asks us to confront the "detestable putrescence" of the dead body, and more emphatically, his mesmerist's communion with wasting flesh.

This confrontation resounds with historically situated implications. The medical proximity to Valdemar's body evokes the twin peril of the nineteenth-century corpse: the prospect of breathing or touching its pestilence. Antebellum America redefined the corpse as "a potential source of disease, pollution, and danger."[25] Early nineteenth-century medical literature warned that decomposing bodies posed serious risks to public health. In 1823, for example, the Massachusetts Medical Society cautioned that "'the earth of cemeteries in time becomes so filled with putrid matter and effluvia, as to endanger the health and the life of all those exposed.'"[26] Dead bodies were believed to spawn earthly cesspools and atmospheric pollution.[27] Putrid gases were also a documented danger of dissection. More explicitly, the early nineteenth century feared "the odor, or miasma, of decomposition."[28] The miasma theory of disease held that airborne remnants of decay—foul-smelling particles of putrefying matter—were agents of illness and death. In 1819, *The Eclectic Repertory and Analytical Review, Medical and Philosophical* informed its readers that when a Dr. Chambon "laid open the abdomen of a subject considerably advanced in decomposition," a "horrible gas immediately issued forth, and nearly overwhelmed the demonstrator and four others." One of the observers fainted and died three days later, two "remained long ill," and the dissecting physician suffered a fever and "copious perspiration."[29] Physically touching the corpse had even more lethal implications. "More dangerous still," Michael Sappol purports, "was the prospect of direct bodily contact with 'the terrible poison of the putrefying human body.'"[30] Handling the corpse meant risking pain, psychological disturbance, illness, and death. For the nineteenth century, the corpse was noxious waste and a biohazard.

Hence, Valdemar threatens his caretakers with his immediate presence. Their sickened reaction to Valdemar's wasting, however, runs counter to medical sensibilities. Medical students were taught to master their own bodies when they encountered the corpse.[31] Strikingly, in "Valdemar," disgust bursts through this professional mettle, shattering training and experience. This reaction haunts the scene, indexing failure, rift, and rupture. Why does *this* body incite medical disgust? And what exactly does P's disgust signify? What does it reveal about Valdemar's body, P's body, and the connection between their bodies? The answers to these questions are manifold, reaching into the corpse's sticky properties, Valdemar's queer subjectivity, and the cadaver's allure. Thus, the next three sections examine P's disgust as a subjective conundrum and a psychosocial tell. As we shall see, P's disgust is a meter of inadmissible intimacies and refused desires.

STICKINESS

Theories of disgust suggest that P cannot manage his revulsion because Valdemar's corpse "sticks" to him. Valdemar's body tangles with P's own corporeal grossness, and it rouses a dread of incorporation and human closeness. Here, I examine the adhesive power of the corpse. I argue that two privileged elements of Valdemar's body—pus from his eyes and his open mouth—threaten P with penetration and abjection. As a result, "Valdemar" dramatizes the terrors of the contact senses: the dread of bodily secretions, openings, and nearness.

The narrative emphasizes the viscous properties of Valdemar's body just before his total liquefaction. As Valdemar's eyes descend, "this lowering of the pupil was accompanied by the profuse out-flowing of a yellowish ichor (from beneath the lids) of a pungent and highly offensive odor" (414). William Miller explains that this "ichor" has a unique capacity to disgust. Such substances nauseate because they remind us of bodily fluids and waste products (mucus, snot, semen, feces, etc.); because they connote the "mess of gooey, oozey, slimy, smelly things" that thrive under the skin; and because they *stick*—they "leave filmy, clammy, or oily substances" on the body.[32] Syrupy substances cement us to our own body's disgustingness as well as others.' Thus, the discharge from Valdemar's eyes reinforces the corpse's stickiness, the possibility that his deathly ooze will cling to the bodies around him.

When Valdemar first enters into death's throes, the narrative sketches another insidious and captivating change, this one in his mouth. Indeed, Valdemar's mouth and tongue have been the objects of sustained critical attention.[33] The narrative reads: "The upper lip, at the same time, writhed away from the teeth, which it has previously covered completely; while the lower jaw fell with an audible jerk, leaving the mouth widely extended, and disclosing in full view the swollen and blackened tongue" (412). As he dies, Valdemar's mouth becomes gruesomely and hyperbolically exposed; it grows wider, revealing his teeth and his engorged, discolored tongue. This development turns Valdemar's body into a "deathbed horro[r]" of extraordinary proportions (412). Essential to eating and sex, the mouth functions ubiquitously in the disgust response. Paul Rozin positions the mouth "at the core of disgust."[34] According to Miller, the mouth is associated with a full range of disgusting channels, fluids, and actions: oral sex, excessive eating, chewed food, saliva, phlegm, etc. Miller classifies the mouth (along with the vagina and the anus) as an "ingesting organ."[35] And McGinn argues that ingestion drives disgust. McGinn postulates that the disgust mechanism rejects an object "not just on you, but also *in* you." The "ingestion of the disgusting object—on the tongue, the lips, in the throat, inside the stomach" is especially vile. Thus, the mouth becomes "that most sensitive of bodily zones."[36] Nineteenth-century physiognomy likewise reinforced the association between the mouth and the "animal" elements of human existence, making the mouth a nexus of sensual appetites, base instincts, and destructive immoderation.[37] When Valdemar's mouth becomes disgusting then, the story summons the panic of consumption and assimilation. His mouth reminds us that Valdemar's body is an ingestible entity and that contact with it would mean a mortifying incorporation.

Disgust itself represents a proximity problem and an identity issue. Menninghaus aptly designates the experience of an unwanted nearness as "the fundamental schema of disgust."[38] In McGinn's terms, disgust teems with aversions to "physical propinquity." Thus—our contact senses—smell, touch, and taste—stimulate its revulsions. The disgusted subject cannot bear the corporeal truths that their senses communicate. Just as notably, disgust makes us hostile to *increasing* intimacy: "the closer something comes, the greater the disgust reaction."[39] Disgust is so contact sensitive that it can stream through "sympathetic" channels, refusing objects and bodies that have had historical, cursory, or associative contact with the abhorrent.[40]

Disgust creeps into the essence of an object and the body, holding them both in a formative grip. Ahmed concludes that disgust "*over takes* the body" and "*takes over* the object."[41] Disgust initiates a holistic renegotiation of matter and meaning. The disgusting body simultaneously commands attention and compels expulsion. In Miller's words, disgust is "the uneasiness, the panic . . . that attends the awareness of being defiled."[42] The disgusting entity permanently plagues what it touches. According to Daniel Kelly, it has "the ability to infect other items with its offensiveness; it can pass on its disgustingness and contaminate otherwise pure and undisgusting entities."[43] The reach of the awful implicates us in its awfulness: "The disgusting object has left its mark on you, shaping you, transforming you."[44] Disgust mobilizes a dread of physical violation and subjective degradation. Under its sway, we patrol borders. As Miller reasons, "Disgust helps mark boundaries of culture and boundaries of the self."[45] Implicitly, the disgust reaction fears disgust itself. It fears disgust's sensations, operations, and effects; it fears disgust's portability and pliability; it fears disgust's capacity to attach to other objects and bodies. It fears a terrible becoming. It is afraid that intimacy is identity, that we are what we touch, what we eat, what we metabolize.

In its attention to ichor and orifice then, "Valdemar" activates terrors of stickiness, ingestion, and transformation. Valdemar's viscosity and distended mouth agitate the worry that his body—in all its atrociousness—might adhere to, infiltrate, or abase adjacent bodies. Contact with Valdemar jeopardizes the soma and the psyche. By this logic, P violently rejects what might happen to his body—and his subjectivity—as he manages Valdemar's death. With his repugnance, P refuses the touch of decomposition and any change that touch might instigate.

QUEERING VALDEMAR

Provocatively, nightmares of transformation also infiltrate nineteenth-century conceptions of corpse contact. Authoritative discourses postulated that regular communion with dead bodies could corrupt individual character. Detractors claimed that the cadaver could "incite desire (necrophilia), inspire contempt for humanity, or lead [medical] students to reject Christianity . . . and so jeopardize their immortal souls."[46] Paradoxically, however, nineteenth-century America also gravitated to the corpse, even its detachable parts and decay. Antebellum death rituals necessitated a sustained closeness with the recently dead body: Loved ones reverently washed, shaved, and dressed the corpse in a shroud or winding sheet. The body remained at home for one to three days and was constantly attended.[47] Mourners braided the corpse's hair into "bracelets, broaches, watch chains, and other jewelry items."[48] Posthumous mourning pictures—paintings and photographs—were "taken from the physical remains before burial," capturing dead bodies upright, in chairs, in the arms of family members, holding books, or in their "last sleep."[49] Poe kept locks of his dead wife's hair in a sheaf of paper, and he commissioned a postmortem mourning portrait of Virginia that shows "how her head fell and her eyes and lips relaxed in the moments following her death."[50] Scholars implicate postmortem pictures in a pervasive cultural urge to deny or domesticate death, but this archive also documents a coincident attraction to morbidity.[51] A circa 1843 photograph depicts a dead woman in profile with dried blood running from nose to neck; an image dated 1846 portrays a mother cradling a child obviously stiff with rigor mortis; and a number of pictures showcase visibly emaciated children—pale, gaunt, skeletal, and grotesque.[52] These images reveal a keen preoccupation with dead corporealities.

This enthrallment outlasted funeral rites and burials. Laderman affirms that nineteenth-century culture exhibited a "consuming interest in detailed descriptions" of terminal disease and "a powerful desire to observe bodily decay."[53] Lewis Saum notes the excessive "physiological detail" that pervades accounts of death in antebellum letters.[54] Nineteenth-century diarists also tracked quotidian signs of decomposition in the recently deceased; mourners lifted coffin lids to see putrefaction in the faces of lost loved ones; indeed, Emerson opened his late wife's coffin a full year after her death.[55] The culture also romanticized more fleshly reunions with corpses. In a *New York Weekly Museum* story, "The Dead Infant" (1816), a desolate mother tears the lid from her child's coffin, takes him home, and refuses to part with his body. Debilitated by grief, "she once more pressed him with redoubled force to her breast, again kissed his putrid cheek—and slept her final sleep."[56] Laderman emphasizes the affective dimensions of this attachment to the disintegrating body, noting that "the feeling of loss—the overbearing absence associated with the death of a close relation—often led to a fixation on the corpse."[57] But the historical record indicates that something more salacious also drove this mania. The residents of Salem, Massachusetts, for example, turned the disinterment of a former minister into a public spectacle: The community gathered to see the unburied corpse "'which was exposed in a high state of putrefaction.'"[58] Sensational literature amplified the cadaver's lascivious potential, representing it in lurid, sexualized terms.[59] The nineteenth-century corpse titillated and teased.

Disgust can also seduce its subjects.[60] Disgust and desire circle one another, suffused with reciprocal urgencies and compulsions. Miller theorizes that the disgusting "can attract as well as repel" and that the disgusting "has the power to allure."[61] Ahmed remarks that "disgust is deeply ambivalent, involving desire for, or an attraction towards, the very objects that are felt to be repellent."[62] And Kristeva defines the abject as "a vortex of summons and repulsion."[63] Disgust agitates clashing yet interconnected sensations, working through an oscillation between desire and renunciation, craving and queasiness. Other theorists posit a more coercive relationship between disgust and desire, arguing that disgust circumvents and contains unruly hungers. Miller maintains that disgust prevents the activation of "unconscious desires, barely admitted fascinations, or furtive curiosities." Kolnai says that "we shun what is disgusting only because otherwise we should take hold of it, something which must not happen." McGinn likewise claims that disgust operates to restrain "infinite, unquenchable" wanting.[64] By this reasoning, P's disgust expels Valdmar's body *and* the desires it rouses.

In what follows, I excavate the yearnings that Valdemar's corpse activates. More concretely, I examine the queer signifiers written into Valdemar's character and a tragically formative relationship between queerness and disgust. For my purposes, "queer" describes bodies that exist outside binary, heterosexual, procreative, and conventionally human frameworks. Eve Kosofsky Sedgwick says queer extends to "the open mesh of possibilities, gaps, overlaps, dissonances and resonances, lapses and excesses of meaning when the constituent elements of anyone's gender, of anyone's sexuality aren't made (or can't be made) to signify monolithically."[65] Carla Freccero explains that queer names the deviant and "the force of that deviation"; queer "is what is strange, odd, funny, not quite right, improper."[66] Queer denotes subjectivities and materialities that flummox the norm. Valdemar represents this kind of queerness: He is sexually perplexing and physically strange, and he lives the queer subject's raw exposure to the machinations of disgust and death.

Valdemar is discernibly queer—in cultural and corporeal terms. Presumably an immigrant, Valdemar translated the Polish versions of Schiller's *Wallenstein* and Rabelais's *Gargantua*, and he currently resides in Harlem, New York. The allusion to Rabelais's tale aligns Valdemar with a bawdy, fantastic fiction and with queer forces and bodies.[67] William Benemann, moreover, substantiates the early American association between the immigrant and homoerotic networks of men in Europe's urban centers, noting that male-male sexual subcultures and practices might have been more familiar to the "foreigner" in this era.[68] Analyzing a series of newspaper attacks against American "sodomites" in 1842, Jonathan Katz likewise underscores the assumption that "acts of sodomites . . . were not native to America or natural to Americans" and affirms the emergence of New York's queer "underworld."[69] More pointedly, Leland Person recovers editorial accounts of "male cruising behavior" at Five Points and other city streets.[70] Thus, Poe marks Valdemar's queerness with geographic cues, making him both a New Yorker and an immigrant. In addition, P calls Valdemar a "friend," a term that extended to sexualized love between men in the eighteenth and early nineteenth centuries. As Richard Godbeer testifies, early American "romantic friendships" could be "physically affectionate and yet nonerotic" or they could be sexually intimate, passionate, and loving.[71] Benemann defines early American male friendship as a "complex web of profound affection and sexual attraction," an arena where platonic affinity could flow into erotic fervor.[72] Shadowed by the "bugger," the "sodomite," the "molly," or the "mouche," the term "friend" was the only word available to affirmatively yet covertly name sexual relationships between early American men.[73] Its identifying presence in "Valdemar" actually makes it that much more difficult to determine the affiliation between P and Valdemar: acquaintance? comrade? lover?

Other elements of Valdemar's character code queer, as well. He lives alone, apparently wifeless and childless, and he is notably odd: "particularly noticeable for the extreme sparseness of his person—his lower limbs much resembling those of John Randolph, and, also, for the whiteness of his whiskers, in violent contrast to the blackness of his hair—the latter, in consequence, being very generally mistaken for a wig" (408). Valdemar is physically strange: excessively thin, with dissonant or abnormal bodily features. John Randolph (1773–1833), the referent in this description, was a Virginia plantation owner and congressman. He was notorious for his flamboyant dress, delicacy, effeminacy, and irregular legs. As David Johnson's biography records, Randolph's contemporaries described him as a "'flowing gargoyle,'" "'pale, meager, ghostly,'" and "'grotesque.'"[74] His legs were long and heavy, thickening toward the ankles, and he had stark black hair. He drank copiously and used drugs liberally. He chronically suffered from innumerable illnesses and ailments, and he died of tuberculosis. He never married, though he was rumored to suffer from unrequited love or to have a secret wife. Benemann documents his intense romantic friendships with three different men during his youth. For most of his lifetime, Randolph was presumed unmanly, impotent, or celibate. At his death, a physician attributed his sexual apathy to his underdeveloped testicles. The scandal that came in the wake of this revelation squashed further explanation, and we do not know "whether the examination revealed him to be a hermaphrodite, or a suffering from undescended or malformed testicles or some other disease or trauma."[75] Randolph's race politics were just as puzzling: He owned almost four hundred slaves and virulently defended the institution, but he questioned the ethics of slaveholding, considered his slaves friends and family, and his will provided for their manumission and resettlement.[76] The stark contrast between Valdemar's white whiskers and black hair metaphorically writes Randolph's race confusion into Valdemar's body. And the analogy to the senator's "lower limbs" implicitly aligns Valdemar with Randolph's malformed legs, atypical genitals, and confounding sexuality. Holistically, the allusion to Randolph amplifies Valdemar's queerness, punctuating his bachelorhood, childlessness, physical oddity, and sexual opacity.

P's medical objectification of Valdemar's body further queers—and, indeed, enfreaks him—in physical and social terms. Gabrielle Foreman illuminates the historical relationship between "medical knowledge generation and white uses of black bodies."[77] My own work shows that "queer bodies like Valdemar's became the object of relentless medical scrutiny and violation in the nineteenth century."[78] While Nadja Durbach reinforces the historical synapses between freak shows and medical inquiry in the same epoch, medical schools—especially in the South—disproportionately relied on enslaved, black corpses to teach the fundamentals of anatomy. And "nineteenth-century

displays of human oddities regularly used the language of science and medicine" to substantiate claims that their particular freaks were "both rare and
genuine." The corpses of indigenous and black people were museum attractions well into the twentieth century. Julia Pastrana's dead body—billed
as "the Nondescript," "the Gorilla Woman," or the "Ugliest Woman in the
World" during her lifetime—was exhibited at London's prestigious art gallery, 191 Piccadilly. The museum assured prospective spectators that "'her
skin is as fresh and her body is as plump, as if she were alive.'"[79] Similarly,
the body of an enslaved man named Fortune was first dissected by his physi-
cian-slave master, his skeleton preserved by the family, and his bones eventually became "the most popular exhibit for decades" at the Mattatuck Museum
in Connecticut.[80] More fundamentally, "relegating the dead body to any
secular, economic, or scientific purpose" in this epoch was both ethically and
sexually suspect. "It was especially barbaric to put the cadaver on display . . .
: pundits considered dissection 'a rape of the body,' another 'skin trade' akin
to slavery and prostitution. According to nineteenth-century principles, P's
desire to turn Valdemar's body into experimental matter, to convert his death
into a scientific exhibition, suggests something rapacious in his character."[81]
Altogether, the graphic, medicalized display of Valdemar's corpse intensifies
the racial amalgamations, gender/sexual difference, and social alienation that
queer him.

Thus, it follows that Valdemar embodies the queer subject's liability to
be judged disgusting. Martha Nussbaum asserts that because sex enacts an
exchange of otherwise disgusting substances (semen, sweat, saliva, vaginal
fluids, etc.) and because sex "marks us as bodily beings," disgust often infiltrates social conceptions of sexuality. "In almost all societies," Nussbaum
expounds, "people identify a group of sexual actors as disgusting or pathological." As a result, disgust operates as a powerful "mechanism of stigmati-
zation."[82] Multiple theorists acknowledge that the United States historically
stigmatizes homosexuality in this way, cataloging it as sick and revolting.[83]
Any deviance from heterosexuality, Rozin attests, is often classed "as
unnatural, inhuman, and therefore disgusting."[84] More narrowly, Nussbaum
contends that the gay male body catalyzes disgust (especially for other men)
because it is "imagined as anally penetrable," because it invokes the menace
of semen and feces infiltrating the body, and because "nonpenetrability is a
sacred boundary against stickiness, ooze, and death."[85]

The nineteenth century pilloried male sexual intimacy with similar justifications and a terrifying zeal. Frederick Hollick's 1852 treatise on venereal
disease described male-male sexuality as a "disgusting affection."[86] And
Jonathan Katz reinforces sodomy's disgusting connotations in this era:
"Because of its unspoken link with anal intercourse, sodomy was an especially frightening term, redolent of excrement, dirt, corruption, crime, and

death." Male-male sexuality was reviled for its extramarital, nonreproductive, and unnatural effects. The nineteenth century deemed it "'abominable'" and punished it with religious censure and brutal prison sentences.[87] As a queer subject, therefore, Valdemar figures a singular repugnance: the disgust reserved for the sexual deviant. His life as a corpse symbolizes and amplifies the logic of sexual disgust. Like homosexuality, the cadaver represents nonreproductive sex, a perverted object choice, stickiness, secretion, infiltration, and death.

Yet onanism may have constituted the grossest sex offense in the 1830s and 1840s. David Leverenz reads "Valdemar's" climax—the "ejaculations of 'dead! Dead! absolutely bursting from'" Valdemar's black tongue—as a "grotesque masturbation fantasy" where a white man discovers that "he has been masturbating with a black man's penis."[88] Revealingly, the masturbating body most notoriously materializes the antebellum interstices between sex, disgust, and death that Valdemar represents. Tissot's pivotal treatise on masturbation, *Onanism*, opens with the fatal invocation: "Our bodies are constantly wasting." Further tangling sex and death, Tissot lists masturbation as an aggravating cause of consumption, the disease that kills Valdemar. Tissot's case studies, moreover, include spectacles of autoerotic horror that percolate with ooze, stink, and cadaverousness. After a year of unrelenting self-pollution, one young man constantly secretes seminal fluid; his body appears "dry, emaciated, pale, dirty, exhaling a disagreeable odor, almost motionless"; a "bloody discharge issue[s] from his nose"; his eyes are "watery, dim, and fixed"; he suffers from diarrhea and voids "his feces involuntarily." Like Valdemar, Tissot's onanist lies seeping, deteriorating, and dying. Indeed, Tissot concludes: "I found him more like a corpse than a living being."[89] Sylvester Graham's *A Lecture to Young Men* disseminated these terminal sexual pathologies to a mass American audience.[90] His catalog of the masturbator's physical distresses spans almost ten pages and includes "purulent discharges from the anus"; "feeble and languid" circulation; a "small, slow" pulse, "gushing of blood from the mouth and nostrils"; fistulas that "discharge great quantities of foetid, loathsome pus"; "a general wasting of the body and deterioration of all its tissues and substances"; "dry and brittle" bones; decaying "black and loose" teeth; "pale, flassid [sic], and often ulcerous" gums; numbness of the whole body; and "a general withering, and impotence, and decay" of the genitals.[91] Advanced onanism sinks the body into its most disgusting parts—its orifices, excretions, and rot—and, like Valdemar, the afflicted live on the edge of bodily death. Just as importantly, Graham's masturbator literally yearns for death, feeling suicidal pinnacles of "self-contempt, and disgust": "He would give worlds to be annihilated. His life is intolerable. And he often determines, and still fears to throw it off."[92] As an incorrigible sex offender, the onanist becomes ugly morbidity.

Foucault maintains that the sociomedical wars against masturbation were integral to the nineteenth-century "deployment of sexuality" and the evolution of the "abnormal individual."[93] Analyzing this history, Ladelle McWhorter perceives that the onanist will become the "late nineteenth century's sexual predator[s]"—the "black rapist," the "syphilitic whore," the "sex-crazed imbecile," the "female sexual invert," and the "homosexual child molester."[94] Thomas Laqueur says that the most relentless and unifying objection against solitary sex was that it reflected and fueled "unnatural" desires.[95] Aberrant, nonprocreative, and oppositional, the onanist represents a historical shade of queerness. Sedgwick sees the masturbator as "a powerful form of *sexuality*" that runs "fully athwart the precious and embattled sexual *identities* whose meaning and outlines we always insist on thinking we know."[96] "Valdemar" traces the ghastly corporealities that were essential to this sexuality and its history. Through Valdemar's physicality, the story somatizes a vital connection between sexual deviance, disgust, and death. "Valdemar" reminds us that the corpse—the disgusting body, the dying body—lies entombed within the historical queer body, waiting for its awful life to begin.

Thus, Valdemar's cadaverous subsistence anticipates the modern relationship between queerness and social death. Sarah Ahmed recognizes that queerness gets "read as a form of 'non-life'—with the death implied by being seen as non-reproductive." Because queerness constitutes a failed ontology—an aborted heterosexuality or a barren sexuality—"then queers are perhaps even already dead and cannot die."[97] Dominant culture sees queerness as nonprocreative, infertile, and therefore lifeless (or alive only with the certainty of extinction). Lee Edelman argues that queerness is so constitutionally opposed to "social viability" that it exists in death, abjection, and the absence of futurity.[98] Judith Butler likewise posits a critical link between sexual aberration and an unlivable life; as Butler writes, the anomalous "I" becomes "unknowable, threatened with unviability, with becoming undone altogether."[99] Cultural legibility and validation are crucial to an ontological survival—to the I's ability to thrive in its social location. Relegated to invisibility and sterility, queer people are social corpses. When Valdemar becomes the cadaver, his body makes the queer subject's cultural annihilation literal and material.

NECROSEXUAL INTENSITIES

Because mesmerism worked through a kinetics of intense desire and gravitation, P becomes increasingly implicated in Valdemar's queer, terminal corporeality. Poyen listed "intimate connexion [sic] with the magnetizer" among the definitive characteristics of the phenomenon.[100] Townshend identified "attraction towards the mesmerizer" as a signature characteristic of sleepwaking, describing patients compelled to follow him, mirror his movements, and repulsed by anyone else's touch.[101] Mesmerism defined the "rapport" between magnetizer and somnambulist as relationship of affective absorption and interdependence.[102] In an especially acute state of rapport, for instance, a young male patient seized Townshend's hands and refused to release him: "[E]very effort that I made to free my hands only made him grasp them more firmly. . . . " Townshend writes, "I had raised a spirit which I could not quell, and the work of my hands had become as unmanageable as the creation of Frankenstein."[103] Townshend observed an even more pronounced and eroticized affinity between Mr. K and a seventeen-year-old boy named "Theodore." Under K's influence, Theodore refused to let K go even "a short distance from him." If K tried to leave the room, Theodore "dragged him back with considerable agitation, which was only calmed by the mesmerizer caressing him." Theodore grew increasingly demonstrative in his devotion to K: "On all occasions, he testified to the strongest attachment to K frequently leaning his head upon the shoulder of the latter, and running to him . . . on the slightest motion of his hand."[104] K's encounter with Theodore registers the (homo)erotic implications of mesmeric encounters. In magnetic sleep, Theodore becomes insistent on K's physical nearness, effusive, and affectionate. Magnetic attraction held both mesmerist and somnambulist in its grip, fostering desires it could not reliably predict or subdue.[105]

In this final section, I analyze the erotics of the affiliation between P and Valdemar. Remarkably, P's magnetic occupation of Valdemar reaches its zenith as Valdemar becomes the corpse; thus, I argue that their intimacy surges with both homosexual and necrosexual attractions. Magnetic sympathies of volition and sensation further entangle P in an erotic link to Valdemar's cadaverousness. In its sleep state, Valdemar's body effectively mirrors—and potentially divulges—P's yearnings and inclinations. Hence, P's disgust rejects more than an unwelcome communion with queerness, putrescence, and death. It also refuses an uncomfortable proximity to his own desires.

Practitioners and pundits decried the sexual potency of the magnetic bond. Standard mesmeric intimacies—"passes" over the body, touching, eye-gazing, attraction, obedience, dependence, and suggestion—constituted real sexual dangers. As Louis Rostan wrote in 1825, "The somnambulist develops toward her magnetizer a gratitude, an attachment without boundaries. She will freely follow him as a dog follows his master. The path is not long from there to true passion. . . . How does one resist repeated touches, tender looks, daily meetings, protestations of interest . . . ?"[106] Mesmerism exposed patients to powerfully erogenous stimuli, yearnings, and impulses. Joseph Deleuze naively describes the orgasmic effects of magnetic sleep when he cautions prospective magnetizers against "any act of impudence" with patients: "It often happens," Deleuze explains, "that the first impression of magnetism produces a crisis, accompanied with convulsive motions, stiffness of the limbs, and fits of laughing or crying." In one episode Deleuze cites, after four to five minutes of long passes and placing his hands on a woman's stomach, the patient "cried out 'O, what an agreeable sensation!' One minute after she was seized with convulsive movements; her limbs were stiffened; her neck became swollen; and she threw her head back, uttering shrieks." When the convulsions subsided, "a laughing fit succeeded," she "gradually became calm," and told Deleuze that "she felt very well, and . . . she did not believe she had suffered."[107] Magnetizers, too, felt the wanton impact of the bond. Some mesmerists admitted sexual misconduct; others were accused of it.[108] And while mesmeric discourse tried to desexualize or heteronormalize this threat, its queer potential was encoded in the conception of magnetic rapport and attraction.

"Valdemar" subtly but steadily evokes the erotics of mesmeric contact as Valdemar recedes into an ever more cadaverous condition. Not satisfied with observing unmistakable "signs of the mesmeric influence" in Valdemar's eyes, P "continued the manipulations vigorously, and with the fullest exertion of the will, until I had completely stiffened the limbs of the slumberer, after placing them in a seemingly easy position." Valdemar's prostrate body— "stiffened" and arranged in an "easy position" by P—exhibits an erotic receptivity here. The description goes on to emphasize his body's relaxed approachability: "The legs were at full length; the arms were nearly so, and reposed at a moderate distance from the loins. The head was very slightly elevated" (411). Valdemar lies quiet, open, and amenable. P's subsequent observation posits a connection between this tranquil pliancy and living death. Three hours later, "[Valdemar] lay in the same position; the pulse was imperceptible; the breathing was gentle (scarcely noticeable, unless through the application of a mirror to the lips); the eyes were closed naturally; and the limbs were as rigid and as cold as marble" (411). Without a discernible pulse or breath, and with a pseudo rigor mortis settling in, Valdemar's body approximates death. Tellingly, once Valdemar enters this deathly repose, P achieves full magnetic rapport with him: "As I approached M. Valdemar, I made a kind of half effort to influence his right arm into pursuit of my own, as I passed the latter gently to and fro above his person. In such experiments with this patient I had never perfectly succeeded before, and assuredly I had little thought of succeeding now; but to my astonishment, his arm very readily, although feebly, followed every direction I assigned it with mine" (411). P realizes mesmerism's signature identification with Valdemar—full bodily rapport—when Valdemar becomes the undead corpse. In other words, the more Valdemar embodies death, the closer P gets to a complete, embodied intimacy with him. Because mesmerism relied on intense psychosomatic attractions between mesmerizer and patient, the fusion between P and Valdemar hums with homoerotic and necroerotic energies.

In *Desiring the Dead*, Lisa Downing advocates for a more capacious definition of necrophilia, one that goes beyond sex with a dead body. Downing agilely challenges the reductive assumption that necrophilia means simply "sexual intercourse with the corpse," venturing that it extends to an encounter "between the living erotic imagination" and the outlawed object of its desire. Downing recasts necrophilia "as a desirous and idealizing relation to death."[109] Underscoring such nuances, Patricia McCormack purports that the necrophile "enter[s] into a desiring intensity with the corpse." P's magnetic link to Valdemar's dying and dead body represents that "desiring intensity," that "desirous . . . relation to death."[110] Indeed, the pronounced physical evolutions that mark Valdemar's descent into death come *after* P establishes a mesmeric affinity with him. And when Valdemar's hand no longer moves under P's direction, "the vibratory movement of his tongue" continues to affirm P's mesmeric hold on him (413). Valdemar consistently tries to answer P's questions, and the more sexualized body parts—the tongue, the mouth—remain attuned to P. Just as suggestively, Valdemar persists in an exclusive, monogamous communion with P. "To queries put to him by any other personal than myself he seemed utterly insensible—although [I] endeavored to place each member of the company in mesmeric rapport with him" (413). Because mesmerism works through circuits of captivation and desire, these bodily ties resonate with necrosexual synergies. P sustains a mesmeric connection with Valdemar's increasingly cadaverous subjectivity because magnetic gravitation remains alive between them. In that sense, P becomes the necrophile, sustaining a "desiring intensity" with P's rotting flesh.

Mesmerism produced confusions of experience, volition, and identity that exacerbate this intensity, further catching P in a necrophilic attachment to Valdemar's body.[111] Mesmerism created what Townshend called a "sensitive and motive sympathy" between magnetizer and sleepwaker.[112] In effect, the mesmerist's sensations and yearnings surged through his patients. Townshend observed that somnambulists experienced an ability to taste, touch, feel, and smell anything the mesmerist encountered. Townshend describes patients' bodies and facial expressions moving with their mesmerist's, wincing with a mesmerist's injury, and correctly naming his sensate experiences (e.g., the taste of wine, coffee, brandy, and water; the smells of flowers and tobacco; the feel of household objects). For Townshend, this reciprocity testified to mesmerism's ability to propel the desires, and by extension, the intentions, of its subjects. As Townshend wrote, sleepwaking subdued and redirected individual will: "It cannot, if it would, rise to freedom [because the will's] . . . motive force, desire, is evidently changed, since, as I have shown, the sleepwaker adopts . . . the likings and dislikings of the mesmerizer." Mesmerism facilitated extraordinary projections of inclination, agency, and being. In response, Townshend theorized: "There is an identification between the mesmerizer's will and [the somnambulist's]." The "attractive force" between them pulls so strongly that the patient "exists [there] even more than in himself."[113] Townshend saw mesmerism as a psychosomatic byway, one that relocated a sleepwaker's axis of sensation, volition, and subjectivity. Under magnetic influence, the somnambulist internalized the mesmerizer's thoughts, feelings, and aims, living more in the force of the rapport than in their own body or mind.

Plausibly then, P's connection to Valdemar could reveal as much or more about what P wants—what he wills, what he fantasizes—than it does about Valdemar's desires. Jonathan Elmer deciphers the syntactical affinity between P's objectives and Valdemar's: When P fails to "re-compose" his patient because of a "total abeyance of the will," he does not specify whose will defies re-composition[114]: Does Valdemar resist P's effort to restore the trance and preserve the integrity of his body? Or does Valdemar's liquefaction manifest P's deepest craving and intention? Because magnetic subjects reflected the desires and sensations of their mesmerists, the sleepwaker is an unruly vehicle of sexual truth. As R. S. owned in *The Confessions of a Magnetizer* (1845): "You assume her hands, which are clasped in your own, you look intently into the pupils of her eyes. . . . Then is her mind all your own, and she will evince the most tender solicitude and care for your good. . . . [S]omnambulists will stop at no point beyond which they may afford you pleasure should you indicate it by thought or word."[115] Somnambulists offered their physicians whatever pleasures they requested—in "thought or word." Their symbiotic relationship with the magnetizer suggests that even subterranean desires might be sensed and sated.

Hence, P's disgust rebukes an unwanted intimacy with his own desire. Ahmed notes that disgust does not simply repel the ingestion of an external, alien other; it rejects the awful inside us: "What threatens from the outside only threatens insofar as it is already within."[116] That interior menace may be the pull of a homosexual or necrosexual yearning. Or it may the profligate, indiscriminate force of desire itself. Sianne Ngai observes that "desire seems capable of being vague, amorphous, and even idiosyncratic in ways that disgust cannot." In other words, "Disgust is urgent and specific; desire can be ambivalent and vague."[117] P's disgust both defines and refuses his desire. Indeed, it clarifies and repudiates what Tim Dean terms "the impersonality of desire." Dean suggests that deviant desires may "remind us of how desire itself remains potentially anti-normative, incompletely assimilable . . . inimical to the model of the person, fundamentally impersonal."[118] Dean asserts that desire has to be trained to attach to human bodies, live bodies, gendered bodies, adult bodies, genitals, genital intercourse, and so on. Fundamentally, desire can be staunchly indifferent to the identity of its objects or our own subjectivity.

The "impersonality of desire" resonates with antebellum understandings of sex and sexuality; for early America, desire was inherently omnivorous and "impersonal." This cultural epoch comprehensively scorned all pre- or extramarital impulses, including masturbation. And "sodomy" denoted any non-procreative or "unnatural" sexual act between men, women, animals, and children.[119] Early American desire was opportunistic, voracious, and undifferentiated. Sexual transgression, moreover, was not an expression of a distinct identity or targeted orientation; it signified more ubiquitously, evidencing original sin and the innate depravity of the human condition. As Katz writes, "an urge to perform sodomy was not . . . restricted to a particular, small minority of Americans: it was considered a general propensity of fallen humans."[120] In other words, while both "sodomy" and "buggery" named criminal and sinful male-male sexual activity, "sodomite" and "bugger" were not fixed or interior identities with a coherent sexual objective.[121] Laqueur, moreover, contends that the masturbation wars gained unprecedented cultural traction because self-pollution exposed the undifferentiated desires that prowl—sly and insatiable—within the subject. The onanist always wants "more and more"; his desire is always "out of control"; masturbation only produces "more desire, not its fulfillment."[122] P's disgust, therefore, revolts against an intrinsically nebulous desire—a desire that wants indiscriminately and expansively, a desire that may fuck death itself.

In its rancid body, "Valdemar" materializes ominous cultural affinities between desire and disgust, sex and death. These affinities will generate a profound ontological paradox. Foucault privileges this period as the antecedent to a fateful arrival: "the point where we expect our intelligibility to come from what was for many centuries thought of as madness; the plenitude of our body from what was long considered its stigma and . . . wound; our identity from what was perceived as an obscure and nameless urge." Foucault recognizes that the modern sexual subject owes his life to a historically stigmatizing, wounding, and inchoate force. More primally, his identity is steeped in death. The nineteenth-century sexual regime makes a "Faustian pact" with its subjects: "to exchange life in its entirety for sex itself, for the truth and sovereignty of sex. Sex is worth dying for. It is in this (strictly historical sense) that sex is indeed imbued with the death instinct."[123] "Valdemar" archives a culture that did not go gently into this darkness. This historical change state was met with shudder and recoil. Indeed, P's disgust haunts contemporary sex and sexuality with seductive yet lethal truths. Desire will open us to the corpse. It will liquefy and putrefy us. It will leave us dead on the bed. Yet some bodies—queer bodies—live the bond between sex and death uniquely, excessively, and traumatically.

NOTES

1. An earlier version of this chapter appeared as, "Cadaverous Intimacies: Disgust, Desire, and the Corpse in Edgar Allan Poe's 'Valdemar,'" *Criticism* 58, no. 4 (Fall 2016): 565–92.

2. "An Account of the Dissection of a Young Man, Who Died Dropsical . . . ," *Philadelphia Medical Museum*, Feb 4, 1806, search.proquest.com/americanperiodicals.

3. A search of the *American Periodicals* database on November 29, 2012, elicited over 4,500 articles devoted to dissection published between 1800 and 1850, including pieces on the dissection of an alligator, an orangutan, a possum, individual arms and legs, an opiate overdose, children with congenital differences, victims of pertussis, dyspepsia, tuberculosis, and cholera, and so on.

4. Originating with the work of Franz Anton Mesmer in the 1770s, animal magnetism (subsequently mesmerism) held that a magnetic fluid connected planets, the earth, and human bodies. Mesmer believed that this fluid could be manipulated to cure illness. Mesmer's predecessors refined his practice and his suppositions, emphasizing the induction and impact of a trance, or "magnetic sleep" state, in patients. This evolution led to extraordinary medical and psychological phenomenon, including telepathy and medical clairvoyance. For more on the emergence and history of animal magnetism in the United States, see Robert C. Fuller, *Mesmerism and the American Cure of Souls* (Philadelphia: University of Pennsylvania Press, 1982), 16–47.

5. Chauncey Hare Townshend, *Facts in Mesmerism with Reasons for a Dispassionate Inquiry into It*, 2nd ed. (London: T. G. Wiegel, 1844), 112.

6. Adam Crabtree, *From Mesmer to Freud: Magnetic Sleep and the Roots of Psychological Healing* (New Haven: Yale University Press, 1993), 173.

7. Charles Poyen describes Cynthia Ann Gleason's diagnostic abilities in *Progress of Animal Magnetism in New England* (Boston: Weeks, Jordon & Co, 1837), 144–47. Adam Crabtree explains that Poyen popularized magnetism in the United States, demonstrating its wonders across the Atlantic seaboard in 1836 and publishing *Progress* in 1837. Joseph Deleuze wrote the "most widely read compendium of magnetic practice," and "its influence was particularly great in the United States" (*From Mesmer to Freud*, 131, 135). My study draws on both Poyen's and Deleuze's texts, but it relies primarily on Chauncey Hare Townshend's *Facts in Mesmerism*, published in 1840 and "issued in several subsequent British and American editions" (*From Mesmer to Freud*, 149). As Bruce Mills notes, Poe read and was deeply influenced by Townshend's work (*Poe, Fuller, and the Mesmeric Arts: Transition States in the American Renaissance* [Columbia: University of Missouri Press, 2006], 44).

8. Robert Fuller notes that when "Valdemar" was first published, "debates raged over the factuality of Poe's story. . . . Newspapers and magazines were inundated with letters from readers demanding assurance that Poe's account was wholly fictional" (*Mesmerism and the American Cure*, 38).

9. Kenneth Silverman argues that a "peculiar cluster of dead-alive persons" populate Poe's poetry and fiction, and "the question of whether the dead remain dead" propels his later writings (*Mournful*, 76). Ruth Mayer affirms, "More than any other author of the nineteenth-century," Poe dramatizes "the traumatic fears released by the

popular frenzy concerning apparent death" ("Neither Life Nor Death: Poe's Aesthetic Transfiguration of Popular Notions of Death," *Poe Studies/Dark Romanticism* 29, no. 1 [June 1996]: 2). And Judith E. Pike contends that Poe's writings reveal "a profound ambivalence towards the dead body" that pervaded the cult of mourning and that they "reinvest the dead body with the corporeality" which this cult "attempts to eradicate" ("Poe and the Revenge of the Exquisite Corpse," *Studies in American Fiction* 26, no. 2 [Autumn 1998]: 1).

10. Edgar Allan Poe, "The Facts in the Case of M. Valdemar," in *The Selected Writings of Edgar Allan Poe*, ed. G. R. Thompson (New York: W. W. Norton, 2004), 412, 413, 414. Hereafter cited parenthetically in the text.

11. Silverman, *Mournful*, x; Thomas Ollive Mabbott, ed., *The Collected Works of Edgar Allan Poe, Volume III: Tales and Sketches* (Cambridge: Balknap Press, 1978), 1228, Edgar Allan Poe Society of Baltimore, www.eapoe.org/works/mabbott/tom3t027.htm, last modified October 20, 2012; Jonathan Elmer, *Reading at the Social Limit: Affect, Mass Culture, and Edgar Allan Poe* (Stanford: Stanford University Press, 1995), 123.

12. David S. Reynolds illuminates Poe's mastery of the sensational: "Poe brought control and intentionality to sensational themes that appeared more chaotically in lesser texts." More concretely, Poe used "exaggeration" to cultivate grotesque and horrific affects (*Beneath the American Renaissance: The Subversive Imagination in the Age of Emerson and Melville* [New York: Alfred A. Knopf, 1988], 230–31, 231).

13. Gregory J. Seigworth and Melissa Gregg, "An Inventory of Shimmers," *The Affect Theory Reader* (Durham: Duke University Press, 2010), 2.

14. Winfried Menninghaus's study of disgust documents the history of triggers that my argument elucidates, including "repugnant defects of skin and form, loathsome discharges . . . repellent sexual practices, [and] an obscene, decaying corpse" (*Disgust: The Theory and History of a Strong Sensation* [Albany: SUNY Press, 2003], 7). More narrowly but pertinently, William Ian Miller sees modern disgust-inducers ("tactility," "purity," "bodily shame," and "group definition") already operative in Charles Darwin's *The Expression of the Emotions in Man and Animals* (1872) (*The Anatomy of Disgust* [Cambridge: Harvard University Press, 1997], 169, 3).

15. Gustavus T. Stadler, "Poe and Queer Studies," *Poe Studies/Dark Romanticism* 33, no. 1–2 (2000): 20.

16. Person, "Queer Poe," 7, 8.

17. Of course, Michel Foucault's three-volume *History of Sexuality* is a foundational and formative work in the field. The other scholars I cite in this essay—Jonathan Katz, Heather Love, Eve Kosofsky Segdwick, Jennifer Terry, and so on—likewise testify to the vibrancy of queer historiography.

18. Heather Love, *Feeling Backward: Loss and the Politics of Queer History* (Cambridge: Harvard University Press, 2007), 1, 29, 21.

19. Colin McGinn, *The Meaning of Disgust* (Oxford: Oxford University Press, 2011), 13. Menninghaus, *Disgust*, 1. Aurel Kolnai, *On Disgust*, Barry Smith and Carolyn Korsmeyer, eds. (Chicago: Open Court, 2004), 53.

20. McGinn, *Meaning of Disgust*, 90, 91.

21. Gary Laderman, *The Sacred Remains: American Attitudes Toward Death, 1799–1883* (New Haven: Yale University Press, 1996), 27.

22. Ibid., 31.

23. Martin Willis holds that P "differentiates" himself from the medical professionals in the story, although he is the "primary scientific figure in the tale" (*Mesmerist, Monsters, and Machines: Science Fiction and the Cultures of Science in the Nineteenth Century* [Kent: Kent State University Press, 2006], 118, 119). But it's more accurate to read P as scientist, medical practitioner, and mesmerist. Since its inception, mesmerism was a "system of healing," used to treat a seemingly infinite range of illnesses, including respiratory disorders, headaches, injury, hysteria, convulsions, and so on (Crabtree, *From Mesmer to Freud*, 109, 110–13). And Alison Winter explains that "there were no definitive medical orthodoxies to police the profession and to define a medical 'heterodoxy,'" during this interval. Winter documents mesmerism's presence in nineteenth-century hospitals, sickrooms, and research settings. While mesmerism would foment more pernicious "contests over scientific and medical authority" later in the century, in the 1830s and 1840s, it was a medical practice *and* a science of the mind (Winter, *Mesmerized*, 6, 9). As a magnetist, then, P has both medical and scientific authority.

24. Megan Stern, "'Yes:—no:—I have been sleeping—and now—now—I am dead': Undeath, the Body, and Medicine," *Studies in History and Philosophy of Biological and Biomedical Sciences* 39, no. 3 (2008): 348, 347, 348.

25. Alan C. Swedlund, *Shadows in the Valley: A Cultural History of Illness, Death, and Loss in New England, 1840–1916* (Amherst: University of Massachusetts Press, 2010), 172.

26. Quoted in Laderman, *Sacred Remains*, 70.

27. This notion of toxic putrescence premised "the exile of the dead from the space of the living" and the rural cemetery movement inaugurated by Boston's Mount Auburn Memorial Park (Ibid., 70).

28. Swedland, *Shadows in the Valley*, 172.

29. M. Percy, "On the Dangers of Dissection," Eclectic Repository and Analytical Review, Medical and Philsophical (January 1819), search.proquest.com/americanperiodicals.

30. Michael Sappol, *A Traffic of Dead Bodies: Anatomy and Embodied Social Identity in Nineteenth-Century America* (Princeton: Princeton University Press, 2002), 79.

31. An 1830s journalist trumpeted stoic medical students who "'wallow in the filth of the dissecting room, with a cheerful and animated countenance, and sustain the most offensive effluvia without a qualm, for the sake of unraveling the morbid condition of some rotten viscous'"(quoted in Sappol, *Traffic of Dead Bodies*, 80). Nineteenth-century physicians were primed in affective implacability. Sappol explains that clowning circumvented a medical student's sensitivities: "alcoholic jollity, morbid humor, dissecting room antics, and body snatching were very much part of a fraternalist medical school culture." More specifically, "pranks involving body parts were common. Students courted disaster by throwing pieces of their dissections at visitors, displaying severed limbs in windows, or taking bodies and body parts home. Classmates dared each other to snatch bodies from graveyards or even from

death vigils." The medical students' reckless camaraderie hardened more professionally suspect emotions. Turning corpses into "sport" evidenced strength, control, and
an imperviousness to the dead body (*Traffic of Dead Bodies*, 81, 84, 83).

32. Miller, *Anatomy of Disgust*, 60, 62, 53, 58.

33. David Leverenz reads P's reaction to Valdemar's tongue as a "grotesque masturbation fantasy" where a white man discovers that "he has been masturbating with
a black man's penis" ("Spanking the Master: Mind-Body Crossings in Poe's Sensationalism," in *A Historical Guide to Edgar Allan Poe*, ed. J. Gerald Kennedy [Oxford:
Oxford University Press, 2001], 118). And Adam Frank underscores Poe's "blatant
depiction of the disgusted and disgusting face" here, arguing that Valdemar's facial
characteristics—"upper lip up, mouth distended, tongue out"—reflect "the overly
legible expression of disgust" ("Valdemar's Tongue, Poe's Telegraphy," *ELH* 72, no.
3 [2005]: 655).

34. Paul Rozin et al., "Disgust," in *Handbook of Emotions*, eds. Michael Lewis and
Jeannette M. Haviland (New York: Guilford Press, 1993), 576.

35. Miller, *Anatomy of Disgust*, 98.

36. McGinn, *Meaning of Disgust*, 41, 42.

37. Lucy Hartley, *Physiognomy and the Meaning of Expression in
Nineteenth-Century Culture* (Cambridge: Cambridge University Press, 2001), 34.
Lavater's *Physiognomy* postulated that the shape and size of the lips could signify "an
inclination to pleasure," "coldness, industry, a love of order," "sensuality and indolence," "anxiety and avarice," "consideration, discretion, and firmness," or "courage
and fortitude." The color and configuration of the teeth could evidence "weakness and
pusillanimity," "sickness," or "some mental imperfection." And visible upper gums
were associated with "much cold and phlegm" (Ellis Shookman, ed., *The Faces of
Physiognomy: Interdisciplinary Approaches to Johann Casper Lavater* [Columbia,
SC: Camden House, 1993], 71–74, 75–76).

38. Menninghaus, *Disgust*, 1.

39. McGinn, *Meaning of Disgust*, 41, 43.

40. Rachel Herz, *That's Disgusting: Unraveling the Mysteries of Repulsion* (New
York: W. W. Norton, 2012), 106.

41. Sara Ahmed, *Cultural Politics*, 84.

42. Miller, *Anatomy of Disgust*, 2.

43. Daniel Kelly, *Yuck!: the Nature and Moral Significance of Disgust* (Cambridge:
MIT Press, 2000), 19.

44. McGinn, *Meaning of Disgust*, 43.

45. Miller, *Anatomy of Disgust*, 50.

46. Sappol, *Traffic of Dead Bodies*, 79.

47. For more on antebellum death rituals, see Laderman, *Sacred Remains*, 27–38.

48. Ann Schofield, "The Fashion of Mourning," in *Representations of Death in
Nineteenth-Century US Writing and Culture*, ed. Lucy E. Frank (Burlington, VT:
Ashgate, 2007), 162.

49. Laderman, *Sacred Remains*, 77.

50. Adam C. Bradford, *Communities of Death: Whitman, Poe, and the American
Culture of Mourning* (Columbia: University of Missouri Press, 2014), 30.

51. Jay Ruby notes that "last sleep" imagery dominates postmortem photography from 1840–1880. This portraiture reinforces the belief that people did not die and that death was an eternal rest and release (*Secure the Shadow: Death and Photography in America* [Cambridge: MIT Press, 1995], 65, 63). For more on postmortem photography, see Michael J. Steiner, *A Study of the Intellectual and Material Culture of Death in Nineteenth-Century America* (Lewiston, NY: Edwin Mellon Press, 2003), 59–110.

52. See, for example, "Malnourished Girl with Flowers on Blanket," "Close Up of a Dead Woman with Blood," "Mother Holds Daughter with Rigor Mortis While Father Mourns," "Child Dead from Dehydration due to Intestinal Disease"; Stanley B. Burns, *Sleeping Beauty: Memorial Photography in America* (Altadena, CA: Twelvetree Press, 1999), 15, 16, 20, 23.

53. Laderman, *Sacred Remains*, 75, 76.

54. Lewis Saum, "Death in the Popular Mind of Pre-Civil War America," in *Death in America*, ed. David E. Stannard (Philadelphia: University of Pennsylvania Press, 1975), 34.

55. Laderman, *Sacred Remains*, 76.

56. "The Dead Infant; or, the Agonizing Mother," *New York Weekly Museum*, 4, no. 9 (June 29, 1816): 135, proquest.com/americanperiodicals.

57. Laderman, *Sacred Remains*, 74.

58. Quoted in Ibid., 76.

59. As Laderman puts it, sensational literature fed a cultural appetite for "lust," "adventure," and "dismembered and rotting corpses" (*Sacred Remains*, 79).

60. Carolyn Korsmeyer summarizes a range of theoretical explanations for the "magnetism of disgust" in her study of "aesthetic disgust" (*Savoring Disgust: The Foul and the Fair in Aesthetics* [Oxford: Oxford University Press, 2011], 113–36).

61. Miller, *Anatomy of Disgust*, x, 111.

62. Ahmed, *Cultural Politics*, 84.

63. Julia Kristeva, *Powers of Horror: An Essay on Abjection*, trans. Leon S. Roudiez (New York: Columbia University Press, 1982), 1.

64. Miller, *Anatomy of Disgust*, 110; Kolnai, *On Disgust*, 77; McGinn, *The Meaning of Disgust*, 124.

65. Eve Kosofsky Sedgwick, *Tendencies* (Durham: Duke University Press, 1993), 8.

66. Carla Freccero, *Queer/Early/Modern* (Durham: Duke University Press, 2006), 18.

67. A bawdy, fantastic fiction, *Gargantua* chronicles the life, education, and exploits of its giant protagonist. Gargantua embodies excess, irreverence, and immensity. As an adult, Gargantua builds the Abbey of Desire: an open-air convent with a pleasure garden, a theater, swimming pools, and playing fields. The Abbey houses both women and men; it allows residents to come and go freely, to marry, to acquire riches. Its constitution stipulates only "do what you will" (Francois Rabelais, *Gargantua and Pantagruel*, trans. Burton Raffel [New York: W. W. Norton, 1990], 124).

68. William Benemann, *Male-Male Intimacy in Early America: Beyond Romantic Friendships* (New York: The Haworth Press, 2006), 29.

69. Jonathan Katz, *Love Stories: Sex Between Men Before Homosexuality* (Chicago: University of Chicago Press, 2001), 49, 45.

70. Person, "Queer Poe," 11.

71. Richard Godbeer, *The Overflowing of Friendship: Love Between Men and the Creation of the American Republic* (Baltimore: Johns Hopkins University Press, 2009), 6.

72. Benemann, *Male-Male Intimacy*, xvii.

73. Benemann contextualizes these terms in *Male-Male Intimacy*, chapters 2 and 4.

74. David Johnson, *John Randolph of Roanoke* (Baton Rouge: Louisiana State University Press, 2012), 2.

75. Benemann, *Male-Male Intimacy*, 193.

76. Jennifer Terry illustrates that in early medical discourses, "the homosexual was viewed as having the same characteristics that distinguished 'primitive' races from their 'advanced' European counterparts, namely degeneracy, atavism, regression, and hypersexuality. In this respect, race functioned as both an *analogous* and *synonymous* rubric for conceptualizing sexuality in its deviant homosexual form" (*An American Obsession: Science, Medicine, and Homosexuality in Modern Society* [Chicago: University of Chicago Press, 1999], 36).Thus, Randolph's racial attachments and confusions magnify his queerness.

77. P. Gabrielle Foreman, "New England's Fortune: An Inheritance of Black Bodies and Bones," *Journal of American Studies* 49, no. 2 (May 2015): 289.

78. Suzanne Ashworth, "Experimental Matter, Unclaimed Death, and Posthumous Futures in Poe's 'Valdemar,'" *Poe Studies* 49 (2016): 59.

79. Nadja Durbach, "'Skinless Wonders': 'Body Worlds' and the Victorian Freak Show," *Journal of the History of Medicine and Allied Sciences* 69, no. 1 (January 2014): 54, 39.

80. Foreman, "Fortune," 288.

81. Ashworth, "Experimental Matter," 60.

82. Martha Nussbaum, *From Disgust to Humanity: Sexual Orientation & Constitutional Law* (Oxford: Oxford University Press, 2010), 17. Nussbaum offers a more extensive analysis of disgust and legal edicts against homosexuality, obscenity, sodomy, and necrophilia in *Hiding from Humanity: Disgust, Shame, and the Law* (Princeton: Princeton University Press, 2004), 107–57.

83. Kelly, *Yuck*, 31; McGinn, *The Meaning of Disgust*, x; Herz, *That's Disgusting*, 182–83.

84. Rozin et al., "Disgust," 587.

85. Nussbaum, *From Disgust to Humanity*, 18.

86. Quoted in Benemann, *Male-Male Intimacy*, 139.

87. Katz, *Love Stories*, 52, 56, 64.

88. Leverenz, "Spanking the Master," 118.

89. Samuel August Tissot, *A Treatise on the Diseases Produced by Onanism* (New York: Collins & Hannay, 1832), 1, 17, 19, archive.org/details/57110430R.nlm.nih.gov.

90. Helen Lefkowitz Horowitz notes that Graham, a well-known temperance reformer, lecturer, and writer, "brought Tissot's concerns to the attention of many

Americans" in the 1830s (*Rereading Sex: Battles over Sexual Knowledge and Suppression in Nineteenth-Century America* [New York: Vintage Books, 2003], 93).

91. Graham, *Lectures*, 94, 97, 100, 101, 112, 113.

92. Ibid., 114.

93. See Foucault, *History of Sexuality*, 103–14, and *Abnormal: Lectures at the College de France 1974–1975*, trans. Graham Burchell (New York: Picador, 1999), 55–80.

94. Ladelle McWhorter, *Racism and Sexual Oppression in Anglo-America: A Genealogy* (Bloomington: Indiana University Press, 2009), 172.

95. Thomas W. Laqueur, *Solitary Sex: A Cultural History of Masturbation* (New York: Zone Books, 2003), 209.

96. Eve Kosofsky Sedgwick, "Jane Austen and the Masturbating Girl," *Critical Inquiry* 17, no. 4 (Summer 1991): 826.

97. Ahmed, *Cultural Politics*, 156.

98. Edelman, *No Future*, 9.

99. Butler, *Undoing Gender* (New York: Routledge, 2004), 3.

100. Poyen, *Progress*, 63.

101. Townshend, *Facts in Mesmerism*, 68–69.

102. As Adam Crabtree explains, "The rapport between magnetizer and somnambulist . . . allows two beings that have the same physical constitution to modify each other's magnetic fluids" (*From Mesmer to Freud*, 74).

103. Townshend, *Facts in Mesmerism*, 56, 56–57.

104. Ibid., 48.

105. Adam Frank reasons that "mesmerism offered Poe and his contemporaries a medium at once spiritual and material in which an individual's sensations or feelings could be imagined to be connected to those of others and to larger social networks." Just as pertinently, Frank reinforces Poe's interest in mesmeric connections between male bodies as well as magnetic "excess or loss of control" ("Valdemar's Tongue," 639).

106. Quoted in Crabtree, *From Mesmer to Freud*, 98.

107. Joseph Phillipe Francois Deleuze, *Practical Instruction in Animal Magnetism*, trans. Thomas C. Hartshorn (New York: D. Appleton & Co, 1843), 49, 50, books.google.com.

108. For more on the sexual scandals and anxieties that shadowed magnetism, see Whorton, *Nature Cures*, 110, and Crabtree, *From Mesmer to Freud*, 89–105.

109. Lisa Downing, *Desiring the Dead: Necrophilia and Nineteenth-Century French Literature* (Oxford: Legenda, 2003), 3, 5.

110. Patricia McCormack, "Necrosexuality," *Rhizomes* 11, no.12 (Fall 2005–Spring 2006): par. 12, http://www.rhizomes.net/issue11/maccormack/index.html.

111. As Alison Winter writes, mesmeric "influences bound human beings to each other intimately, if invisibly. It was commonly claimed that communication consisted of the transfer of vital fluids between two bodies, that people's minds and bodies touched each other immaterially in mysterious ways. Demonstrations could display forms of interpersonal communication and influence that seemed to dissolve the boundaries between two people or to subsume one person's identity in another's"

(*Mesmerized: Powers of Mind in Victorian Britain* [Chicago: University of Chicago Press, 1998], 119).

112. Townshend, *Facts in Mesmerism*, 119.

113. Ibid., 135, 136, 199.

114. Elmer, *Reading*, 123.

115. Quoted in Crabtree, *From Mesmer to Freud*, 99.

116. Ahmed, *Cultural Politics*, 86.

117. Sianne Ngai, *Ugly Feelings* (Cambridge: Harvard University Press, 2005), 335, 337.

118. Tim Dean, *Beyond Sexuality* (Chicago: University of Chicago Press, 2000), 238, 240.

119. John D'Emilio and Estelle B. Freedman, *Intimate Matters: A History of Sexuality in America* (New York: Harper & Row, 1988), 30. With one qualification: "the term sodomy was not applied to sexual relations between women" (D'Emilio and Freedman, *Intimate Matters*, 30).

120. Katz, *Love Stories*, 67.

121. Benemann, *Male–Male Intimacy*, ix–x.

122. Laqueur, *Solitary Pleasures*, 237, 239.

123. Foucault, *History of Sexuality*, 156.

Chapter Four

Resentment

"After my treatment on yesterday and what passed between us this morning, I can hardly think you will be surprised at the contents of this letter. My determination is at length taken—to leave your house and indeavor [sic] to find some place in this wide world, where I will be treated—not as *you* have treated me—"[1]

—Edgar Allan Poe, *letter to John Allan*, March 19, 1827

Poe made this proclamation to his foster father, John Allan, two months after he returned home from his first, and only, year at the University of Virginia, and within hours after he was banished from Allan's Richmond estate. That year prefaced the disintegration of Poe's relationship with John Allan, and a heart-wrenching experience with a mercurial patriarch. It began with financial struggles. Allan sent Poe to school without enough money to cover room, board, and books. Poe quickly went into debt, borrowing money at exorbitant interest to pay for "wood, washing, and other necessaries."[2] Allan sent funds periodically, but never enough. Poe resorted to gambling for income, and his crises mounted. He returned home insolvent, and Allan refused to support him for another term.

In Richmond, the hostility between Poe and Allan erupted into a two-day row. Allan ordered Poe out of the house, and Poe immediately wrote a letter to his foster father that enumerated his grievances against him. Poe accused Allan of mistreatment, sabotage, and emotional indifference. One cannot underestimate the pain of this alienation for Poe. Parentless by the age of two—and separated from his brother and sister—John Allan's rejection was a second orphaning. Poe's closing lines in that first, fateful letter show how much he still wanted John Allan's approval, despite his anger. He said he hoped to get a job, support himself, save money, and re-enroll at university. Some part of Poe forever remained the prodigal son, yearning for a paternal mercy that would never come.

For the next six years, Poe erratically corresponded with Allan, and those surviving letters center this chapter. The correspondence begins in 1826, when Poe arrived at university, and it ends in 1833, a year before John Allan's death. For my purposes, the letters represent three chronological and yet distinct intervals. First, a pivotal year from May 1826 to March 1827, which culminates in Poe's expulsion from Allan's home and the "grievance" letter described above. Second, two years of tentative, temporary reconciliations, from December 1828 to January 1831, when Poe sought admittance to West Point and Allan's favor. This period ends with Poe's dismissal from the academy and the longest letter Poe writes to Allan, a blistering indictment of his abuses. And third, February 1831 to April 1833, a final, tortured two years when Poe pleaded with Allan for money.

Collectively, the letters document the affective intricacies of grievance and resentment. My argument excavates the tangled relationships between resentment, time, and unjust harm. Here, I examine how resentment works on and through memories of powerlessness and loss. In his resentment, Poe fixated on the past, on specific events in his short life as Allan's ward. I show that Poe's bitterness emerged within a relationship of patriarchal subordination, and that behind his resentment, Poe nursed an agonizing oedipal grief. In response, Poe worked hard to re-establish himself as Allan's ward and protégé. He tried. He aimed to be a good Southern son. But Poe failed to recognize the obstinacy of Allan's contempt. He continued to believe in the prospect of reconciliation. So he remained vulnerable to compounding frustrations and rejections. More tragically, his attempt to heal the oedipal fracture—to change John Allan—miscarried. Thus, he was left only with grief, only with the phantom of a lost ideal. As resentment theory anticipates, Poe found some reparation in victimization. As a victim of unconscionable injury, Poe assumed a powerful moral authority. He arbitrated ethical right, wrong, and justice itself. Just as potently, his fictions teach us that there is also recompense in the fantasies his resentment inspired: fantasies of protest, reconciliation, or revenge.

In methodological terms, I situate the letters in biographical, cultural, and theoretical contexts. More concretely, I explore the events of the past that tangle with the acrimony between Poe and John Allan. The injuries that Poe named over and over in his letters centered on Allan's failures as a guardian and surrogate father. He castigated Allan for derailing his education, reputation, and professional prospects. With more vitriol, he brooded on Allan's refusals to save him from poverty. In this disgruntlement, Poe expresses the sensitivities of a masculinity alive with the principles of postrevolutionary American manhood and Southern honor. But Allan answered injury with injury, admonishing his foster son with his own grievances. Allan's retaliation reflects select principles of Southern parenting, particularly its vexed relationship with the white supremacies of self-willed boys and the edicts of self-reliance. Historical and theoretical conceptions of resentment further illuminate the hostility in the letters. As we shall see, the letters reinforce the significance of *injury*—an unjust wounding—in the persistence of resentment. In addition, resentment discourses emphasize the peril of the Allan-Poe feud for Poe. Resentment theory holds that without resolution—without the exorcism of an apology, forgiveness, or revenge—bitterness will sicken the subject. Indeed, resentment is a pathology of re-feeling. Because resentment refuses to forget, the subject relentlessly re-experiences an original injury. Preoccupied with prior harms, Poe sought redemption through worldly achievement, turning to manly exertion to win Allan's love. When that effort failed, he simmered with the affects of resentment, including grief, rage, and indignation.

FRACTURE

Poe entered the University of Virginia in 1826, the year after it opened. The school was the dreamscape of its chancellor, Thomas Jefferson. Jefferson designed the college "to form the statesmen, legislators, and judges, on whom public prosperity and individual happiness are so much to depend."[3] Poe's matriculation fulfilled the pledge John Allan made to Poe's paternal grandfather when the orphaned child became his ward.[4] It also represented a perilous rite of passage. In the South, more than the North, university arbitrated a boy's entry into manhood. Founded in an era of increasing factionalism, Southern universities were pre-confederate microcosms. They nurtured "state pride and regional defensiveness," and they educated a moneyed demographic: the sons of planters, politicians, doctors, and lawyers.[5] As Lorri Glover explains, "The price of attending these schools ensured a gentry clientele. Virginia ranked as the most expensive school in the United States by 1840."[6] At university, the South's elite young men were urged to increase the future value of their characters. As Timothy Williams explains, learning to be a man—to "elevate mind over temperament, restraint over impulse, and independence over dependence"—was the purpose of college.[7] Parents were explicit about the stakes of this interval, warning sons that success or failure would permanently define them. As his son left for college, for example, Kentucky lawyer and Supreme Court justice Thomas Todd cautioned that debauchery now would mean "'respectability is forever gone, no exertion can produce a reformation and you will sink into contempt & misery.'"[8] Recklessness at school could forever exile a man from a viable masculinity.[9]

Poe and his contemporaries, moreover, were uniquely measured by the mettle of the men who birthed the nation. The questions that shadowed their rise were: "Could boys born of the generation after the founders live up to the high standards set by their fathers? Would they be faithful stewards of the Republic?"[10] Postrevolutionary men were conditioned to be "republican machines" (in the words of Benjamin Rush), ever ready to serve state and country. In Poe's era, the begetters of American independence represented the pinnacle of manly achievement. As a result, masculine identifications were directed "vertically . . . toward abstracted and idealized founding fathers."[11] American men "idealized the dying generation of revolutionary fathers" and worked to create a politics of "brothers."[12] In other words, these men experienced American manhood with a decidedly filial disposition: "National manhood was symbolically and structurally oedipalized."[13] That dynamic fueled insecurities about the fitness of American sons for the pressures of nation-building. As revolutionary patriots aged and died, unprecedented anxieties emerged about the nascent men who would shoulder the fate of the United States.

For Poe then, university was a crucible of his manly potential as well as his political worth. While his academic performance attested to his intellectual and creative promise, his disgrace became a dark omen. As this section illustrates, Poe's disastrous year in Charlottesville rendered him an outcast, suddenly impoverished and wounded by Allan's scorn. More importantly for my purposes, this year would prove formative in the advent of Poe's resentment. In future years, Poe would remember this time as an unforgivable collision of another man's neglect, obstruction, and betrayal.

Initially, Poe flourished at school. He excelled in French, Italian, and Latin. He wrote poems and sketched in charcoal. He earned the highest academic honors, debated formidably in the Jefferson Society, and excelled as an athlete. His surviving letters home reinforce both a determination to succeed and honest trepidations. Anticipating exams, he says: "I have been studying a great deal in order to be prepared, and dare say I shall come off as well as the rest of them, that is—if I don't get frightened" (Ltr-004). He also voices his hope that John Allan might come to watch his oral exams, like other fathers: "Perhaps you will have some business up here about that time, and then you can judge for yourself" (Ltr-004). In sum, Poe writes as a dutiful, hopeful son.

But university would rapidly become a site of humiliation and failure. Poe's financial disadvantage quickly translated into social disadvantage. As Glover shows, Poe's relative poverty would have been uncomfortably visible to his peers. Early American men "understood that appearance, most obviously fashionable dress, informed reputation." Wealthy men wore pristine white linen collars and cuffs; their suits were made of silk, satin, or velvet. Poorer men wore cruder, cheaper fabrics. No man secured status or respectability without appropriate dress, even in college. As one student put it, "'The boys if they have not as good clothes as the rest are never satisfied and are always laughed at.'" Southern men were especially fixated on appearance; clothing evidenced and determined a "man's merit." So much so that "boys counted clothing expenses as essential as books and boarding" and "obsessed over acquiring the proper clothing." Southern college students regularly requested "new shoes, coats, hats, and waistcoats" to keep pace with fashion imperatives.[14] In his first letter home, Poe thanked Allan for providing "uniform coat, six yards of striped cloth for pantaloons & four pairs of socks," noting that "the coat is a beautiful one & fits me exactly" (Ltr-003). But Allan was not an indulgent benefactor. And without resources for a more abundant wardrobe, Poe would have been immediately vulnerable to social demotion. Indeed, Poe later scorned Allan for "the mortification" of making him appear like a "beggar" before his classmates (Ltr-028). "It was then that I became dissolute," Poe accused, "for how could it be otherwise?" Financial deprivation premised a shameful lowering at university. Without money, Poe was classed as riffraff.

That said, drinking, gambling, and financial recklessness—the vices that debased Poe—were rife at Southern colleges. A number of researchers testify to the ubiquity of cards and liquor in Southern university cultures.[15] Even at Northern schools, Southerners surpassed "the misbehavior of northern boys," drinking and gambling more than their counterparts. In addition, Southern boys regularly squandered their fathers' money. They "treated finances as a manifestation of their autonomy. Adolescents spent money wildly to entertain themselves, to impress their peers, and out of youthful imprudence." This profligacy was believed to be a byproduct of Southern conceits. According to Southern matron Martha Ramsey, the spoiled sons of plantation owners "carry their idleness, their impatience of control, their extravagance, their self-consequence" with them to university.

Young Southern men were accustomed to indulgence, and their lavishness rarely resulted in disownment. When Virginian Edward Taylor went to Harvard in 1819, for example, he paid for a servant, a livery stable, hats, shoes, clothing, furniture, and a trip to Washington. He spent "as much on clothes as tuition." Despite these excesses, Edward's father continued to pay his expenses. While some parents chastised their sons' immoderation, many simply gave them the exorbitant sums they requested, eager to accessorize a young man's reputation. Some patrons even regretted not being able to offer more. In addition, parents often let students manage all the money allocated to their education, responding to wastefulness with only encouragement and advice: "They hoped these tactics would give young men the opportunity to independently correct any problems, avoid conflict, and build confidence." Occasionally fathers threatened to cut off improvident sons, but most boys knew that such warnings expressed more exasperation than resolve. Glover notes, "only chronically dreadful misbehavior provoked the severing of kinship bonds."[16] By his culture's standards, Poe's dissipation was common enough. Most families would have judged it a predictable imprudence, one that would right itself with time, good counsel, and experience.

While Poe's difficulty at school was typical then, John Allan's response was not. It is possible that Allan was abiding by university policies governing student expenses. Southern colleges, including the University of Virginia, advised parents to give only a modest subsistence to their sons. In 1827, Virginia "required students to deposit all funds with a university proctor, forbade boys from spending more than $100 per session on clothes and $40 for 'pocket money,' and specified that student dress should always be 'uniform and plain.'"[17] Such rules, however, were consistently and flagrantly broken, and the Poe-Allan letters make no mention of Allan's compliance with university guidelines.

This historical context weights Poe's castigation of Allan with a certain validity. He navigated his only year at college under duress. He endured financial scarcity, social demotion, and paternal apathy. Allan's disdain for the crushing realities of this crisis added insult to injury, and Poe's eviction from the Allan estate was the final indignity. In response, Poe wrote to Allan with unmitigated gall. He indicts Allan for denying him a much-coveted education; for thwarting his rise to "eminence in public life"; for saying he had "no affection" for him; for "continually upbraiding [him] with eating the bread of idleness"; for taking delight in "exposing" his blunders before those who could "advance [his] interest in the world"; and for subjecting him "to the whims & caprice, not only of [Allan's] white family, but the complete authority of the blacks—" (Ltr-005). In total, the letter prosecutes Allan for treachery and cruelty.

Confronted with these allegations, Poe's contemporaries would have asked questions about Allan's intention and impact. The seventeenth and eighteenth centuries understood resentment as a reasonable response to "actual and purposeful" harm. Moralist philosophers Joseph Butler and Adam Smith saw resentment as a moral sentiment, an ethical reaction to a personal or cultural wrong.[18] Butler defined resentment as "a weapon . . . against injury, injustice, and cruelty." He claimed that resentment kindled "self defence," preventing hurt in circumstances where passivity means "certain destruction."[19] And Butler maintained that resentment "brings the offender to justice," driving a desire for punishment that "the cool consideration of reason" does not.[20] In addition, the moralists held that resentment was integral to a judicious reckoning with both the self's worth and its wounding. They argued that resentment had powerful sympathetic properties, believing it could animate empathy for suffering outside the self. By this logic, resentment could be entirely altruistic, turning into "indignation" for the mistreatment of others. Indeed, Adam Smith maintains that resentment prompts us to punish the evil-doer, to "return evil for the evil that has been done."[21] This chastening acts as "recompense" for injustice. Smith also suggested that resentment could be principled and constructive. It can operate as a legitimate response to unfairness or violation, and ultimately, it can preserve human dignity. More recently, Leon Wurmser has extended the connections between resentment and self-worth. In Wurmser's analysis, the incitements to resentment in the aggrieved subject are: "not being recognized, not being listened to, not being seen in his individuality, subjectivity, and identity, not being acknowledged and respected for himself and being treated as a mere tool." Wurmser contends that resentment insists on a fundamental human right: "the right to be respected as an individual and as an autonomous person."[22] Such conditions return us to issues of injury and accountability in the Poe-Allan conflict: Did Allan do Poe wrong? Did he treat Poe unfairly or maliciously? Was he culpable for damages to his foster son?

By Southern standards, the devastation of a man's education and reputation were egregious blows. An aristocratic Southern son had an obligation to enhance familial prestige. Young men became students of reputation in college, learning the nuances of cultivating respect and admiration. The Southern gentry delineated "public status" as "the ultimate value of a university education." In Southern family systems, societal measures of a boy's character mattered more than his academic performance. Reputation was so exalted in the South it assumed sacred proportions: "Worshipping at the altar of reputation, southern gentlemen . . . raised their sons to judge the morality of behavior not by religious tenets but according to public perceptions."[23] As Bertram Wyatt-Brown confirms, reputation was an essential component of Southern honor: "Those who lacked honor also lacked reputation."[24] Social judgments arbitrated a man's integrity. If credible then, Poe's contentions—that Allan sabotaged his schooling, his ethos, and his prospects—were terrible harms.

It was equally egregious to subject a white Southern son to an enslaved person's authority. Recall that Poe accused Allan of surrendering him to the "the complete authority of the blacks" in his household. By nineteenth-century measures, such a committal constituted a flagrant race betrayal: "To be man in the eyes of Southern elites was to be white, autonomous, and the master of others."[25] White boys learned early and often to exercise racial dominance. Certain chores, like shoe polishing or laundry, were beneath a son's station. Parents "gave" their boys enslaved children to "master" the habitual command of white supremacy. Many students brought enslaved servants with them to university. If Poe was subordinate to enslaved domestics as he claimed, then Allan violated a crucial tenet of white parenting and white man-making.

Given the affronts to personhood that Poe alleged, his bitterness can be understood as an assertion of his individual worth. As Rushdy illustrates, eighteenth-century moralists maintained we feel resentment because we value ourselves enough to begrudge an act of malice. This thinking persists in twentieth-century assessments of resentment. Peter Frederick Strawson connects resentment to "an expectation of, and a demand for, the manifestation of a certain degree of goodwill or regard on the part of the other."[26] In this paradigm, as Rushdy indicates, resentment must be "appreciated as a source of our considered conception of how we respect ourselves and others—ourselves for what we deserve, and others for their moral accountability." As a judicious response, resentment "helps constitute our sense of ourselves as having certain rights, [and] our sense of others as possessing particular responsibilities." More pointedly, anyone who does not feel resentment after injury lacks "the moral self-esteem" to know—and defend—his own dignity.[27] Thus, Poe's grievances testify to his capacity to grasp his self's significance and resist its denigration.

Poe's umbrage was also a political legacy. Poe, like other men of his generation, came by his egoism honestly, internalizing the hubris of the new republic. He was personally and culturally identified with revolutionary manhood. His grandfather, David Poe, was a career soldier, the assistant deputy-quartermaster general for the city of Baltimore, and a major in the revolutionary army. At fifteen, Poe was part of a procession of junior riflemen that followed Marquis de Lafayette's carriage through the streets of Richmond, and his company was reviewed, in full uniform, by the Revolutionary War hero himself. Poe's grievance letter—written after his eviction from Allan's household—was patterned after the Declaration of Independence, listing the offenses against him in terse, tight paragraphs.[28] Later in their turbulent relationship, Poe told John Allan, mistakenly and piquantly, that he was actually the grandson of Benedict Arnold (Ltr-014). In another instance, he imagined himself like William the Conqueror crossing the English Channel: "I have thrown myself on the world, like the Norman conqueror on the shores of Britain &, by my avowed assurance of victory, have destroyed the fleet which could alone cover my retreat—I must either conquer or die—succeed or be disgraced" (Ltr-007). Poe aligned his life project with men who make war and nations. His personal grievances with John Allan, then, reverberate with presumptions of Southern pride and American independence.

Indeed, resentment itself was political capital in the nineteenth century. As Javier Moscosco details, resentment was pivotal to the rise of egalitarian ideologies.[29] Writing in the early twentieth century, German philosopher, Max Scheler, theorized a formative connection between resentment and democratic principles. Scheler explained that resentment thrives in contexts where the expectation of "equal rights" co-exists with acute power differentials. Scheler saw the French Revolution as a culmination of historical resentments, driven by a force that "demands . . . the political and even the socioeconomic equality of all men." Scheler was especially conscious of the role of power in the genesis of resentment: It is the sentiment of a "weaker party" that simultaneously "places himself on the same level as his injurer"; and it "must therefore be strongest in a society like ours, where approximately equal rights (political and otherwise) or formal social equality, publicly recognized, go hand in hand with wide factual differences in power, property, and education."[30] Scheler's observations similarly implicate early America in a politics of resentment. In the new republic, democratic ideals clashed with pernicious hierarchies and oppressions. All men believed themselves equal—entitled to liberty and happiness—but inequality was their lived reality. Most men subscribed to an ideal of democratic personhood they would never realize.[31]

Poe can be understood as this lesser-but-equal subject in the dissidence with Allan. His charity case wardship exacerbated the conventional power differential between father and son. The University of Virginia conflict exposed enduring poverties of care and caretaking between them. Allan's insensitivity to Poe's financial precarity at school, his contempt for his ward's predicament, and his annulment of home and guardianship caught Poe in stark inadequacies. This penury came when Poe had the hope and expectation of enoughness. Whatever his recent debacles, John and Frances Allan were "Ma" and "Pa" to Poe. He anticipated paternal affinity and a margin of error, but he received condemnation and rejection. Poe's grievances emerged in a vortex of insufficiency and inferiority. In this sense, his injuries had validity. The harms were real. In response, Poe fomented a resentful avowal of his individual and social value. His declarations aligned with a cultural logic that made resentment a personal currency and a national politics.

INJURY FOR INJURY

John Allan did not receive his foster son's indictment with compassion or contrition. Instead, he felt a reciprocal harm, and his own sense of injury pervades his answering letters to Poe. Allan's reactive ire was premised on select tenets of antebellum Southern parenting. Here, I situate Allan's letters in these historical parenting philosophies. Although Allan refused to give Poe the Southern son's liberal allowance—and he withheld paternal understanding when Poe blundered—his parenting aligned with an ideology of child rearing that conditioned white boys to racialized ascendancies. Even as children, white men could not be forced into obedience. Only slaves were subject to compulsion. White boys, in contrast, knew radical forms of self-rule and self-will. Southern fathers tried to coax their sons into right action with emotional maneuvers and conditional love. Indeed, their sons knew that they could misbehave their way out of familial acceptance. Love and belonging were secured only through good conduct. Allan's letters attest to Poe's failures. As Allan saw it, Poe refused to learn through admonition, and he courted Allan's rejection with his failures and disgrace.

On March 20, 1827—a day after he ordered Poe out of his house—Allan explained that his previous censures were paternal guidance. For example, "the charge of eating the Bread of idleness," he wrote, "was to urge you to perseverance & industry in receiving the classics, in presenting yourself in the mathematics, mastering the French &c. &c. . . . " With rebuke, Allan sought to prod Poe into more diligence. More poignantly, he says, "It is only on this subject that I wish to be understood, your Heart will tell you if it is not made of marble whether I have not had good reason to fear for you, in more ways than one." According to Allan, his admonishments were inspired by fear. His intent was rectification, not alienation. "I should [be] justly chargeable, in reprimanding you for faults had I . . . any other object than to correct them," he declares. Allan writes as an aggrieved guardian, a father who tried to influence a wayward son.

Allan was not alone in his reliance on reprimand as an expression of watchful correction. Glover's work confirms the primacy of emotional coercion in Southern parenting tactics. "Commanding correct behavior through physical force or threats (not coincidentally the lynchpins of slave mastery) simply did not fit with southern family values. Slaves, not future patriarchs, were commanded, threatened, and physically compelled to action."[32] Punishment was racialized in the South. Certain forms of discipline contradicted a white Southern son's supremacist birthright. Without recourse to force, parents trusted affective manipulation—especially guilt and emotional withdrawal—to discipline an errant boy. Allan's letter reflects the Southern assumption that white boys could be cajoled into virtue.

That said, if a son grew recalcitrant, Southern patriarchs disavowed responsibility for their child's choices. As Glover explains, parents felt obliged to launch their boys, but they were not accountable for their misconduct. The South's devotion to white masculine autonomy meant that even in childhood and adolescence, a boy's character and decisions were his own. In addition, a Southern family could not abide a young man's debasement. Personal reputation had profound implications for a family's status: A son's depravity could sully a family's name for generations. As Glover summarizes, "Adults placed enormous pressure on young sons, repeatedly telling them that their actions affected their relatives' future." If a boy failed to realize his duties to familial honor or distinction, parents withdrew affection and belonging. Ignominy necessitated rejection. Glover notes that fathers especially emphasized the contingent relationship between a son's behavior and paternal acceptance. One planter cautioned his son with the story of a "chronic ne'er do well from Charleston who so alienated his family that, when he died, his father refused 'to put on mourning for him.'" Kentucky Congressman Henry Clay told his fifteen-year-old son, "You bear my name, you are my son, and the hopes of all of us are turned with anxiety upon you."[33] Conscientious fathers primed their sons to understand the gravity of name, worldly success, and social esteem. They also ensured that their sons knew a family's love was subject to a contract of accomplishment and respectability.

John Allan's response to Poe's grievance letter signals that this contract has been broken. Allan relinquished Poe to his own judgment, saying that he was "not at all surprized [sic]" at anything Poe might say or do. In Allan's account, he and his wife, Frances, gave support, concern, and education until Poe renounced their care. Allan asserts that they "watched with parental solic-itude & affection over your tender years affording you such means of instruc-tion as was in their power & which was performed with pleasure until you became a much better judge of your own conduct, rights & priveledges [sic] than they. . . . " Essentially, Allan maintained that Poe refused to be governed.

Allan also prophesied that Poe was destined for mediocrity. He acknowl-edged that he taught Poe "to aspire, even to eminence in Public Life," but he scorned the sincerity of Poe's dedication to that aim: "I never expected that Don Quixotte [sic], Gil Blas, Jo: Miller & such works were calculated to promote the end." Allan's allusions here are loaded with cynicism. *Don Quixote* (1605) famously tells the story of a Spanish nobleman who reads so many romance novels he loses his mind and quests to revive medieval chiv-alry across the land. *Gil Blas* (1715–1735), a French novel, chronicles the immoral misadventures of its protagonist as he seeks his fortune. *Joe Miller's Jests* (1739) was the first in a series of vulgar joke books that were ubiquitous in the eighteenth and nineteenth centuries. With mocking literary references then, Allan condemned Poe as a sluggard.

Allan closed his letter with a final dismissal and a parting insult. "Your list of grievances require no answer," he says, "the world will reply to them." With more invective, he writes, and "& now that you have . . . declared for you own Independence—& after such a list of Black charges—you Tremble for the consequences unless I send you a supply of money." Allan answered Poe's grievances with more grievance, with his own criticisms and dissatis-factions. He could not endure the grumblings of an intractable ward.

Allan's counterclaims left the two men deadlocked. Historical and current thinkers hold that resentment can resolve itself in one of three ways: valida-tion, forgiveness, or revenge. As Rushdy explains, "To feel resentment is to feel the need for repentance or apology, and to feel apologetic is to feel the need for forgiveness, and to feel the need for forgiveness is to recognize the need for a peaceful resolution."[34] Such a resolution can come through the wrongdoer's avowal and atonement. If amends go unmade, however, punish-ment will suffice. Scheler argues that retaliation likewise settles resentment. But resentment persists when vengeance is denied or suppressed.[35] By this logic then, the Poe-Allan stalemate constitutes a critical obstruction. If Allan refused Poe corroboration and apology—and if revenge was unobtainable— Poe would be left to relentlessly seethe. In other words, a standoff could relegate Poe to a perilous irreconcilability.

The tenacity of this frustration makes resentment dangerous in past and present paradigms. Joseph Butler stipulated that resentment turns malignant if "someone feels it without reasonable cause or indulges in it beyond reasonable measure."[36] Taken to a rancorous extreme, Adam Smith argued that resentment turns men into "wild beast(s)" intent on destruction.[37] Scheler characterized resentment as a "self-poisoning of the mind" that steeps the psyche in "hatred, malice, envy, the impulse to detract, and spite."[38] Indeed, Rushdy notes that one of the "most resonant models of resentment" in the nineteenth and twentieth centuries diagnosed resentment as a disease, "an unforgiving and incurable spiteful illness."[39] Nietzsche embraced this vision of resentment, depicting the resentful man as polluted and corrupt: "His soul *squints*; his mind loves dark corners, secret paths and back-doors . . . he knows all about keeping quiet, not forgetting, waiting, temporarily humbling and abasing himself." For Nietzsche, the psyche of the resentful man is "a teeming mass of worms."[40] Leon Wurmser likewise contends that the "inner life" of the resentful subject settles into an "enduring bitterness, in the simmering indignation about others, the world, or fate."[41] Resentment clings and broods. It fixes the psyche on the injury.

Scheler underlines the inescapable grip of resentment, noting that the French term *ressentiment* re-inscribes the original Latin "re-sentire," which means to "re-feel." The resentful subject feels the same wounding over and over. He remains caught in selective memory, repetitively recalling a decisive hurt. Nietzsche reinforces the resentful man's power of recall, saying pain is "burnt in memory."[42] As Paul Hogget notes, the resentful subject "cannot forget."[43] And thus, he cannot evolve. He cannot age out of grievance. Allan's indifference, then, makes Poe vulnerable to these pathologies of resentment. Resentment discourses predict that he could be immobilized in bitterness. More fundamentally, he could find a self in wrath. Antagonism could become identity.

BEGINNINGS

Poe certainly stayed resentful, railing against his foster father, his deprivation, and his thwarted future. In the correspondence, the impacts of resentment are measured by Poe's obsessions with the past. The acrimony between Poe and John Allan suggests that resentment requires memory. It must be recollected. It needs a history, and not just any history: It necessitates a past defined by subordination and disregard. Just as importantly, it demands a devotion to that past powerlessness. In this sense, resentment evidences a nineteenth-century phenomenon that Dana Luciano calls "affective time-keeping," a temporality of feeling that deviates from linear, progressive time. Grief's time, for example, moves "at a different pace from ordinary time: it was *slower*, more capacious, almost spatialized, enabling contradictory feelings . . . to be indulged at once and without traumatic contradiction" (italics added).[44] Similarly, resentment works through slow time, through a repetitive re-feeling of bygone injuries. In the process, it endlessly revives the other as an abuser and a traitor. Thus, it holds the other in an economy of liability and obligation. The other becomes *one who owes* the subject, the one obligated to tender remedy or reparation.

The resentment between Poe and Allan kept time with their personal and interpersonal histories. In other words, their mutual animus tangled with the events of their individual and shared pasts, and it eventually created its own affective timeline. As I show here, Allan's miserly provisions for Poe at college—as well as his punitive anger at Poe's grievances—reflect Allan's hardworking adolescence and mercantile rise. Both Poe and Allan were subordinate "sons" in a benefactor's home. Allan believed himself self-made and self-reliant. He fostered Poe out of altruism and ambition, forming a tentative family unit with a probationary heir. In his early childhood, Poe was keenly attached to the only parents he knew. He could not have grasped the complexities of his ancillary position in Allan's heart and home.

John Allan was a Scottish immigrant. He came to Virginia at sixteen. He lived and worked for his uncle, William Galt, one of Richmond's most prominent entrepreneurs. Allan met his future business partner, Charles Ellis, while clerking in Galt's shop. When Allan was twenty-one, they launched the House of Ellis and Allan, a tobacco export and mercantile firm. At twenty-three, Allan married Frances Valentine. The couple lived over the store with Frances' sister, Nancy. Edgar entered the family six years later. It was not a silver spoon household. The Allans moved at least four times in fourteen years, including a five-year relocation to London when Allan attempted to establish a London House of Ellis and Allan. Before 1825, when the death of William Galt made Allan one of the richest men in Virginia, he circled financial ruin twice: once in 1819 and again in 1822. The first crisis came in London with the collapse of the British tobacco market and the failure of Virginia state banks. Allan begged his partner, Ellis, for money to pay rent, feed his family, and appease their creditors. He was dejected at the prospect of insolvency but determined to press on: "'I always say If we are doomed to Fall let us Fall like men.'" The second crisis bankrupted the business. Allan survived only because "Galt bought the firm's assets and took him in as a secret partner."[45] Still, Allan considered himself a rags-to-riches success. He belonged more to "that group of English, Scottish, and Irish merchants, usually younger sons, who came over before the Revolution," than he did to Richmond's planter class.[46] He subscribed to the practical wisdom of *Poor Richard's Almanac*, and frequently used words like, "'fortitude,' 'correctness,' 'undeviating firmness,' 'perseverance,' 'good habits,' [and] 'prudence.'"[47] He was not a man to suffer entitlement or indolence gladly. He did not forgive reckless hubris in himself, and he would not forgive it in his orphan charge.

Just as significantly, John Allan became Poe's guardian as an act of charity. His wife, Frances, was among the benevolent women who attended Eliza Poe's sickbed. Allan had a reputation for philanthropy; he was said to never deny a beggar at his door.[48] The Allans took three-year-old Edgar Poe into their home in December 1812 but did not adopt him. Their fostering recalls a history of indentured servitude and apprenticeships for orphans in early America. Traditionally, members of an extended family adopted orphaned children. Lorri Glover's study of Southern kinship networks testifies to the commitment uncles, aunts, cousins, and grandparents made to parenting parentless children. Before the emergence of orphanages, "when parents died, sibling and kin stepped in to raise the children who were left behind."[49] Indeed, Poe's brother, William Henry, went to live with his paternal grandparents. But his sister, Rosalie, was placed with another Richmond family (like Poe). Such arrangements attest to how destitute and alone the Poe children were after their mother's death. Fostering occurred only when a family system abandoned its most vulnerable charges. Early America's version of foster care rehomed poor orphaned children with "local farmers, householders, or heads of business—whomever would take them."[50] These placements constituted a work contract. Even when asylum adoption occurred, indenture was typically a motive. An adopted child might be returned to the orphanage because parents were disappointed in their charge, and adoption usually constituted a lesser emotional bond. As Susan Porter writes, "Patronage was not parentage."[51] An adopted family rarely rivaled a biological family in its love or commitment to a child.

John Allan's adolescence under William Galt's stewardship familiarized him with the distinctions between foster child, adopted son, and familial ward. Galt patronized the sons of several Scottish relatives, helping them immigrate to Richmond and training them in his business. He later adopted three orphaned Galt brothers, the children of "the woman he loved but could not win," calling the boys his "sons" and himself their "Virginia father."[52] As a result, Allan carried the bitterness of an inferior son. He begrudged Galt for giving one of his other wards more extensive schooling than he received, believing he "had stronger claims."[53] Like Allan, Frances was also parentless as an adolescent, orphaned at the age of ten and raised by a guardian.

Biographical controversy persists over the Allans' decision to foster but never adopt Poe. What seems clear is that they both knew—and lived—the implications of such a choice. In the end, Poe was their ward, not their son.

That said, Poe's station in the Allan family took years to define. The evidence from the first years of his fostering suggests a relationship of fondness. Frances's marriage with John was childless (although he fathered two illegitimate children after Frances died and three children with his second wife). Hence, it seems likely that John and Frances welcomed the opportunity to provisionally parent the dark-eyed boy. Poe's name was entered into the family Bible. As mentioned previously, he called Frances and John "Ma" and "Pa." The Allans had suits cut and tailored for him. Poe summered with them at White Sulphur Springs in the Virginia mountains. Allan sent Poe to a private teacher and the Richmond schoolmaster. At six and a half, Poe moved with Frances and Allan to England. For the first two years of their London stay, Poe went to boarding school about three miles from their flat, and Allan received reports that affirmed his fatherly status: "Your Son I am glad to say is well & happy."[54] Just as tellingly, Poe was called "Master Allan" in England.[55] Available data indicates that the Allans presented Poe to the world as their child in this interval.

Other registers testify to Poe's love and need for his foster parents. One story holds that when Poe went to boarding school in Irvine, Scotland—Allan's birthplace—Poe became despondent. On the journey, he complained incessantly. At school, he moped, refused to study, and promised to run back to England. Allan sent William Galt's adopted son, James, to supervise him and sleep in his room. James believed that without his restraint, Poe would have tried to get back to London on his own, although he was only seven years old.[56] Poe's discontent persisted when Allan sent him to Reverend Bransby's boarding school at Stoke Newington. Clearly, Poe became lonely, angry, and scared away from home.

But the Allans did not, or could not, offer their ward parental devotion and caretaking. Allan was consumed with work. His business required frequent trips to Bristol, Liverpool, and Manchester. And even when he was in London, Allan was entirely preoccupied. He described himself as a "stranger in my own house." His letters to America only mentioned Poe in perfunctory terms, as "quite well" or "a fine Boy." Frances was often ill. She "suffered one misery after another: bad cold and sore throat, swollen face, headaches, croup, attacks of 'Catarrh,' a fall." She frequently took to her bed. She also traveled to try different remedies: a water cure, country exercise, the sea air. Her letters home do not ask after Edgar or send her love to him. Similarly, when friends and family wrote to Allan, they remembered only Frances and Aunt Nancy with no mention of Poe. And of course, Poe went unadopted. In contrast, his sister, Rosalie, believed that her adoptive mother was her birth mother until the age of ten and "was christened by the Mackenzie family, who formally gave her their name."[57] Poe had a more ambiguous status in the Allan household: part probationary son, part ward, part charity case.

When Poe was fifteen, four years after the Allans returned from London, ambiguity in the father-son relationship turned to acrimony. In November 1824, Allan complained to Poe's brother, Henry, in a letter.[58] He said that Poe "does nothing & seems quite miserable, sulky & ill-tempered to all the family." Allan read Poe's irritability as thankless indifference: "The boy possesses not a Spark of affection for us not a particle of gratitude for all my care and kindness towards him." Allan further expressed a baffled exasperation: "How we have acted to produce this is beyond my conception."[59] He writes as if he was seeking absolution from Henry, desiring "to Stand as I ought to do in your Estimation," and attributing Edgar's misbehavior to the influence of his "associates" in Richmond. With self-martyring undertones, he adds, "Had I done my duty as faithfully to my God as I have to Edgar, then had Death come . . . [it had] no terrors for me." Allan was both puzzled and bruised by his foster son's gloom. He could not see or acknowledge the impact of Poe's liminality in his household. He believed he gave Poe more than he himself received: a nuclear household, a "Ma" and "Pa," an enviable education, a guardian's interest and care. He did not calculate that Poe might want, need, or expect more.

Biographers speculate about the reasons for Poe's truculence.[60] Whatever the instigation, Poe's childhood was a crucible for resentment. As John Allan's ward, Poe was the lesser, neglected child. He could never command the fidelities and prerogatives of biological kinship. He was never John Allan's son or heir. He was always obliged to remember his home and family were almsgivings—never assured. Scheler theorizes that resentment intensifies if it smolders in "lasting situations which are felt to be 'injurious' but beyond one's control." In other words, resentment escalates if the "injury is experienced as a destiny."[61] As Allan's ward, Poe knew a subjection he could not outmaneuver. His marginalization accrued in the accidents of his birth, his orphaning, and his fostering.

Poe likely experienced certain injuries as destiny then, and his yet bitterness was exacerbated because he believed he was promised another fate. Poe opens an 1830 diatribe with the assertion that his victimization began with Allan's fostering: "Did I, when an infant, sollicit [sic] your charity and protection, or was it of your own free will, that you volunteered your services on my behalf?" Although Poe was three when his mother died (painfully young, but not an "infant"), the hyperbole establishes his innocent passivity in the arrangement of "charity and protection" that John Allan made with his family. Contrary to fact, Poe claims that his grandfather, his "natural protector at the time," had more than enough money to raise him, and he was "his favourite grandchild." Then Poe underscores the outrage of Allan's broken oath, say-ing, "the promises of adoption, and liberal education which you held forth to him in a letter which is now in possession of my family, induced him to resign all care of me into your hands." According to Poe, Allan had pledged him paternity. He secured his guardianship through a contract of care with his grandfather. "Under such circumstances, can it be said that I have no *right* to expect anything at your hands?" Poe demands (Ltr-028).

Javier Moscoso maintains that eighteenth- and nineteenth-century con-ceptions of resentment turned on "an obsession with a broken promise." Resentment grows when an earned or expected grace does not materialize. The question that sustains resentment is: "Why not me?"[62] Why wasn't I saved from a disastrous fate? Why wasn't I rewarded with love, money, acco-lades, or power? Poe came of age in a barrage of "why not me" questions. Why didn't his mother live to raise him? Why wasn't he taken in by family? Why couldn't Frances and John Allan love him completely? Why didn't they adopt him? And so on. Poe's wardship caught him in an interminable "why not me." He grew up in an elsewhere between belonging and unbelonging, advantage and deprivation.

The history of Poe's childhood tarries with the resentment he would feel later, just as Allan's personal past channeled through his own anger. Their rancor emerged over time and fixated on events from previous intervals: Poe's ingratitude, Allan's stinginess, Poe's dissipation, and Allan's reneg-ing. Yet Poe's spite emerged within a singular dynamic of subjugation. He was beggared by accidents of class, age, and death. His fostering presaged a deliverance that never materialized. Instead, he confronted repeated and intractable power differentials.

DISILLUSIONMENT

Leon Wursmer calls the violations Poe experienced "soul-blind" mistreat-ments. Wurmser recognizes that when resentment emerges in love rela-tionships, "we may feel betrayed and cruelly misunderstood." As a result, resentment extends to a "deep sense of aggrievement, of injustice, of help-less rage." Intriguingly, Wurmser and other thinkers argue that behind this resentment is grief. Wurmser writes that this "deep hurt and sadness" finds its origins in loss: in "betrayal" or a "break" in a critical relationship.[63] For Michael Feldman, the pain of this treachery and fracture resonates with a prior oedipal grief. Feldman suggests that an unfair injury in love relation-ships revives an original "oedipal disappointment": the disillusionment with father and mother, the ejection from a primordial intimacy, the forfeit of an erotic ideal. This oedipal rift is "unbearable."[64] As John Steiner clarifies, the oedipal disruption "introduces the child to new realities that are experienced as profoundly shocking and can lead to a deep sense of hurt, of injustice and of betrayal." The oedipal ejection from wholeness and continuity is devastating: The "child feels that a promise has been broken, so that he is not only wronged but betrayed."[65] Poe's childhood as an unadopted son resonates with this oedipal grief. As a perpetual foster child, Poe losses were multiplied. He was banished from both an infantile oneness with the maternal and a formative affinity with the paternal. His young adulthood as an outcast deepened his confrontation with oedipal betrayal. Dispossessed of foster father, foster mother, home, and education, Poe felt both abandoned and aggrieved.

Still, it took four years for the pain of expulsion to become entrenched antagonism, a period that Poe spent in the army and at West Point. Poe enlisted in May 1827, two months after his exodus from Richmond. Biographical evidence suggests that Poe found soldiering a humiliating necessity. He falsified his name and age in his papers. A letter from his colonel illuminates the fiction Poe created to explain his service. Poe presented himself as Allan's "protégé," adopted "as his son and heir." The colonel believed that Poe made "considerable progress in his studies" at the University of Virginia, but "in a moment of youthful indiscretion he absconded,—and was not heard from by his Patron for several years." In that time, he "became reduced to the necessity of enlisting. . . . "[66] Later, Poe would hide his military past, telling people he was in Europe or "invent[ing] other episodes" to conceal it. Poe communicated minimally with Allan during these two years. A regular correspondence resumed only when Poe sought early release from his five-year enlistment. He needed Allan's approval to receive an honorable discharge.

This interim was pivotal, a time of industry and effort. Here, I illustrate *how hard Poe worked* to please Allan, to make him proud. He tried. He quested to be a worthy Southern son—ambitious, reliable, and accomplished. He made strategic appeals to Allan's personal currencies and the touchstones of Southern masculinity. Although Poe re-secured an unpredictable assistance from Allan, he never recovered his affection. Poe underestimated Allan's capacity for condemnation and doubt. When Allan sporadically answered his calls for help, he acted out of a distant, altruistic concern, not love. But Poe failed to read the relationship accurately. He continued to believe they might reconcile. As a result, he was exposed to accumulating rejections and frustrations. His attempt to heal the oedipal break—to change John Allan—aborted. Thus, only grief and the ghost of a lost ideal remained.

When Poe contacted Allan again in December 1828, he was tactical. He attended closely to matters of reputation and achievement. He wrote directly to Allan's assumption that he was irreparably "degraded and disgraced," countering, "I am altered from what you knew me & am no longer a boy tossing about on the world without aim or consistency" (Ltr-007). Now he swore that he was alive with ambition: "I feel that within me which will make me fulfil [sic] your highest wishes & only beg you to suspend your judgment until you hear *of* me again" (Ltr-007). Poe had, in fact, matured and evolved. He distinguished himself in the military, rising to the highest rank a noncommissioned officer could earn. He felt secure in his accomplishments. "[A]t no period of my life, have I regarded myself with a deeper Satisfaction—or did my heart swell with more honourable Pride," he trumpets (Ltr-007). He implicitly tried to resolidify Allan's paternal interest in him, saying he told his lieutenant "that your wishes for me (as your letters assured me) were, and had always been those of father & that you were ready to forgive even the worst offences." But, all in all, the letter relies more on forecasts of triumph than emotional appeals. "You will perceive that I speak confidently—but when did ever Ambition exist or Talent prosper without prior conviction of success?" (Ltr-007). To win Allan's favor, Poe invoked the standards of Southern masculinity that his university days were supposed to cultivate: initiative, reputation, and achievement.

When Allan did not reply to his first letter, Poe multiplied the proofs of his redemption and ambition. He proclaimed a newborn allegiance to purity: "There is that within my heart which has no connection with degradation—I can walk among infection & be uncontaminated" (Ltr-008). He also prophesied that familial glory would follow Allan's forgiveness: "My father do not throw me aside as degraded[.] I will be an honor to your name" (Ltr-008). He twice reminds Allan that he had been his "son," and plaintively invokes ties of love and belonging: "If you let the love you bear me, outweigh the offence which I have given—then write my father, quickly." But again, he petitions Allan primarily on testaments of his success. "[M]y character is one that will bear scrutiny & has merited the esteem of my officers," he reiterates. More dramatically, he predicts a martyred fame for himself: "Neglected—I will be doubly [ambi]tious, & the world shall hear of the son whom you have thought unworthy of your notice" (Ltr-008). Poe sought to show himself deserving of Allan's pardon, as if he knew an unqualified absolution was impossible. Essentially, Poe negotiates for Allan's renewed interest in him: "Forgive me because I have changed," he tacitly asks, "forgive me because I will rise."

Feldman observes that resentment often inspires a yearning to change its circumstances or its object. The resentful subject "argues over and over that *his object* must change," Feldman asserts. This conviction can become a delusional belief, "like a character out of Kafka the patient persuades himself that the object will eventually soften, or see the justice of his case and change. . . . " As Feldman further explains, the object's transformation represents a seductive recompense. "There is often a powerful, palpable 'if only' implied" in this argument, "if only you realized something, if only you changed, if only you restored me to my proper place . . . ," then love or justice would prevail.

If only you would see and act differently, "you would release the goodness, the love and gratitude of which I am capable."[67] Poe's letters to Allan reflect the force of this longing. He writes to alter his situation and vindicate himself. He writes to recover lost affection and remake the relationship. In Sally Weintrobe's words, "the aim of the grievance is not to destroy the object but to change it."[68]

But Allan did not change. He stonewalled Poe's request to leave the army, writing to Poe's lieutenant, "he had better remain as he is until the termination of his enlistment."[69] Allan had no heart for forgiveness. He had been an ambivalent guardian in Poe's childhood, and his ward's creditors had hounded him in the years since Poe's departure. Allan would not be enticed into granting Poe amnesty with predictions of future victories.

Allan was only moved to assist Poe again when his prospects improved. In early February 1829, Poe wrote that he had an opportunity to secure a cadet's appointment at West Point. He also took full responsibility for the University of Virginia debacle. "I never meant to offer a shadow of excuse for the infamous conduct of myself & others at that place," he concedes. He says only, "I have no excuse to offer for my [con]duct except the common one of youth[fulnes]s . . . " (Ltr-009). This contrition may have gratified Allan's need for penance, if he had one, but apology and officer's candidacy alone did not rouse his sympathies. Three weeks after Poe sent this amends, Frances Allan died. In her last days, she asked to see her foster son. Poe got leave, but Frances died before he made it to her bedside. Presumably, Frances's death and his bereaved presence in Richmond quieted Allan's temper. When Poe returned to Fort Monroe, they had made a fragile peace. Poe began studying for his entrance exams, "anxious to retrieve [his] good name" and especially his foster father's "good opinion."

It seems plausible that Poe's quest for officer's candidacy—rather than tender sentiments—revived Allan's benevolence. Elite Southern men respected military service. According to Glover, veterans of war were considered worthy successors of the revolution. More practically, soldiering enabled social mobility. While the military was not as enviable a profession as business, law, medicine, or planting—and not a permanent career for gentry men—the army provided uplift for working-class boys.[70] Given these connotations, Allan likely saw the wisdom of Poe's objective. As an officer, Poe would have financial stability and social esteem. He would settle into a suitable and sufficient life. Always the pragmatist, Allan solicited letters of recommendation for Poe from prominent citizens, including a former governor of Virginia and the speaker of the House of Representatives.

Allan wrote his own recommendation letter as well, addressed to the Secretary of War. Revealingly, he carefully delineated his relationship to Poe: "Frankly Sir, do I declare that He is no relation to me whatever." He advocated for Poe because "every Man is my care, if he be in distress." Even more tellingly, he told the secretary about Poe's scandalous past: "He left me in consequence of some gambling at the University at Charlottesville, because (I presume) I refused to sanction a rule that . . . others had adopted there, making Debts of Honour of all indiscretions."[71] Although Poe never read this declaration of Allan's emotional detachment, his boundaries are stark and plain. Allan did not write as father or guardian. He endorsed Poe as he would every man. The few surviving letters between Poe and Allan from these months are records of networking and nepotism. They both tallied the contacts they made to advance Poe's candidacy. Allan advised Poe to enhance his application with an official certificate of his grandfather's service in the Revolutionary War and to "be prudent and careful." He wrote in succinct, professional terms. Whatever the armistice between them, Allan made no proclamations of love or protection.

The delicate truce broke when Poe was waitlisted for admittance to West Point and worse, when he asked Allan to finance the publication of his book-length poem, *Al Aaraaf*. A Philadelphia firm agreed to publish the text if an investor contracted to repay any potential losses. Poe approached the request to Allan as a business proposition. He outlined the money matters, stipulating that cost of publication would total $100, although "it is more than probable that the work will be profitable" (Ltr-013). He framed the venture as a fast track to social prominence. "At my time of life there is much in being *before the eye of the world*," he reflects, "if once noticed I can easily cut a path to reputation" (Ltr-013). At the very least, he specifies that the book cannot "disadvantage" his future or "other objects" on his immediate horizon.

Allan was unconvinced. He summarized his reply at the bottom of Poe's letter, "strongly censuring his conduct—& refusing any aid." Allan did not object to Poe publishing his poetry; he objected to Poe's maneuvers for money. He withdrew into indifference again, declaring, "I am not particularly anxious to see you."[72] A month went by, and Poe wrote once more, this time, all obedience and apology. He immediately clarified his deference to Allan's will: "I did intend, but forgot to say . . . [that] I should by no means publish it without your approbation" (Ltr-014). More emphatically, he reaffirmed his resolve to prosper as well as his dedication to an officer's vocation. He said that he was driven only by bootstrapping ambition: "In whatever errors I may have been led into, I would beg you to judge me impartially & to believe I have acted with the single motive of trying to do something for myself." He swore he had "left untried no efforts to enter" West Point and still "hope[d] to succeed" (Ltr-014). In sum, Poe returned to more steadying appeals to his manly diligence. He was the postulant making his own way in the world.

This petition might have worked had Poe ended it here, with his determination to become an army officer. Regretfully, however, he asked for

money again, insisting "it is only a little that I now want." Then, he offered
an unfortunate rationalization. He explained that a cousin, Edward Mosher,
had robbed him while they shared a hotel room. And, although he had "been
moderate in [his] expenses," he used Allan's recent support to pay a substitute
soldier at Fort Monroe. Poe said he could document the theft with a letter
from Mosher. But his reckoning of the army substitute's fee seemed suspicious to Allan. Poe had stipulated previously that a replacement cost twelve
dollars. Typically, a commanding officer arranged for both the substitute and
his renumeration, enlisting the first recruit who volunteered and paying him
the requisite twelve-dollar fee. But Poe's colonel and lieutenant were on fur-
lough when his dismissal came through, and he had to "scuffle for [him]self."
He negotiated a private deal with a proxy, Sergeant "Bully" Graves, giving
him twenty-five dollars and a note for an additional fifty. If Poe had explained
this contingency when he left his post, Allan might have been less wary of its
truth at this juncture. But "to a man like Allan, so exact in his accounts . . . this
concealment amounted almost to a crime." Later, Louisa Allan, Allan's second wife, reiterated Allan's assumption that Poe had squandered the money
he provided earlier. According to Louisa, Sergeant Graves, uncompensated
and cranky, eventually wrote to John Allan for the fifty dollars still owed
him. Louisa maintained, "Mr. Allan sent the money to the man, and banished
Poe from his affections; and he never lived here again."[73] The purported theft
and the exorbitant cost of the substitute—not to mention the petition for more
money—rankled John Allan. Again, he retreated into silence.

In response, Poe presented himself as an apprehensive, conciliatory son.
"I am sometimes afraid that you are angry & perhaps you have reason to
be—but if you will but put a little more confidence in me—I will endeavor to
deserve it" (Ltr-015). Here, Poe's diffidence tempers his prior arrogance. He
voices confusion and doubt. "I am sure no one can be more anxious, or would
do more towards helping myself than I would—if I had any means of doing
it" (Ltr-015). He goes on to accentuate his need for rescue, saying that "without [Allan's] assistance" he has no way to rise. He writes as a dependent, as
a boy eager for help and counsel. Variations on the word "anxious" appear
three times in the short letter: He is "anxious to return home," "anxious to
abide by [Allan's] directions," and longing to be released "from a great deal
of anxiety" with an answering letter. He closes with a self-martyring summation of his suffering: "I think I have already had my share of trouble for one
so young" (Ltr-015).

The letters Poe sent for the next five months, from July 1829 to January
1830, testify to his continued, often urgent, need for money. When Allan
obliged, he did so begrudgingly. "I . . . am truly thankful for the money you
sent me," Poe acknowledged once, "notwithstanding the taunt with which
it was given 'that men of genius ought not to apply to your aid'" (Ltr-016).

Poe's need for Allan's charity meant he had to be simultaneously grateful and chastened. Thus, his letters diligently record the receipt of funds and the exigencies they answered: "I received yours this morning which relieved me from more trouble than you can well imagine," he confided in August 1829. "I was in a most uncomfortable situation—without one cent of money—in a strange place . . . " (Ltr-019). After leaving Fort Monroe, Poe settled in Baltimore to wait out West Point's selection process. As Silverman explains, Poe was essentially "stranded in Baltimore, a city of some eighty thousand inhabitants, about five times as many as Richmond. He stayed now at a hotel, now at a boarding house, now with his father's family."[74] But the Poe family gave no refuge. Poe found his grandmother "extremely poor & ill (paralytic)," his aunt Maria "still worse," and his brother "Henry entirely given up to drink & unable to help himself, much less me—" (Ltr-019). He hoped that Allan might send five dollars a week for "board, lodging, washing . . . [and] mending" until the West Point acceptance came through. He promised that if his entrance was delayed again, "I can do with much less." He would live on "10 even 8$ a month—any thing with which you think it possible to exist" (Ltr-019). His requests are contrite, keenly sensitive to Allan's reactions. "I am not as so anxious of obtaining money from your good nature as of preserving your good will," he confesses. With palpable apprehension, he says, "I am extremely anxious that you should believe that I have not attempted to impose upon you . . . " (Ltr-019). Poe's declarations did little to reassure Allan or reclaim his patronage. In November, Poe was forced to plead for help because he was "almost without clothes." This letter opens plaintively, "I wrote you about a fortnight ago and as I have not heard from you, I was afraid you had forgotten me" (Ltr-022). At long last, Allan sent eighty dollars, sufficient for certain "expenditures"—for which Poe was "truly thankful"—but not enough for the clothes he sorely wanted.

Poe's poverty in these years was real. After his first break with Allan, he was homeless and hungry in Richmond at eighteen years old. "I am in the greatest necessity, not having tasted food since Yesterday morning. I have no where to sleep at night, but roam about the Streets—I am nearly exhausted— I beseech you. . . . I have not one cent in the world to provide any food" (Ltr-006). Allan was unmoved by his ward's destitution. He returned the letter with only the words "Pretty Letter" written on the back. He did not provide sustenance, and Poe disappeared. He might have gone overseas or simply north to Boston.[75] To elude creditors, Poe used aliases based on his brother's name, Henry Leonard or Henri Le Renner. He published his first volume of poems in 1827, but writing was not a livelihood. By 1828 he was making ten dollars a month in the military.[76] When he decided to leave the army at the end of that year—and before his decision to enter West Point—he was willing to risk precarity again. But he thought, "I can struggle with any difficulty" and the "prime of my life would be wasted" in a five-year commitment to soldiering (Ltr-007). With youthful exuberance and naivete, Poe left Fort Monroe.

After six weeks, however, Poe resolved to enter West Point. Allan's stinginess persisted even as Poe quested for an officer's training because he continued to believe that Poe was swindling him. In July 1829, Poe felt obliged to justify himself once more. "I think it my duty to say something concerning the accusations & suspicions which are contained in your letter," he wrote (Ltr-016). He re-accounted for the costs of his substitute and his frugal rationing of Allan's previous aid. He also reasserted his dogged dedication to the West Point application. "On receiving your last letter, I went immediately to Washington, on foot, & have returned the same way . . . " (Ltr-016). Quinn reinforces that the walk to Washington attests to Poe's "determination to obtain the appointment."[77] Still, Allan remained sour and wary. Three months later, Poe wrote, I "am grieved that I can give you no positive evidence of my industry & zeal . . . unless you will write to M[ajor] Eaton himself who well remembers me and the earnestness of my application" (Ltr-020). He vowed the admission would come by the next term: "I am as certain of obtaining it as I am of being alive" (Ltr-020). With more indignation, he presented Allan with a moral ultimatum: "If you find this statement to be incorrect then condemn me," he declared, "otherwise acquit me of any intention to practice upon your good nature." He sermonized that he now felt "above" such manipulations, and he tried to coax Allan into a renewed relationship with testaments to his diligence and virtue (Ltr-020).

Yet Poe also repeatedly grumbled about Allan's continued hostility. "I am conscious of having offended you formerly—greatly," he acknowledged in July 1829, "but I thought that had been forgiven, at least you told me so" (Ltr-017). He maintained his reborn innocence: "I know that I have done nothing since to deserve your displeasure," he wrote on July 26, 1829, and again on August 4, "I repeat that I have done nothing to deserve your displeasure" (Ltr-017, Ltr-018). He also tried to reason Allan out of his disgruntlement: Because he had made "every endeavor" to enter West Point and because his admittance was delayed by Allan's inaction, it was "therefore unjust to blame [him] for a failure" (Ltr-018). Poe felt that Allan's rancor was irrational and unethical. He went on to allege that Allan's silence defied standards of human decency: "If you are determined to do nothing more on my behalf," he proclaimed, "you will at least do me the common justice to tell me so" (Ltr-018). Again, he martyred himself against the persistence of Allan's disdain: "Perhaps the time will come when you will find that I have not deserved ½ the misfortunes which have happened to me & that you suspected me unworthily" (Ltr-018). By October 1829, he began to express a weariness at Allan's obstinate alienation: "I am sorry that your letters to me have still with them a tone of anger as if my former errors were not forgiven"

(Ltr-020). More despondently, he acknowledged that reconciliation seemed increasingly elusive to him, "if I knew how to regain your affection God knows I would do any thing I could—" (Ltr-020).

The West Point odyssey was a time of exertion and apology for Poe. He tried to avoid a catastrophic oedipal break. He tried to earn exoneration. His later resentment was predicated on this Sisyphean effort—on the hard, thankless work of attempting to change an unchangeable love object. Worse, their affective positions were intransigent: Poe was the repentant son; Allan the unforgiving father. We cannot minimize the significance of Poe's material and affective labor in this interval. Because of these efforts, his resentment was hard-earned. It became an emotional entitlement, the recompense for the allowances and care that Allan denied him. In time, Poe would come to feel that he had a *right* to his grievances. His anger was legitimate; his resentment was justified. As a result, his resentment not only becomes that much more uncompromising, it also assumes more subjective weight. To release resentment—forget or forgive—would have necessitated intolerable negations of Poe's self and his reality. His resentment validates his history, his truth, and the lived experience of his attempt at redemption. It also proves his personal value, confirming that he merited Allan's fealty and support.[78]

BETRAYAL

When Poe finally earned admission to West Point in 1830, Allan allowed him to return home. He bought him four blankets and saw him off at the steamboat docks. Their letters resumed. Poe writes as a freshman again, sounding like an earlier self, like the university student eager to make a father proud. "The examination for admission is just over—a great many cadets of good family &c have been rejected as deficient," he crows (Ltr-026). His confidence returned, and he affirmed his earnestness: "I find that I will possess many advantages & shall endeavor to improve them" (Ltr-026). Three months later he certified, "I have a very excellent standing in my class—in the first section of every thing and have great hopes of doing well" (Ltr-027). He also punctuated the rigor of the cadet's trial: "Of 130 Cadets appointed every year only 30 or 35 ever graduate—the rest being dismissed for bad conduct or deficiency [,] the Regulations are rigid in the extreme" (Ltr-026). Poe did not exaggerate here. A cadet's regimen began with reveille at 5 a.m. and alternated between study, drills, parade, and guard duty until ten o'clock lights-out. By January exams, his class of 104 cadets was reduced to eighty; Poe placed seventeenth in mathematics and third in French. He thrived in military culture: "With its supervisors and comrades, set meals and routines, punishments and rewards," the academy was the most fraternity he had ever known.[79]

But Poe arguably wanted a father as much or more than a battalion of brothers. His longing for Allan's affection persisted. He still addressed Allan as "Dear Pa," asked for answering letters, and signed himself, "yours affectionately" and "I remain respectfully & truly Yours." Nevertheless, he reencountered a familiar neglect that fall. John Allan remarried in October 1830, taking Louisa Patterson as a second wife. The wedding was held at the Patterson family home in New York, close enough to West Point that Allan might have visited. He did not. Poe confessed his sadness at the omission to Allan: "I was greatly in hopes you would have come on to W. Point while you were in N. York, and was very much disappointed when I heard you had gone on home without letting me hear from you" (Ltr-027). Allan's disregard recalls his indifference to visiting a younger Poe at university or attending his exams. Poe sent perfunctory "respects" to the new "Mrs. A," but the letter is brief and dispirited. It ends with the dejected reiteration that he was "very much in hopes that the beauty of the river" would have "tempted" Allan to come see him, as if he knew only the Hudson could entice Allan, not his former foster son (Ltr-027).

Poe's gloom intensified a few weeks later when Allan wrote him a scathing letter. Allan was outraged at learning Poe had disparaged him to his army proxy, Sergeant Graves. In an effort to explain a neglected debt, Poe wrote Graves that Allan had not made good on the money because he was often drunk.[80] Graves sent the letter to Allan. Allan was furious, and the insult magnified their estrangement. On January 3, 1831, Poe shot off a venomous four-page reply to Allan's renunciation, the longest letter in the correspondence. It retches with years of suppressed hostility. He casts himself as a long-suffering victim, refusing to assume guilt for "all that has been alleged against me, and which I have hitherto endured, simply because I was too proud to speak." Breaking this persecuted silence, Poe blasts Allan for his obstructed young life. While he notes Allan's miscarriage of the adoption pact, Poe broods on his lost education. Indeed, the University of Virginia fiasco fuels his bitterness. "You may probably urge that you have given me a liberal education. I will leave the decision of that question to those who know how far liberal educations can be obtained in 8 months at the University of Va . . . " (Ltr-028). Poe felt entitled to the education that, as he alleged in earlier letters, Allan had promised to provide. He believed he had been denied a patrimony.

According to Poe, the entire university crisis was Allan's fault. "I will boldly say that it was wholly and entirely your own mistaken parsimony that caused all the difficulties in which I was involved while at Charlottesville." He accused Allan of answering his requests for money and books "in terms of utmost abuse," as if he were "the vilest wretch on earth." He presents a strict re-accounting of his financials, saying that the humiliation of accruing debt defied "the known rules of the institution." He insists that John Allan's miserly allocations left him only "one dollar in pocket." He goes on to explain that he tried to "retrieve [his] character" with a loan from James Galt, but Galt refused to lend him money; he "then became desperate, and gambled—until I finally i[n]volved myself irretrievably." He acknowledges his intemperance, but declares, "I call God to witness that I have never loved dissipation. . . . But I was drawn into it by my companions." Poe attributes his fall from grace to the seductions of "friendship" when "no one on Earth . . . cared for me, or loved me" (Ltr-028). He further blames Allan for prohibiting his return to university, claiming his "reformation had been sure" if he were given this second chance. Allan's final crime against him was another form of withholding. Faulting Allan's indifference, Poe claims he was denied an occupation: "I waited in vain in expectation that you would, at least, obtain me some employment." Consequently, he "left home," dispossessed by Allan's betrayals (Ltr-028).

The rest of the letter makes quick work of the next four years. Poe repackaged his stint in the army as a steady rise to officer's candidacy. "After nearly 2 years conduct with which no fault could be found—in the army, as a common solider—I earned, myself, by the most humiliating privations—a Cadet's warrant which you could have obtained at any time for the asking" (Ltr-028). Poe further alleges that Allan made him suffer the humiliations of the protracted West Point admissions process. He enumerated the events surrounding Frances's death and the months at West Point as additional instances of infidelity: "I came home, you will remember, the night after the burial. . . . You promised to forgive all—but you soon forgot our promise." In Poe's reckoning, Allan turned traitor again. "You sent me to W point like a beggar. The same difficulties are threatening me as before at Charlottesville—and I must resign" (Ltr-028). As Poe saw it, Allan was a serial offender, responsible for the cycle of poverty and adversity that plagued him.

Poe then fashioned himself as a conscientious objector, pledging to boycott his military obligations until he got free of West Point. "From the time of writing this I shall neglect my studies and duties at the institution—if I do not receive your answer in 10 days—I will leave the point without [it] . . . " (Ltr-028). But the terms of this projected protest were a partial fabrication. Records indicate that Poe had already committed to chronic disobedience before he threatened Allan with neglect of duty. In December, and several days before he wrote to Allan, he had a total of 106 demerits, ranking as one of the worst delinquents in his class. In January, after he sent his ultimatum to Allan, he accumulated an additional sixty-six infractions; the cadet behind him only had a total of twenty-one. John Allan did not send the requisite permission that would have enabled Poe's official resignation—and authorize thirty dollars of final compensation. Instead, he wrote on the back of Edgar's

invective letter, calling it "the most barefaced one sided statement" and concluding "I do not think the Boy has one good quality." On January 28, 1831,
Poe faced a general court martial, charged with "gross neglect of duty" and
"disobedience of orders."[81] The court found him guilty on all counts.

Less than a month later, however, Poe wrote to Allan—sick and miserable—for money again. He said he left West Point two days before, "without
a cloak or any other clothing of importance." And worse, he "caught a most
violent cold and am confined to my bed." His desolation was complete: "I
have no money—no friends—I have written to my brother—but he cannot
help me." Totally forsaken, Poe forecasted his own death: "I shall never rise
from my bed—besides a most violent cold on my lungs my ear discharges
blood and matter continually and my headache is distracting." In closing, he
begged for help: "Please send me a little money—quickly—and forget what
I said about you—" (Ltr-029).

Allan did not respond. His new wife was pregnant with their first child. In
August 1831, Louisa gave birth to John Allan Jr. This child was, of course,
Allan's legitimate, biological son and heir. In psychoanalytic terms, the oedipal loss was irreparable for Poe. Silverman speculates that Poe had not heard
about the birth when he wrote the most poignant expression of grief in the
correspondence, which makes the sorrow in the letter that much more acute
and prophetic. It was over between them. Poe lamented: "When I think of the
long twenty-one years that I have called you father, and you have called me
son, I could cry like a child to think that it should all end in this" (Ltr-032).
His words pitch with regret and self-recrimination. "When I look back on the
past and think of every thing—of how much you tried to do for me—of your
forbearance and your generosity, in spite of the most flagrant ingratitude on
my part, I can not help thinking myself the greatest fool in existence." He
feels blighted: "I am ready to curse the day I was born" (Ltr-032). And he
surrenders to loss. "I am not the damned villain even to ask you to restore
me to the twentieth part of those affections which I have so deservedly lost,
and I am resigned to whatever fate is allotted me" (Ltr-032). Although Poe
does not explicitly ask for reunion, he still registers his longing for reparation and Allan's "affections." Whatever resignation he claims is incomplete
and ambivalent.

In the aftermath of this fracture, grief and grievance—and ultimately
resentment—were all that remained. With resentment, Poe would sustain
his attachment to Allan, holding him in bonds of acrimony. Indeed, Hogget
fittingly recovers the relationship between grief, grievance, and resentment.
Associated with grief (a "deep and intense sorrow or mourning") and grieve
(to "cause grief" or "suffer grief"), grievance names a state of melancholy
bitterness. In both its origins and persistence, grievance is analogous to
resentment. Like resentment, grievance begins in injury or offense, a "cause

for complaint."[82] And grievance can become chronic. As Steiner expounds, in resentment an "injury smolders on as a grievance . . . held on to and nursed."[83] Grievance holds the injury close, and it holds the injurer even closer. Feldman theorizes that "the inevitable experiences of disappointment and injury give rise to the grievance as a means of denying the reality of loss."[84] Grievance defends against an irreparable break. In this sense, grievance and resentment are grief denied. As Weintrobe's contends, "Nursing the grievance keeps alive the possibility of restoring the relationship with the idealized object, if not now, then at some point in the future." Grievance's tirades—"berating the idealized object that has fallen from grace"—are attempts to restore an "exclusive and possessive relationship with the ideal object." Anger and indignation become intimacy. Indeed, "grievance can be clung to and nursed like a babe in arms."[85] When Poe lost John Allan, lost him over and over again, he lost a singular, oedipal intimacy. With resentment, however, he could refuse mourning. With resentment, he could reattach.

In this defiant clinging, resentment recalls melancholia's investment in grief. As we see in chapter 3, melancholia also refuses to release the lost object, encrypting it in a maelstrom of love, hate, and desire. Through incorporation, the melancholic assimilates the lost object in the ego, forever yearning for its return and retaliating against its absence. Elizabeth Wilson reminds us that "melancholic responses to loss are often malicious. . . . This is a scene of intense bitterness—simultaneously painful and enjoyable. The depressive is both miserably desperate for attachment and elated by the destruction of the object for which she yearns." The melancholic's self-torments are actually aggression against the love object, designed as punishment for an unforgivable abandonment. As Wilson asserts, there is nothing harmless about the melancholic's internalizations: "Taking in an object—even a loved one—involves devouring and damaging it."[86] Melancholia enacts a spiteful hostility against loss. It consumes what it loves; it cannibalizes what it wants and cannot have.

The parallels between melancholia and resentment raise troubling questions: If resentment likewise refuses to grieve the broken attachment, is it responsible for a similar wreckage? Does it also destroy its object? Does it implicate the subject in sadism and death? Or are there more subjective resources in resentment? Is there more creativity in a grief that becomes grievance? Is there more agency or mobility in resentment?

VICTIMIZATION

Provocatively, the answers to these questions come in the delicious martyrdom resentment finds in reattachment. Resentment discourses suggest that the resentful subject embraces his victimization. As Hogget notes, "grievance is intimately connected to the belief that one is the wronged victim." Grievance knows that persecutions can be unjust and undeserved. As a victim, the resentful subject "is innocent and powerless," morally correct and good. Hence, the other bears the stigma of guilt and evil. "One of the great consolations of victimhood," Hogget writes," comes in "the fantasy that, having been wronged . . . the victim is 'in the right.'" In other words, victimization nurtures a compensatory moral "superiority": the reassuring conviction that "one may have been misunderstood, unfairly treated, even abused, but one would never do those things oneself." The resentful victim recognizes the reality of unwarranted suffering. He perceives both his own oppression and the oppressor's culpability. More actively, these recognitions propel a "drive to make moral judgements."[87] The resentful subject believes he has a heightened ability to see and act ethically. The victim becomes moral authority. The subject "takes up a righteous position in this powerful alliance" between grievance and victimization. This position is strengthened by the conviction that they alone possess "some potent and unassailable truth."[88] In sum, the victim arbitrates moral wrong, moral right, and veracity itself.

Certainly, Poe felt John Allan's abuses intensely. With a victim's acumen, he crafted a pattern of blame in his letters. Two days after he left West Point, Poe revised the reasons for his dismissal, faulting Allan's disdain rather than his own decision to fail out. "I have been dismissed—when a single line from you would have saved it," he railed. "The whole academy have interested themselves in my behalf because my only crime was being sick—but it was of no use," he begrudged. (Ltr 029). In this letter, the principled dissenter becomes the virtuous sufferer. According to Poe, Allan's negligence destroyed his hard-earned caliber in the academy: "I refer you to Col Thayer to the public records, for my standing and reputation for talent—but it was all in vain if you had granted me permission to resign—all might have been avoided" (Ltr 029). Once again, Poe felt that Allan had denied him a just due, an entitlement of assistance. Poe also blamed John Allan for the poverty he endured after the court martial. Once he paid the academy what he owed for board, laundry, and books, Poe had twenty-four cents. If Allan had authorized his formal resignation, he would have left the academy with a requisite thirty dollars.[89] And Quinn notes that most cadets received an allowance from home to supplement a military stipend and rations; Poe, of course, did not.[90] From a place of deprivation, Poe railed against Allan's callousness: "[I]n my present circumstances a single dollar is of more importance to me than 10,000 are to you and you deliberately refused to answer my letter" (Ltr 029). Poe attributed methodical, purposeful malice to Allan's denials. He saw it as a pattern of intentional harm.

Just as importantly, Poe delineated the ethical reasons that he warranted saving. He called on more humanistic values to revive Allan's altruism. "I now make an appeal not to your affection because I have lost that but to your sense of justice" (Ltr-029). He asked Allan to intervene "not for my sake [but] for the sake of humanity" (Ltr-034). And he asked Allan to help him in the name of bygone love and God's favor, "for the sake of what once was dear to you, for the sake of the love you bore me when I sat upon your knee and called you father do not forsake me this only time—and god will remember you accordingly" (Ltr-035). These are potent moral justifications, petitions based on principles of justice, human dignity, paternal care, and religious reward. When Allan answered such requests with silence and denial, he reinforced his status as a victimizer.

Although Poe marshaled more universal ethics, many of his solicitations were deeply personal, based on the exigencies of his poverty and the obligations of past attachment. He vividly described the realities of his penury, and he took to hyperbole to show that Allan's repudiation meant he was punishing an innocent. In November 1831, Poe wrote urgently to Allan for financial aid, saying he had been arrested for debts he had taken on for his recently deceased brother. Here, Poe exaggerates his difficulty. No evidence of the arrest exists. But alleging arrest, especially for a dead brother's arrears, enhanced Poe's status as an irreproachable victim.[91] In the letters Poe writes to Allan between 1831 and 1833, he pleads for money with all the righteousness of the afflicted. "How often you relieved the distressed of a perfect stranger less urgent than mine," he inveighed, "and yet when I beg and intreat you in the name of God to send me succor you will still refuse to aid me" (Ltr-034). Allan's general inclination to charity galled Poe when his own scarcities were more personal and proximate. He claimed to understand Allan's disaffection, but not his financial disownment: "I know that I have offended you past all forgiveness, and I know that I have no longer any hopes of being again received in your favour, but, for the sake of Christ, do not let me perish for a sum of money which you would never miss, and which would relieve me from the greatest earthly misery . . . " (Ltr-034).

Allan's relative ease made Poe's own anguish impossible to assimilate. "You are enjoying yourself in all the blessings that wealth & happiness can bestow," he accused, "and I am suffering every extremity of want and misery without even a chance of escape, or a friend to whom I can look up to for assistance" (Ltr-034). Poe saw his victimization as absolute, made that much more profound by Allan's abundance. Indeed, Allan's privilege ignited the surges of vengeful and moralistic indignation that Poe occasionally expressed. "I have not strength nor energy left to write half what I feel—You one day will feeel [sic] how you have treated me" (Ltr-029). Poe wished for retribution. Just as importantly, he felt sure of the difference in his own character: "I feel at the very bottom of my heart that if you were in my situation and you in mine, how differently I would act" (Ltr-034). Poe knew Allan's wealth and philanthropic reputation. He knew Allan had both the resources and the inclination to help a person in need. In Poe's mind, the bygone love between them gave his distress a priority—a subjective significance—that another postulant could not claim. It made Allan's indifference that much more immoral. It was one thing to refuse a stranger; quite another to refuse the orphan Allan took into his care.

To punctuate his despondency, Poe abased himself. In December 1831, he fell on his proverbial knees before Allan: "If you wish me to humble myself before you I am humble—Sickness and misfortune have left me not a shadow of pride. I own that I am miserable and unworthy of your notice, but do not leave me to perish without leaving me still one resource" (Ltr-034). All hubris gone, Poe presented himself as a lowly supplicant. Later that month, he insisted on his unprecedented desolation: "No person in the world I am sure, could have undergone more wretchedness than I have done for some time past" (Ltr-035). By April 1833, he claimed Allan's miserliness would be the death of him: "If you will only consider in what situation I am placed you will surely pity me—without friends, without any means consequently of obtaining employment, I am perishing—absolutely perishing for want of aid" (Ltr-036). He maintained that his deprivation was an unjust purgatory: "And yet I am not idle—nor addicted to any vice—nor have I committed any offence against society which would render me deserving of so hard a fate. For God's sake pity me, and save me from destruction" (Ltr-036). Poe depicted his victimization as abjection. He begged for aid. He pleaded for pity. He risked emasculation to gain redemption.

Whatever Poe magnified in his letters, poverty certainly imperiled him over and over. Jacksonian America was a world of extreme financial volatility, banking failures, and crushing economic depressions. As Jill Lepore puts it, "Indigence cast a shadow over everything [Poe] attempted."[92] Allan, in contrast, was one of the richest men in Virginia. In 1825, he inherited three quarters of a million dollars—more than twenty million dollars in today's currency—from his uncle and benefactor, William Galt. Thus, Allan's wealth was just as material as Poe's destitution. Poe made no mistake there.

In his relationship with his foster father, Poe navigated stark disparities of capital, power, and attachment. When he claims a victim's status, he effectively redefines the relationship between masculinity and vulnerability. In this redefinition, the letters do their most subversive work. As Erinn Cunniff Gilson signals, in the most reductive cultural paradigms, vulnerability is a "condition of weakness, dependence, passivity, incapability, and powerlessness." This understanding of vulnerability "dominates the sociocultural imaginary of the industrialized, capitalist Western parts of the world, especially the

United States." It also dominates the most pervasive historical segregation of masculinity and femininity. Vulnerability is feminized and sexualized: "Women and sexual minorities have historically been subject to systemic violation, exploitation, objectification, and commodification."[93] In contrast, invulnerability is masculinized, seemingly synonymous with agency, power, control, and autonomy.

Gilson complicates this simplistic, gendered logic of vulnerability. She argues first that invulnerability—as an ideal or an imperative—perpetuates a dangerous fallacy: "Inasmuch as the capacity to be affected by and affect others is central to what it is to be alive, the achievement of full mastery, complete control, and utter impenetrability both is impossible and belies this reality." In other words, vulnerability pervades the human condition. We persist in states of interconnection and interdependence that make us inexorably susceptible to one other. Ideologies of invincibility or impermeability are social fictions. In addition, Gilson holds that vulnerability is never a permanent or fixed reality. It is a "condition of potential," it manifests in multiple, fluid, "ambivalent and ambiguous ways." Most importantly, vulnerability always and only emerges at intersections of power—in power struggles or power exchanges—that can "create, entrench, sustain, or contest inequity."[94] Our exposure to each other constitutes a horizon of possibility as well as an ethical and political responsibility.

For Gilson, a reconsideration of vulnerability requires a simultaneous reassessment of victimization. When we understand vulnerability as more complex and ambiguous than we ever imagined, we can better discern "the coexistence and intertwining of passivity and activity, strength and weakness, assertion and receptivity, agency and the absence of control" in any experience of precarity. In complexity and ambiguity, rigid dualisms break down, and vulnerability cannot be confined to subjective deficiency. Thus, the term "victim" itself must expand to denote assertions of power, strength, agency, control, and resistance within or despite oppression. More fundamentally, when a victimizer exploits a shared, human vulnerability, the injury gets re-seen as an unjust and unethical abuse of power. In other words, this reassessment of victimhood enables a clearer, more forceful delineation of "the wrong in exploiting vulnerability." As Gilson explains, "to exploit vulnerability is to appropriate the basic capacity to affect and be affected to a particular narrow end." Victimization happens when vulnerability becomes a mechanism for the violations of power. Victimization happens when power defies a relational, moral, or political right. The predicament is *not* that we are vulnerable. We cannot transcend vulnerability. The predicament is that power *uses* our vulnerability against us. According to Gilson, such recognitions make the victim judge and jury on the damage done to them as well as the meaning of justice. "It is only with such a conception of vulnerability that those who have been victimized are authorized to make sense of their experiences on and in their own terms, and so to be the arbiters of the wrong committed."⁹⁵ A more nuanced understanding of vulnerability empowers victims to name and adjudicate their own pain.

In his letters to Allan, Poe claims a victim's authority to know the harm done to him and to declare the injustice of that wounding. He inscribes a vulnerable white masculinity, a manhood subject to material and emotional scarcities. As J. Gerald Kennedy discerns, "Poe portrayed himself recurrently as an unloved, abandoned child; his deepest need was to re-establish connection with a parent who had not only ceased to give him affection but who had also stopped communicating."⁹⁶ Thus, the letters say something profound about victimization *within* a gender, a race, and a family. The letters expose the impacts of a victim/victimizer dichotomy *between* white men. They expose oppressions that can circulate *inside* white masculinity: abuses that exploit the human vulnerabilities of age, attachment, station, and poverty.

In his relationship with Allan, Poe experienced both affective and economic violations. Allan knew Poe's orphaned and lower-class origins. He knew Poe's losses and grief. He knew his youth, his penury, and his alienation from masculine networks of influence. He denied him affection and assistance anyway. The last time Allan sent Poe financial relief, his former ward was twenty-two. The last surviving words John Allan wrote about Poe were invective, scrawled on the back of an old letter: "it is not upwards of two years since I received the above precious relic of the Blackest Heart & deepest ingratitude alike destitute of honour & principle every day of his life has only served to confirm his debased nature."⁹⁷ In perhaps his worst insult on record, Allan routed Poe in racialized terms. Southern men described the vilest "character deficiencies in racial terms." Incorrigible boys were said to have "'blackened' their reputations." Men "who abrogated the power and the duties their wealth bought them" had likewise "blackened" their natures.⁹⁸ To Allan, Poe had entirely corrupted himself.

Poe purportedly saw Allan a month before he died in 1834. When he entered the bedchamber, Allan "raised his cane as if to strike him and ordered him to leave."⁹⁹ He left his fortune—three plantations and 230 slaves—to Louisa and their three children. His will made no mention of Poe. Poe was twenty-five years old at Allan's death. By then, they had been estranged for seven years.

Poe's alienation from Allan—his dispossession, disownment, and disinheritance—became a bitter legacy. Allan left him with only the resentment that the letters meticulously archive. Intriguingly, this acrimony would ultimately fuel a powerfully productive energy in Poe. A number of thinkers testify to the potentially generative effects of resentment.¹⁰⁰ Without recourse to more direct assertions of power, resentment can find a vital and vitalizing expression in fantasy. In resentment, a subject reimagines the terms of his injury, delivering punishment and redemption to an unjust world. For Poe, the fantasy gave life to the fictions that center this study. In his short stories, Poe imagined men in close, caretaking intimacies with one another, as well as in relationships of violence and vengeance. He imagined men vulnerable to other men, men with the capacity to rescue or destroy each other. He imagined men sickened in their relationships to one another and men victimized by hostile, hateful patriarchs. He imagined men retaliating against loss, pain, and injury. In this, he wrote from the place of fantasy that resentment creates. As Kennedy affirms, "In letters, as in fiction and poetry, he elaborated fantasies of retribution and triumph which carry a metaphysical import, and he inscribed visions of a pastoral paradise where he could be insulated from failure, pain, and death." Indeed, Kennedy discerns a direct line of ascent between Poe's letters to Allan and his later fictions. In the letters, Kennedy writes, "we observe the writer figuring himself as the inevitable victim—of poverty, illness, treachery, or bad luck—and appealing for deliverance from his fate." Thus, "well before publishing his first tale," Poe "had mastered the rhetoric of dread," a "strategy of writing rooted in despair."[101] For Poe, the despair and the dread were more than rhetorical. They were lived affects, inextricable from the relentless re-feeling of grief and grievance his resentment roused. That resentment proffered him a creative plenty—fantasies to inspire fictions—does not diminish the injuries he endured. But he told its stories. And the stories stay with us.

NOTES

1. Edgar Allan Poe, "The Letters of Edgar Allan Poe," Ltr 05, Edgar Allan Poe Society of Baltimore, www.eapoe.org/people/allanj.htm#letters. Hereafter cited by number parenthetically in the text.

2. Silverman, *Mournful*, 33.

3. Thomas Jefferson, "Report of the Commissioners for the University of Virginia to the Virginia General Assembly," 1818, founders.archives.gov/documents/Madison/04–01–02–0289.

4. "John Allan had promised the family of David Poe to afford Edgar the liberal education he had not had himself" (Silverman, *Mournful*, 12).

5. Glover, *Southern Sons*, 55.

6. Ibid., 56–57.

7. Timothy Williams, *Intellectual Manhood: University, Self, and Society in the Antebellum South* (Chapel Hill: University of North Carolina Press, 2015), 6.

8. Glover, *Southern Sons*, 37.

9. Williams argues that no "stigma attached to trying college and failing." Southerners believed that some sons were suited to university; others were not. Yet his

explanation of this ideology reinforces the imperative to succeed in other arenas. Students who did not graduate college "often went on to become highly successful statesman, planters, or professionals." In an era of apprenticeship, students frequently left school to study a specific vocation (*Intellectual Manhood*, 24). Hence, leaving school might not have meant ignominy, but failure or dissipation was a scarlet letter.

10. Glover, *Southern Sons*, 37.

11. Dana White, *National Manhood* (Durham, NC: Duke University Press, 1998), 13, 22.

12. Paul Rogin, *Fathers and Children*, 54, 36.

13. White, *National Manhood*, 22.

14. Glover, *Southern Sons*, 98, 99.

15. Ibid., 73–76. Joseph F. Kett, *Rites of Passage: Adolescence in America, 1790 to the Present* (New York: Basic Books, 1977), 51–59; Williams, *Intellectual Manhood*, 33–34.

16. Ibid., 78, 107, 78, 108, 109, 110.

17. Ibid., 61.

18. Joseph Butler (1692–1752) was an Anglican bishop, theologian, and philosopher. Adam Smith (1723–1790) was a Scottish economist and philosopher. Moral sentiments are commonly understood as affective reactions to moral phenomena, e.g., disgust, resentment, indignation. Adam Smith theorized that sentiment itself—sympathy, or empathy in more contemporary terms—was the basis for all moral action. As Rushdy explains, "The British tradition of philosophy about resentment focused on the emotion as one that could stimulate important social passions (especially the desire for justice) or one that could likewise become a brooding illness. What the British tradition implicitly assumed is that resentment could be expressed in and through individuals as a result of either personal injury to the self or public injury to others (*After Injury: A Historical Anatomy of Forgiveness, Resentment, and Apology* [Oxford: Oxford University Press, 2018], 123).

19. Ibid., 101, 129.

20. Shelby Weitzel, "On the Relationship Between Forgiveness and Resentment in the Sermons of Joseph Butler," *History of Philosophy Quarterly* 24, no. 3 (2007): 239.

21. Adam Smith, *The Theory of Moral Sentiments* (Ann Arbor: University of Michigan Library, 2005), 144, name.umdl.umich.edu/K111361.0001.001.

22. Leon Wurmser, "The Superego As of Herald Resentment," *Psychoanalytic Inquiry* 29, no. 5 (2009): 392.

23. Glover, *Southern Sons*, 41, 19.

24. Bertram Wyatt-Brown, *Southern Honor: Ethics and Behavior in the Old South* (Oxford: Oxford University Press, 2007), 46.

25. Glover, *Southern Sons*, 26.

26. P. F. Strawson, "Freedom and Resentment," in *Freedom and Resentment and Other Essays* (New York: Routledge, 2008), www.ucl.ac.uk/~uctytho/dfwstrawson1 .htm.

27. Rushdy, *After Injury*, 102.

28. See Silverman's discussion of the grievance letter (*Mournful*, 35).

ort4

29. Javier Moscoso, "The Shadows of Ourselves: Resentment, Monomania, and Modernity," in *On Resentment: Past and Present*, eds. Bernardino Fantini, Dolores Martin Maruno, and Javier Moscoso (Newcastle: Cambridge Scholars Publishing, 2013), 22.

30. Max Scheler, *Ressentiment*, trans. Louis A. Coser (Milwaukee, WI: Marquette University Press, 1994), 8, 54, 7, 7–8.

31. Citing Alexis de Tocqueville, Michael Kimmel observes, "The American man was a radical democrat—equal and alone, masterless and separate, autonomous and defenseless against the tyranny of the majority. Each citizen was equal, and 'equally impotent, poor, and isolated'" (*Manhood in America*, 3rd edition [New York: Oxford University Press, 1998], 19).

32. Glover, *Southern Sons*, 29.

33. Ibid., 16.

34. Rushdy, *After Injury*, 117.

35. Scheler, *Ressentiment*, 6.

36. Butler posits that resentment turns pathological in five different ways: if the injury is the product of delusion; if the injury is magnified by narcissism; if the injury is accidental or unavoidable; if the ire is disproportionate to the wound; and if retaliation gratifies meaner instincts (Rushdy, *After Injury*, 130).

37. Ibid., 130, 136.

38. Scheler, *Ressentiment*, 4.

39. Rushdy, *After Injury*, 103.

40. Freidrich Nietzsche, *On the Genealogy of Morals and Other Writings*, trans. Carol Deith, ed. Keith Ansell-Pearson (Cambridge: Cambridge University Press, 2017), 22, 25.

41. Wurmser, "Superego," 396–97.

42. Nietzsche, *Genealogy*, 39.

43. Paul Hogget, "Ressentiment and Grievance," *British Journal of Psychotherapy* 34, no. 3 (2018): 395.

44. Dana Luciano, *Arranging Grief: Sacred Time and the Body in Nineteenth-Century America* (New York: New York University Press, 2007), 5, 6.

45. Silverman, *Mournful*, 21, 27.

46. Arthur Hobson Quinn, *Edgar Allan Poe: A Critical Biography* (Baltimore, MD: Johns Hopkins University Press, 1998), 54.

47. Silverman, *Mournful*, 12.

48. Ibid., 11.

49. Lorri Glover, *All Our Relations: Blood Ties and Emotional Bonds among the Early South Carolina Gentry* (Baltimore: Johns Hopkins University Press, 2000), 43. In addition, Lori Askeland notes that orphaned children were a "constant presence" in America's past. Yet orphanages did not proliferate until the 1830s, when cholera and yellow fever epidemics, immigration, and urbanization caused mass poverty and the splintering of kinship networks (*Children and Youth in Adoption, Orphanages, and Foster Care: A Historical Handbook and Guide* [Westport, CT: Greenwood Press, 2006], 8–9).

50. Askeland, *Children and Youth*, 8.

51. Susan L. Porter, "A Good Home: Indenture and Adoption in Nineteenth-Century Orphanages," in *Adoption in America: Historical Perspectives*, ed. E. Wayne Carp (Ann Arbor, MI: University of Michigan Press, 2002), 40.

52. G. Melvin Herndon, "From Scottish Orphan to Virginia Planter: William Galt, Jr., 1801–1851," *Virginia Magazine of History and Biography* 87, no. 3 (1979): 326.

53. Silverman, *Mournful*, 12.

54. Ibid., 18.

55. Quinn, *Edgar Allan Poe*, 69.

56. Quinn maintains that evidence for Poe's tormented days at Irvine is "slim" (ibid., 67). But Silverman concludes that the account is "chronologically possible, and consonant with Poe's early and later character, and with expressed feelings about his education in England" (*Mournful*, 456).

57. Silverman, *Mournful*, 18, 19, 25.

58. Porter explains that nineteenth-century adoptions were open: "When children were adopted, their relatives were consulted and were expected to know the children's whereabouts" ("A Good Home," 43). Birth parents and family members visited and kept in touch with adopted children. Foster care likely worked on a similar ethic of communication and continuity with biological kindred.

59. Quinn, *Edgar Allan Poe*, 89.

60. Perhaps he was increasingly aware of his tenuous position in the Allan household. Or perhaps he was dejected at the death of Jane Stanard, the mother of a schoolmate who had offered him surrogate love and comfort.

61. Scheler, *Ressentiment*, 8. Scheler posits that certain familial placements can foment resentment. A mother-in-law's situation, for example, particularly the son's mother, "is one which the devil himself might have invented to test a hero." Her beloved child chooses another woman, a woman "who has done nothing . . . and yet demand[s] everything." Worse, a mother must "welcome" this event and "receive the intruder with affection!" Likewise, Scheler observes that a younger child's relation with the first-born son is just as torturous, another familial bond that simultaneously demands love, allegiance, and self-abnegation (*Ressentiment*, 17).

62. Moscoso, "Shadows," 33, 32.

63. Wurmser, "Superego," 387, 389, 387.

64. Michael Feldman, "Grievance: The Underlying Oedipal Configuration," *International Journal of Psychoanalysis* 89, no. 4 (2008): 744.

65. John Steiner, "Revenge and Resentment in the 'Oedipus Situation.'" *International Journal of Psychoanalysis* 77, no. 3 (1996): 435.

66. Quinn, *Edgar Allan Poe*, 134.

67. Feldman, "Grievance," 745, 746.

68. Sally Weintrobe, "Links Between Grievance, Complaint, and Different Forms of Entitlement," *International Journal of Psychoanalysis* 85, no. 1 (2004): 84.

69. Silverman, *Mournful*, 43.

70. Glover, *Southern Sons*, 152–53.

71. Quinn, *Edgar Allan Poe*, 137, 136.

72. Silverman, *Mournful*, 52.

73. Quinn, *Edgar Allan Poe*, 135, 206.

74. Silverman, *Mournful*, 53.

75. John Allan told his sister that "Edgar had gone to Sea to seek his fortunes" (Silverman, *Mournful*, 38).

76. Ibid., 42.

77. Quinn, *Edgar Allan Poe*, 147.

78. Still, given Allan's parsimony—and Poe's yearning for reunion—it baffles that Poe kept complicating the relationship with requests for money. Was he that obtuse? Did his financial crisis compete with the oedipal crisis? Did he confuse with money with love? In later letters, Poe acknowledged that he consistently asked Allan for rescue, offering only a desperate need for a "friend" as explanation: "It is true that when I have been in great extremity, I have always applied to you—for I had no other friend . . . " (Ltr-032). He would repeatedly link his poverty to his affective desolation in subsequent years, saying he was "without friends" who could lend money or help him find a job. In Poe's mind, a "friend" would have acted as a father or a brother, a "friend" would have saved him. Poe's appeals to Allan when he was bereft of any "friend" resonate with a yearning for a patriarchal salvation that pervaded nineteenth-century manhood. Kimmel notes that "the Sons of Liberty carried out a symbolic patricide." To reclaim "their manhood from its British guardians," revolutionary America begot a "new race of men" (*Manhood,* 15, 16). Rogin adds that the self-made man "did not depend on paternal aid"; he "was free of the weight of paternal inheritance." Nineteenth-century men had a singular obligation to birth—and father—themselves. They "idealized the dying generation of revolutionary fathers," Rogin explains, but could not turn to their "living fathers" (*Fathers and Children*, 53, 54). In addition, patricide exacted significant psychological costs, "including the loneliness of the fatherless son." Thus, fathers occupied "an intimate and obsessive role" in Jacksonian culture. Poe's generation "expressed powerful grievances against fathers on the one hand, and powerful need, on the other, to live up to their ideals" (Kimmel, *Manhood*, 16). Intriguingly, as Dana White shows, men tried to resolve this conflict—and recover the absent father—in their friendships. Through fraternal association, men accessed an unparalleled "wholeness"—an intimacy and affection—with other men. These intense emotional bonds worked through "hierarchical structures." In ritualized initiations, "every novitiate [was] 'rescued' by a wiser, older, mystic patriarch, and adopted into the next stage of brotherhood" (*National Manhood*, 178, 183, 185). In his application to West Point, Poe was the novitiate, seeking a homosocial wholeness. His requests for money underscored his need for patriarchal rescue and his desire to be adopted into a deeper fraternity. As he signals, a "friend" would have provided both.

79. Silverman, *Mournful*, 61, 62.

80. Ibid., 63.

81. Ibid., 65, 66.

82. Hogget, "Ressentiment," 396.

83. Steiner, 76.

84. Feldman, "Grievance," 749.

85. Weintrobe, "Links," 84.

86. Elizabeth Wilson, *Gut Feminism* (Durham: Duke University Press, 2015), 75, 78.

87. Hogget, "Ressentiment," 399, 400, 399.

88. Feldman, "Grievance," 745.

89. Silverman, *Mournful*, 67, 35.

90. Quinn, *Edgar Allan Poe*, 173.

91. Quinn speculates that the arrest likely never happened, although Poe certainly had reason to fear prison given the number of debtors in Baltimore's jail (*Edgar Allan Poe*, 190). Three weeks after he got the news, Allan drafted a letter arranging for his "liberation" and sending twenty dollars, but he "neglected" to mail it for another five weeks (Silverman, *Mournful*, 95). Once Allan's assistance arrived, Poe apparently paid the debt and made no contact with Allan for more than a year.

92. As Jill Lepore summarizes, Poe lived through two transatlantic financial collapses: the Panic of 1819 and the Panic of 1837. He was in New York during the second collapse. Riots broke out as people raided the city's shops for food. That fall, nine out of ten Eastern factories closed. Five hundred men answered a single ad for day laborers, desperate to work for a poverty wage of four dollars a month. Poe died at the end of a decade called "the Hungry Forties" across Europe ("The Humbug: Edgar Allan Poe and the Economy of Horror," *New Yorker* [April 27, 2009], www .newyorker.com/magazine/2009/04/27/the-humbug).

93. Erinn Cunniff Gilson, "Vulnerability and Victimization: Rethinking Key Concepts in Feminist Discourses on Sexual Violence," *Signs* 42, no. 1 (Autumn 2016): 74, 75.

94. Ibid., 76–77, 78.

95. Ibid., 88, 89, 91.

96. Kennedy, *Poe, Death, and the Life of Writing*, 95.

97. Silverman, *Mournful*, 96.

98. Glover, *Southern Sons*, 27, 85–86.

99. Silverman, *Mournful*, 97.

100. Without recourse to a more direct axis of power, Nietzsche argues the resentful subject can "compensate only with imaginary revenge." In this sense, resentment can "tur[n] creative and giv[e] birth" (Nietzsche, *Genealogy*, 20). Other theorists reinforce this interplay between resentment and fantasy. Steiner holds that "in the state dominated by grievance, revenge is repeatedly played out in phantasy . . ."(434). And Hogget contends that the resentful subject's exorcises his rage in "endlessly repeating" fantasies: fantasies of revenge, or repossession of the lost object, or redemption for an unjust world. In one case study, for example, a patient exists "almost entirely in a fantasy retreat which provided him both with glimpses of the imagined paradise from which he had been expelled and an attitude of sustained protest against the injustice of what had occurred" ("Ressentiment," 397, 399). Feldman similarly states that "the patient maintains a set of phantasies" in order "to defend himself from the threat of a reality that hates." Until the fantasy assumes "a life of its own" ("Grievance," 745, 749).

101. Kennedy, *Poe*, 91.

Chapter Five

Revenge

Poe died in infamy. Friend and physician Joseph Snodgrass found him at a Baltimore tavern, slumped over in a chair, "stupefied with liquor." His face was "haggard, . . . bloated, and unwashed, his hair unkempt and his whole physique repulsive."[1] He was surrounded by drunk, disorderly men who were entirely indifferent to his distress. Snodgrass arranged for Poe to be transported to Washington College Hospital. He was admitted, came in and out of consciousness for three days, and died on October 7, 1849. Although newspapers recorded the cause of death as "congestion of the brain," people close to Poe knew he drank himself to death. In a diary entry dated October 10, writer and political leader John Kennedy recorded the sordid details of his passing: "On Tuesday last Edgar A. Poe died in town here at the hospital from the effects of a debauch. . . . He fell in with some companion here who seduced him to the bottle. . . . The consequence was fever, delirium, and madness, and in a few days a termination of his sad career in the hospital. Poor Poe!"[2]

Poe immediately became a cautionary tale. Snodgrass told the story of Poe's death in temperance lectures through the 1850s, publishing an account that emphasized his narcosis: "So insensible was he, that we had to carry him to the carriage as if he were a corpse."[3] In his last days, Poe was blackout drunk, lost to the carelessness of dissolute men. Adding to his disgrace, Rufus Griswold—literary critic, editor, and battle-worn Poe detractor—eulogized Poe in a dubious memorial. Griswold acknowledged that Poe's death will "startle many, but few will be grieved by it." He said that Poe had celebrity, but "few or no friends." He summarized Poe's life in reproachful terms, cataloging his dissipation at university, his estrangement from his foster father, John Allan, and his struggles against poverty. Griswold called Poe reckless, arrogant, envious, belligerent, and hostile to the world. Even worse, he depicted Poe as deranged: "He walked the streets, in madness or melancholy, with lips moving in indistinct curses, or with eyes upturned in passionate prayers . . . —or, with his glances introverted to a heart gnawed with anguish, and with a face shrouded in gloom."[4] In 1850, Griswold published a memoir that further distorted Poe's character: He exaggerated his alcoholism, falsely claimed he was expelled from university and deserted the army, suggested he had an illicit affair, alleged that he blackmailed a woman for money, and accused him of indolence. As J. Gerald Kennedy summarizes, Griswold "fixed the poet's image for posterity: Poe would long remain an object of derision, a lonely, amoral lunatic, wandering the margins of American litera-ture."[5] The malice of Griswold's memoir defined Poe's bios for a generation.

This derision was the posthumous culmination of decades of vitriol between Poe and other men. Poe was spectacularly scathing in his literary reviews, and his feuds with nineteenth-century writers, editors, and critics were notori-ous. He clashed with Lewis Gaylord Clark, editor of the *Knickerbocker*, exchanging taunts in contemporary magazines and newspapers for years. In the "Longfellow War," Poe disparaged the acclaimed poet and Harvard pro-fessor as a plagiarist, a didact, and a hack. More scandalously, he caricatured or maligned thirty-eight New York writers in a series of articles printed in *Godey's Lady's Book* between May and November 1846. His opening remarks set the tone for the roasts to come, pronouncing "the most 'popular,' the most 'successful' writers among us . . . busy-bodies, toadies, quacks."[6] In what was christened "The War of the Literati," Poe became the object of retaliatory scorn. Writers like Charles Briggs, Thomas Dunn English, and Hiram Fuller decimated Poe in the press.[7] Twenty years after Poe's death, Charles Briggs bitterly reminisced, "What rendered him so obnoxious to those who knew him intimately were his treachery to his friends, his insincerity[,] his utter disregard of his moral obligations, and his total lack of loyalty and nobleness of purpose." Briggs eviscerated Poe's integrity and humanity, and then went on to impugn his ambitions: "He aimed at nothing, thought of nothing, and hoped for nothing but literary reputation."[8] As late as 1896, Thomas English accused him of "moral idiocy."[9] For most of his adult life and much of his afterlife, Poe incited the anger and retributions of other men. Again, J. Gerald Kennedy captures this truth and its impact: "His urge to locate and confront enemies, to offend and disgust, to mock and mystify, ensured that Poe would remain . . . the obnoxious misfit of American letters."[10]

One of the last short fictions Poe published before his death, "The Cask of Amontillado" (1846), has historically been understood as a purposeful reck-oning with his enemies. Or, more precisely, as a calculated revenge against English, Fuller, Briggs, Clark, and every other combatant who persecuted him. Thomas Mabbott maintains that "The Cask of Amontillado" (printed immediately after the concluding installment of the "Literati" sketches) was a "working out of [Poe's] immediate emotions" in the wake of serial assaults and his "long[ing] for revenge."[11] Kenneth Silverman sees shades of his literati nemeses in the tale as well as John Allan.[12] Its plot seems simple enough. An aging nobleman, Montresor, recounts his lethal revenge against a younger rival, Fortunato, fifty years after his triumph. As Montresor remembers it, he entices Fortunato to follow him into his family vaults for a taste of Amontillado, a Spanish sherry. In an isolated corner of the crypt, Montresor chains Fortunato to a wall and then mortars him in, brick by brick. Fortunato is left to suffocate or starve to death in the tomb, and vengeance is complete. As Richard Dilworth Rust contends, "The Cask of Amontillado" is simultaneously motivated by revenge, about revenge, and the "perfect" construction of a revenge tale.[13]

Whatever its retaliatory genius, a number of critical controversies shadow the fiction. We never know why Montresor reveals the truth of his criminal violence. We never know the transgressions for which Fortunato must be punished. We never know the identity of Montresor's intended confidante: The "you" that he addresses goes unnamed. We never know if Montresor feels guilt or remorse for the murder. We never know if he is rational or gone mad. That said, most scholars agree that the story's silences are intentional and deliberatively provocative. As Elena Baraban notes, in "The Philosophy of Composition," Poe asserts that no part of his craft can be reduced to accident or intuition; his work proceeds "to its completion with the precision and rigid consequence of a mathematical problem."[14] Scholars universally celebrate the mastery of "The Cask of Amontillado"—its "subtle irony, narrative neatness and speed, economy of means, crisp dialogue, structural symmetry, and resonant symbolism"[15]—while critical questions about the narrative's meaning persist.

A series of answers emerge if we situate the story in three cultural and theoretical contexts: one, a recovered history of broken attachment; two, the redemptive force of retaliatory violence for white nineteenth-century men; and three, the power that revenge has over the desolations of time and memory. In this chapter, I revive the record of the shattered friendship between Poe and Thomas Dunn English, arguing first that Montresor's revenge represents an attempt to comprehend bitter grief and loss. Next, I resurrect the history of the "thousand injuries" Poe suffered in the months before "The Cask of Amontillado" was published, as well as the final "insult" of the War of the Literati.[16] This archive illuminates an epoch of shame, scandal, and mortification. In it, we see the astonishing brutalities of male-on-male humiliation. In the presence of this past, we can more fully understand why Montresor does not enumerate Fortunato's trespasses as well as the intelligence of that silence. In his calculated obfuscation, Montresor maximizes revenge's ability to rearrange time and alter memory. With his vengeance, Montresor generates a new past and present, one defined by the renaissance of his power and honor. Through recognition—through a careful manipulation of the perceptions of his enemy and his audience—Montresor resuscitates his masculinity and dominance. Indeed, his revenge is only assured and complete when he tells the story. In its revelation, Montresor achieves a vindication that his author never knew.

ATTACHMENT

Critics have consistently underscored the animosity between Poe and Thomas Dunn English, but neglected the attachment that preceded it. For a time, Poe and English were friends. They met in 1839, when Poe was an assistant editor at *Burton's Gentleman's Magazine* and English one of its contributors. Poe was thirty years old, three years married to Virginia, and aspiring to critical, literary, and financial success. The celebrity that would come with *Tales of the Grotesque and Arabesque* (1840) and "The Raven" (1845) was still on the horizon. English was a physician, lawyer, writer, editor, and politician. Although he was ten years younger than Poe, he was equally ambitious, coveting achievement in writing and politics.[17] Their early closeness can be measured by the trust they shared. In "Reminiscences of Poe," English affirmed the "seven years of intimacy" between them. In the first months of their acquaintance, English saw Poe "at the office and elsewhere, industrious as a beaver." English and Poe talked and visited each other regularly. Indeed, English knew Poe well enough to testify that he was not a "habitual drunkard," but that "his natural sensitiveness, his excessive love of approbation, his domestic afflictions, and his constant struggle with poverty" drove him to drink. He once found Poe so drunk he could not "raise himself from the gutter," and he carried him home. Later, when poverty and scandal plagued him, Poe confided his "discontent" and "forebodings as to his future" to English.[18] Even if English exaggerates their affinity, his recollections only make their estrangement more wrenching.

In this section, I trace the history of the Poe-English attachment as well as the circumstances of their breakup. In the process, the mourning that often predicates revenge is made more visible, both in "The Cask of Amontillado" and Poe's lived experience. As revenge theorists show, vengeance often seethes in the betrayals of an incomprehensible loss. At the same time, it reinforces and enacts tangible intimacies. Montresor's revenge fits this paradigm. It is personal, relational, and powerfully embodied. It engages Montresor's body and the body of his enemy. Ultimately, it adopts Fortunato's body as familial and filial object, albeit a punished one.

Poe's revenge story begins in friendship. In "Reminiscences," English presents himself as a protector and sanctuary to Poe. When Poe's mother-in-law, Maria "Muddy" Clem, heard rumors of Poe's infidelity, she appealed to English to intervene, saying he "had more influence with 'Eddie' than any one else." English defended Poe, assuring Muddy that the relationship was "purely platonic." When the aggrieved brother of an alleged mistress threatened Poe's life, Poe came to English: "He begged me for God's sake to stand as his friend, as he expected to be challenged."[19] When Poe was unable to write a new, original poem for the prestigious Boston Lyceum, he again went to English for guidance. When Poe was struggling to keep *The Broadway Journal* in circulation, he likewise sought English's "advice and assistance."[20] Before they warred against one another, Poe and English were mates and allies.

English attributes their alienation to an adultery scandal. As he tells it, "The Raven" captivated the masses, and Poe became "a lion with a coterie of literary ladies."[21] He was welcomed into New York's literary salons. Often hosted by the poet Anne Charlotte Lynch, the salons included Washington Irving, William Cullen Bryant, Ralph Waldo Emerson, Margaret Fuller, and more, sometimes drawing as many as eighty or ninety artists. In the drawing room, Poe was magnetic, remembered as "polite and engaging . . . quiet and unaffected," with "the bearing and manners of a gentleman." Lynch recalled that many of the women at the salons grew "personally attached, and some *devoted* to him."

Poe soon became entangled in an intense flirtation with Frances Sargeant Osgood. Osgood was one of the most celebrated women poets in nineteenth-century America. She was also married. Evidence suggests that Osgood was enamored with Poe, and seriously considered an adulterous affair, while Poe felt more "conflicted" and "changeable."[22] As the Osgood romance deepened, Poe also gravitated to Elizabeth Ellet, another writer, another married woman. Osgood was jealous, while Ellet was enchanted. By most accounts, Ellet discovered one of Osgood's love letters to Poe when she visited him at his home. She chastised Osgood for her reckless passion and insisted the letter be retrieved. Ellet sent Anne Lynch and Margaret Fuller as emissaries to Poe. On Ellet's directive, the women demanded that Poe return Osgood's letters. Indignant and irritated, Poe gave them Osgood's correspondence and curtly stated that Ellet should be more concerned about her own letters to him.

This insinuation would prove combustible. Although Poe said he immediately regretted the remark, collected Ellet's letters, and left them at her door, Ellet's brother, Colonel William Lummis, felt obliged to defend his sister's honor. Confused or uninformed about where the correspondence was, Lummis ordered Poe to produce the letters or recant and attest to Ellet's virtue. Flummoxed, Poe either told Lummis he had already returned the letters or refused to be subject to the colonel's command. (The biographical data is conflicted here.) In any case, Lummis promised to kill Poe if he did not immediately restore the letters. Angry and terrified, Poe appealed to English, as I mentioned before, asking for English to second him. English refused. Poe then asked for the loan of English's pistol. English again refused. The two men argued, fought, and English apparently beat Poe soundly. As he told it, Poe came at him menacingly. English simply put his fist out to stop him, and Poe ran into it. Poe fell backward, grasped English's arm, and the two men toppled over together. "My blood was up by this time," English remembered, "and I dealt him some smart raps on the face," cutting him severely with his signet ring.[23] Although Poe later claimed he gave English "a flogging which he will remember to the day of his death," Thomas Lane, who witnessed the fight, confirmed that "Poe was drunk and getting the worst of it."[24] They remained bitter enemies until and after Poe's death.

A fuller reckoning with the bygone fondness between Poe and English makes betrayal and grief more visible in the revenge Poe imagines in "The Cask of Amontillado." Montresor sustains a relationship of "good will" with Fortunato as he plans his vengeance (1252). The night that Montresor kills Fortunato, they meet as close consorts: Fortunato greets him with "excessive warmth," and Montresor was "so pleased to see him that I thought I should never have done wringing his hand" (1257). Indeed, Montresor's revenge works through an affectionate seduction, one that relies on an established trust. Montresor coaxes Fortunato to his death through the fidelity between them. He calls him "my friend" six times as they descend into the crypt. He repeatedly expresses concern for Fortunato's severe cough in the dampness of the catacombs. And he lavishly affirms Fortunato's worth and status, diminishing his own. Montresor flatters, "You are rich, respected, admired, beloved; you are happy, as once I was. You are a man to be missed. For me it is no matter" (1259). Previous scholars detect irony and manipulation in these tactics.[25] But there is also an avowal of attachment and regard. Montresor has been hurt and harmed by a *friend*.

This bond makes his revenge an intimate act—personal and relational. Tellingly, the revenge that Montresor designs requires physical and emotional proximities. The two men are alone in the catacombs together for hours, drinking sips of Medoc as they journey through the crypt. And Montresor's revenge is hands-on. He shackles Fortunato to the granite. The stonework is close, bodily labor. As he lays the masonry, he hears Fortunato's "low moaning cry," and later, when Fortunato screams, Montresor echoes him, their voices wailing in unison. He calls Fortunato's name twice before he leaves him. By deliberate, premeditated plan, he buries Fortunato in his family vault, among the bones of his "great and numerous" ancestors (1259). In death, Fortunato becomes akin to Montresor's family, assuming a position reserved for a brother or cousin.

Scholars affirm what Montresor makes literal: Vengeance keeps an enemy closer. As Irwin Rosen asserts, revenge sustains "an enduring object-relational" connection, one that nurtures relationship through "envy, splitting, sadism, greed, spite, and Schadenfreude." In other words, revenge deepens and perpetuates the bonds of malignity: The "experience of revenge is like 'falling in hate.'" This emotional entanglement contributes to the gratifications of revenge. Pleasure arises in an "object tie" with a persecutor that says, "'I will cause you to feel what I have felt, and that will unite us forever.'"[26] Revenge initiates a sinister empathy, an enmeshment of shared feeling. As Eugene Goldwater explains, "Just as sexual union is an instinctual expression of a love relationship, revenge is an instinctual expression of a hate relationship."[27] Revenge materializes an abiding connection to the enemy. Thus, as Judith Shklar indicates, retribution can never be "detached [or] impersonal." For Shklar, "revenge is uniquely subjective," situated in the propinquities of self and other.[28] Revenge may proceed rationally and carefully, but it cannot affectively detach from subject or object.

Revenge also exposes the heartbreak in the avenger's relational past. In Miriam Berger's estimation, revenge is a kind of conversation, a "message about one's experiences and one's history." Berger reads revenge as "a coded personal biography about failed relationships waiting to be deciphered, witnessed, authenticated, mourned properly." Revenge attests to an interpersonal past defined by wounding and infidelity. In this sense, vengeance is a "social feeling": It tells us that "reciprocity, mutual acknowledgement, and connectedness has been disrupted and needs repair."[29] Similarly, Terry Aladjem categorizes revenge as an "affect of broken attachment." According to Aladjem, revenge registers an "obstinate inability to reconcile grief, rage, guilt, indignation" as well as feelings of "ruptured faith."[30] A number of thinkers reinforce the anguish that motivates the vengeful act. Hilary Beattie writes that revenge can be an attempt at "psychic survival in the face of devastating loss or betrayal."[31] Just as fundamentally, vengeance constitutes an effort to "make moral sense of pain, death, and cruelty."[32]

Certainly, Montresor's revenge is a response to accumulated pain. The season of his revenge, the "supreme madness of carnival," reinforces the immanence of his distress (1257). In a Christian tradition, carnival precedes Lent, and Lent ritualizes the need to prepare for the treason and sorrow of crucifixion. We meet Montresor at a temporal moment that presages treachery, persecution, and possible resurrection. In addition, Montresor explains that "the thousand injuries of Fortunato I had borne as I best could, but when he ventured upon insult, I vowed revenge." Although he never specifies this insult, Montresor posits that his injury will go "unredressed" if he suffers an answering "retribution" or if Fortunato does not feel his "wrong" (1256). This logic of revenge attempts to make subjective and ethical sense of harm. Essentially, Montresor has calculated Fortunato's aggregating infractions, his last and most intolerable offense, as well as the necessary reparation. His revenge will mediate the wounds of relational damage.

INSULT

And yet, some violations defy that effort, refusing to conform to any exist-ing moral or rational frameworks. In "The Cask of Amontillado," Poe with-holds explanation of the "thousand injuries" and final "insult" that force Montresor's reprisal, and critics continue to be puzzled by the inscrutability of the abuse.[33] The elusive impetus for the murder means that "The Cask of Amontillado" operates like an unsolved mystery tale. As Baraban reinforces, "The Cask of Amontillado" remains a riddle because it turns on the ques-tion: "Why did he do it?" The unknown motive pushes the reader to "reverse the process of solving the mystery," trying to determine the justification for the murder.[34]

The unknown motive also defies the conventions of the revenge tale. In the archetypal revenge story, motive *must* be discerned. A detailed accounting of the damage done is pivotal to the conventional revenge plot. As Aladjem observes, the psychosocial prospect of "getting even" requires a strict inven-tory of the pain that vengeance will answer. A retaliatory punishment must reckon with "the eye, the blood, the life taken."[35] Goldwater affirms that the "sweetness" of revenge accrues, in part, from its compensatory poten-tial: "Getting even" restores the avenger's self-worth and atones for the pain of his humiliation.[36] "The Cask of Amontillado" seemingly frustrates these expectations.

But that frustration persists only if we divorce the story from its context. For Poe's immediate audience, the mortifications he suffered were well docu-mented. Sidney Moss characterizes the interval from 1845 to 1846 as Poe's "crack up," a time when his afflictions reached "pathological proportions" and his adversaries destroyed him. As Moss puts it, Poe's enemies ruined him "with a vengeance, trumpeting his weaknesses and discrediting his opinions until he was disgraced" and virtually banished from the literary world.[37] In this section, I retrace the history of the professional shame and adulterous scandal that preceded the War of the Literati, the discursive battle between Poe, Thomas Dunn English, Hiram Fuller, and other writers described ear-lier. I also track the vitriol of the War itself. In the process, the singularity of the temporal and affective moment when Poe writes and publishes "The Cask of Amontillado" becomes more visible. In the War of the Literati, other men launched repeated assaults on Poe's body, morality, sanity, and liter-ary competence. Poe felt compelled to fight back, the reprisals escalated, and the bad press reached awful proportions. Here, we see the violence of nineteenth-century male-on-male insult. We see the terms and tactics used to debase the masculine subject.

First, Poe was pilloried for his strange, dissonant performance at the Boston Lyceum in October 1845. Cornelia Wells Walter, editor of the *Boston Evening Transcript*, opened her review of the event with the simple proclamation: "A failure."[38] Offended that Poe read "Al Aaraaf" as if it were a new, unpublished poem—and even more offended when Poe confessed he actually wrote the piece before the age of twelve—the Boston newspapers lacerated him for weeks. The condemnations were ruthless, relentless, and very public.[39]

Second, the Ellet-Osgood calumny broke a few months later, in late January of 1846. Rumors of infidelity and indiscretion further maligned Poe. As Horace Greeley summarized it, gossip was that Poe had "scandalized two eminent literary ladies, and came near getting horsewhipped or pistoled."[40] Desperate to interrupt his dishonor, Poe instructed his physician to deliver an imprudent apology to Ellet. He denied casting aspersions on Ellet's virtue and said that if he had ever made such a wild allegation, he must have been temporarily insane. The bizarre excuse only compounded his difficulties. His "enemies publicized the remark and reinforced his reputation as a madman."[41] This episode destroyed Poe's standing as a gentleman and ruined his social capital in the New York literary scene. As Moss concludes, Poe's opponents capitalized on his shame "until, by word of mouth, letter, and by print, Poe's name became anathema. . . . "[42]

The War of the Literati was actually the third and culminating episode in Poe's steady descent into infamy. In Montresor's terms, it was the insult added to injury. Retaliating against Poe's sketches in "The Literati of New York City," writers mercilessly defamed him. Much critical dialogue has accentuated Poe's vindictiveness in this conflict and others. J. Gerald Kennedy holds that Poe "forged his professional identity through hostile relations, and during his relatively brief career as a magazinist, he managed to offend or antagonize an impressive segment of the American literati, either through slashing reviews, biting journalistic profiles, insulting letters, sober threats, or sodden incoherencies."[43] Similarly, Madeline Wing-Chi Ki writes, Poe was ever ready to "criticize both friends and foes, and to retaliate when others struck." In vengeful literary wars, Poe subscribed to a law of "escalating 'ire for ire.'"[44] Yet these critical conclusions neglect the violence and velocity of the contempt other men felt for Poe. In the war that gutted Poe's ethos, the counterattacks were more malicious and more voluminous than any of Poe's assaults.

Hiram Fuller, editor of New York's *Evening Mirror*, responded to the literati sketches with an especially tenacious fury. In his first disparagement, Fuller bashed Poe's temperament and veracity, saying that Poe's "infirmities of mind and body, . . . his unfortunate habits, his quarrels and jealousies, all unfit him" to render an "honest opinion" of anything.[45] He also ambushed Poe's person, alleging he was only five-foot-one, 115 pounds, and depicting him as physically deformed. The derision is so vicious it is worth quoting in full:

> His face is pale and rather thin; eyes gray, watery and always dull; nose rather prominent, pointed and sharp; nostrils wide; hair thin and cropped short; mouth not very well chiseled, nor very sweet; his tongue shows itself unpleasantly when he speaks earnestly, and seems too large for his mouth; teeth indifferent; forehead rather broad, and in the region of ideality decidedly large, but low, and in that part where phrenology places conscientiousness and the group of moral sentiments it is quite flat; chin narrow and pointed, which gives his head, upon the whole, a balloonish appearance, which may account for his supposed light-headedness; he generally carries his head upright like a fugleman on drill, but sometimes it droops considerably.

Fuller methodically slandered every feature of Poe's countenance, and went on to ridicule his walk as "quick and jerking, sometimes waving" and his hands as "singularly small, resembling bird claws. . . . "[46] The physical pejorative alone was systematic and comprehensive. Fuller then proceeded to impugn Poe's intellect and recititude with equal ferocity. In the seventeen months that the war raged, Fuller wrote more than twenty notices that vilified Poe. In the worst of it, he assailed Poe as a "sad, wretched" imbecile, guilty of "evil living," lying, and malice.[47] As Moss comments, "Editors were horsewhipped, cowhided, or caned for less provocative articles" than Fuller's expositions.[48] In sum, Fuller proved an exceptionally malevolent enemy.

While Fuller was a more prolific combatant, English's indictments were just as incendiary. English attacked Poe's honesty, insight, intemperance, talent, and manhood. In his first "Reply" to his literati portrait, dated June 23, 1846, English asserted his physical dominance, recounting the "sound cuffing" he gave Poe at their last encounter. He charged Poe with conduct "unworthy of a gentleman," plagiarism, and ignorance. English's diatribe ended with an annihilation of Poe's decency and credibility: "He mistakes coarse abuse for polished invective, and vulgar insinuation for sly satire. He is not alone thoroughly unprincipled, base and depraved, but silly, vain, and ignorant—not alone an assassin in morals, but a quack in literature."[49] English's censure was so severe that George Pope Morris refused to reprint it in the *National Press*, and instead wrote, "The reply of Mr. English to Mr. Poe is one of the most savage and bitter things we ever read."[50] Even Griswold was astonished by English's tirade, writing in a letter to a colleague, "I, who have as much cause as any man to quarrel with Poe, would sooner have cut off my hand than used it to write such an ungentlemanly Card, though every word were true. But my indignation of this treatment even of an enemy exceeds my power of expression."[51] John Du Solle, editor of Philadelphia's

Spirit of the Times, judged English's first "Reply" a "literary meat-axe."[52] However, the bitter rancor did not stop there. In a second "Reply," written three weeks later, English called Poe "profligate in habits and depraved in mind."[53] He accused Poe of habitual drunkenness and total corruption. In English's jeremiads, Poe was a hack, a lush, and a degenerate.

Initially, Poe was especially disturbed by the distortion of his physicality, writing to Joseph Fields, editor of the St. Louis *Reveille*, for remedy. "All that I venture to ask of you in case of this attack, however, is to say a few words in condemnation of it," he appealed, "and to do away with the false impression of my personal appearance. . . . You have seen me and can describe me as I am."[54] As we saw in chapter 4, men, particularly Southern men, were measured by their dress and attractiveness. They were also measured by their capacity for intimidation and violence. Poe was so troubled by English's claim to have walloped him, he wrote to ask Henry Hirst for "a fair account of your duel with English" as well as a record of another man "kicking E. out of his office."[55] Clearly, Poe hoped to document moments when English was effectively routed by other men. He sarcastically made good on this intention in his rejoinder. Published four days after English's first "Reply," Poe's retort mockingly enumerated twelve instances where English was thumped, including one Poe gave "him myself, for indecorous conduct at my house," as well as an altercation that saw English knocked to the ground and "pummeled . . . for not more than twenty minutes." In addition, Poe corrected English's account of their recent skirmish, declaring that he was "dragged from his prostrate and rascally carcase [sic]" by a mutual friend who, "with good reason, had his fears for the vagabond's life."[56] The catalog of English's defeats is one of the most sustained passages in Poe's "Reply." It registers his sensitivity to the significance of physical violence for nineteenth-century men as well as his anxiety that his own prowess was in question.

Poe also leveled insults against English's character, calling him a coward, a slanderer, and a plagiarist. He smeared English as a "blackguard of the lowest order," a "blatherskite," a "poor, miserable fool," a "malignant . . . villain," and a "mental imbecil[e]."[57] He mocked his goatee. He compared him to a baboon, a frog, a weasel, a flea, and a fat sheep. But Poe's "Reply" functions primarily as an answer to the specific allegations against him. He defends his personal bravery and brawn, the truth of his literati sketches, and the originality of his poetry and prose.

If the answering press and correspondence are any indication, Poe's "Reply" did little to redeem his reputation or his masculinity. In a letter to Poe, author and friend William Gilmore Simms told him that he was engaged in a "long & manful struggle" with fate and fortune. In this "warfare," Poe could only rely on his "own unassisted powers." Simms worried that Poe's

belligerence was self-defeating, and he counseled that "only your manly resolution to use these powers, after a legitimate fashion" will rally the world's
"regards & sympathy." More explicitly, Simms cautioned: "You are no longer
a boy. 'At thirty wise or never! You must subdue your impulses; &, in particular let me exhort you to discard all associations with men . . . whom you cannot esteem as men." He advised Poe to "remain in obscurity for a while" and
to "learn the worldling's lesson of prudence." Urging Poe to retreat from a
fight that would only ruin him, he warned, "these broils do you no good—vex
your temper, destroy your peace of mind, and hurt your reputation." Lastly, he
appealed to their shared Southern sensibilities to underscore the impropriety
of a protracted quarrel with unequals: "To a Southern man, the annoyance of
being mixed up in a squabble with persons whom he does not know, and does
not care to know . . . would be an intolerable grievance."[58] Simms intuited that
Poe would not win a war of rants and rages. Rather, he would be personally
and professionally devastated by the malice of contemptuous men.

    But Poe would not or could not stand down. He insisted on the exact-
ness of his response. Writing to Louis Godey in July 1846, Poe defended
both its literary and vengeful excellence: "The man, or men, who told you
there was anything wrong in *the tone* of my reply, were either my enemies,
or your enemies, or asses. When you see them, tell them so from me." He
went on to argue that "I have never written an article upon which I more
confidently depend for *literary* reputation than that Reply," saying, "Its
merit lay in being *precisely* adapted to its purpose."[59] More than a year later,
when George Eveleth, one of Poe's devotees, criticized Poe's coarseness in
the "Reply," Poe continued to champion its potency. Eveleth worried that
"in some instances you have come down too nearly on a level with English
himself. . . . You laid yourself liable to be laughed at by answering in such a
spirit, more than you had done if you had kept calm."[60] But Poe maintained
his response was both necessary and formidable. "I do not well see how I
could have otherwise replied to English," he explained. "He is so thorough a
'blatherskite' that [to] have replied to him with *dignity* would have been the
extreme of the ludicrous." In Poe's mind, a more judicious rejoinder would
have given English's attack a significance it did not deserve. Accused of
forgery and worse, moreover, he could not remain silent. "To such charges,
even from the Auto[crat] of all the Asses—a man is *compelled* to answer,"
Poe argued. "There he had me. Answer him I must[.] But how? Believe me
there exists no dilemma as that in which a gentleman [is] placed when he is
forced to reply to a blackguard. If he have any genius then is the time for its
display." To Poe, the complexities of the conflict required the dexterity of a
virtuoso. "I confess to you that I rather like that reply of mine in a literary
sense," he bragged. "It fully answered its purpose beyond a doubt—would to

Heaven every work of art did as much!"[61] Poe believed his reply was both perfectly attuned to English's affront and incisive in its defense.

Despite Poe's audacity, he was sinking beneath poverty, Virginia's worsening tuberculosis, alcoholism, and disrepute. July 1846 was an especially brutal interim in the War of the Literati. Newspapers were covering the feud with headlines like "The Literary War" and "The War still Raging."[62] Contributors were accusing Poe of madness: "Mr. Poe is making many enemies here by his insane writings."[63] Poe knew he was diminished. He wrote to friend and poet Thomas Holley Chivers that his adversaries had become unprincipled predators: "Little birds of prey that always take the opportunity of illness to peck at a sick fowl of larger dimensions, have been endeavoring with all their power to effect my ruin." Believing that his rivals were capitalizing on his misery, Poe lamented that "my dreadful poverty, also, has given them every advantage. In fact, dear friend, I have been driven to the very gates of death and a despair more dreadful than death. . . . "[64] Penury, grief, rage, and shame did their terrible work on Poe's heart and mind. He later explained to Eveleth that, as Virginia hemorrhaged with consumption, he experienced "all the agonies of her death" and a "horrible insanity." He drank himself into oblivion: "It was a horrible never-ending oscillation between hope & despair which I could *not* longer have endured without the total loss of reason."[65]

Indeed, as the War of the Literati raged on, Poe appeared wasted on the streets of New York and even in Hiram Fuller's offices. On July 20, 1846, Fuller reported: "[S]ad, sadder, saddest of all is the poor wretch whose want of moral rectitude has reduced his mind and person to a condition where indignation for his vices, and revenge for his insults are changed into compassion for the poor victim of himself." Disingenuously, Fuller expressed a temporary empathy for the "unhappy man" who had recently called on him at the *Evening Mirror*. Enervated and inebriated, Poe no longer seemed worthy of retaliation: "When a man has sunk so low that he has lost the power to provoke vengeance, he is the most pitiful of all pitiable objects." According to Fuller, Poe arrived in such a state of wretchedness, "that every spark of harsh feeling toward him was extinguished, and we could not entertain a feeling of contempt for one who was evidently committing a suicide upon his body, as he had already done on his character."[66] For a quick, shallow moment, Fuller considered an end to hostilities.

The amnesty did not last. Poe sued for libel three days later, filing his Declaration of Grievances against Fuller and Augustus Clason, owners of the papers that published English's and Fuller's abuse. Fuller and English immediately reunited forces in the serial publication of a novel that cruelly satirized Poe. In it, English introduces a character that is unmistakably Poe: Marmaduke Hammerhead. Hammerhead is the author of the "Black Crow." He says things like, "Quoth the raven—never more," and asks strangers if they have read his reviews of Longfellow. Somewhat predictably, English further characterizes Hammerhead as a drunk, a liar, a malcontent, a womanizer, an egomaniac, and a lunatic.[67] It is a scornful portrayal, and Silverman deems this "the most protracted and probably the most vicious of all the attacks yet made on Poe."[68] From September to October 1846, English featured Hammerhead in six installments of the book, while Fuller continued to fire off brief notices that denounced Poe for plagiarism and lying. In this same interval, Poe's old nemesis, Lewis Gaylord Clark, commented in *The Knickerbocker*, "He is too mean for hate, and hardly worthy scorn."[69] Thus, the counterblows against Poe multiplied. He was buried in hateful, harmful press.

"The Cask of Amontillado" was published in this here and now: November 1846. Just after the closing installment of the "Literati" sketches appeared in *Godey's*. After the final Marmaduke Hammerhead episode covered the front pages of the *Evening* and *Weekly Mirrors*. Before Virginia's death in January1847. And before the libel trial and its verdict in February 1847. In other words, "The Cask of Amontillado" was released at a historical and personal moment when retaliation was required. For Poe, this interim was simultaneously singular and accumulative, exceptional and familiar. In it, he was caught in an unprecedented collision of scandal, enmity, and immanent sorrow. And yet Poe had been embattled, embittered, and mournful for years. In this, he must have felt like his protagonist, Montresor: advanced in age, not a man "to be missed," and no longer "happy" (1259).

TIME, MEMORY, HISTORY

Critics assume that "The Cask of Amontillado" takes focused, purposeful aim at the acrimony of 1846 and particularly Thomas English. Francis Dedmond reasons that the tale finds its "inception" in the Fuller-English grudge and English takes "the brunt of Poe's attack."[70] Richard Rust argues that "Poe used his finest skills and energy to make the story an act of revenge against Thomas Dunn English."[71] Certainly, "The Cask of Amontillado" draws allegorical parallels to the War of the Literati and English himself.[72]

But it also reaches deeper into the past. A fuller reckoning with this context reveals the memory work the story performs. More specifically, it explains why the story refuses to recount the offenses against Montresor as well as the masterful impact of that omission. In this section, I examine Montresor's revenge as a response to historical harms—as a reoccupation of the past and past pain. In his vengeance, Montresor commands time and memory, generating new antecedents, an alternative present, and a different future.

Revenge cannot be understood apart from its temporal interests and aspirations. Terry Aladjem contends that revenge directly intervenes in time, memory, and history. With Nietzsche, Aladjem maintains that revenge enacts "the will's ill will against time and its 'it was.'"[73] Reconsidering the interstice between punishment and memory, Aladjem argues that revenge makes memory, or more pointedly, revenge *remakes memory*. Aladjem illuminates three pivotal "memory effects" in an avenger's punishments. First, his punishment produces "conscience"—guilt or regret—in an enemy. Second, it generates a vindicating power for the avenger, altering how "the punisher is perceived or remembered" and repositioning him as master of fate and foe. Third, it creates "a memorable spectacle" before the world, an exhibition that "aims to reverse the past" in the present consciousness. In Aladjem's assessment, these memory effects distinguish the punitive force of vengeance from other forms of violence. Revenge resists and revises time: It "enlist[s] cruelty to change the past"; it substitutes "one bloody past for another." In other words, retaliatory violence attempts to "to displace the memory of an injury and seemingly reverse its consequence."[74] Revenge aims to dispossess the past of the avenger's disgrace and initiate a new history, one defined by his righteous violence and the restoration of his power.

In "The Cask of Amontillado," this dispossession becomes total erasure. Montresor obliterates the memory of harm well before he kills Fortunato. He dissociates from that past in the story's first sentence, which ends portentously with the resolve to vengeance: "I vowed revenge" (1256). In the story's opening—and its more immediate and protracted past—Montresor plots his reprisal: "*At length* I would be avenged" (1256). Most of the story's chronology centers on the execution of the revenge itself: Montresor's seemingly chance encounter with Fortunato at carnival; their extensive expedition through the tombs; and the work of the murder. Montresor takes his time walling Fortunato into the vault, toiling from dusk until midnight. Just as tellingly, he pauses four times in the effort: once to listen to the sound of the chains as Fortunato struggles against them; once to look at Fortunato in the firelight; once when Fortunato begins to scream; and finally, just before he places the last stone in its position. With each delay, Montresor arrests and controls time. Indeed, when Fortunato screams, Montresor "ceased [his] labors and sat down upon the bones" so that he "might hearken to it with the more satisfaction" (1262). Fortunato confronts death on Montresor's clock.

In its ultimate temporal subversion, at the story's end we learn that Fortunato has been dead for fifty years. Raymond DiSanza suggests that this is "the most chilling aspect" of the tale: "the sudden, unpredictable, understated revelation that the murder, recounted in its every lurid detail, occurred not yesterday or last week, but a full fifty years prior to the telling."[75] This succeeding fifty years amplifies Montresor's long life over Fortunato's slow death as well as the decisiveness of his revenge.

In my reckoning, this last temporal disturbance propels the most power-ful element of the story: the intervention that enables Montresor's revenge to bend time. Recall that Aladjem defines revenge as a temporal disruption that actively renegotiates memory. As Aladjem puts it, "Vengeance entails *an economy of memories of horror*," an economy that reconstructs the apprehension of a painful past. Revenge works directly on the perception of historical wounds, "[p]urging the memory of victims, inducing recognition in offenders, changing the story for those who bear witness in memorable acts of humiliation. . . . " In the process, vengeance transubstantiates historical injury. As it rearranges time and memory, revenge redistributes "pain, horror, grief, and guilt." It transfers "pain from one party to another."[76] Roger Lopez elucidates the psychic rewards of this transference, explaining that while the avenging "I" initially suffers from the original wound, "what I suffer from now is my memory of it." Revenge exorcises the intolerable memory: "By inflicting pain on another, I can rid myself of my own."[77] In other words, revenge has an evacuative, cleansing effect. As Aladjem expounds, retalia-tion rectifies "unendurable memories of suffering by changing the equation of suffering itself." Thus, retaliation "is at once a source of faith, redemption, a wish, and a promise to undo harm and suffering."[78] In this sense, reprisal is optimistic. It amends the ravages of time. In its re-orchestration of the past, revenge generates a different present and a new future.

In the timeline of "The Cask of the Amontillado," the present is all ven-geance, and the gratifications of reprisal secure Montresor's future. When Montresor withholds the historical harm that precedes his revenge, he alters precedent itself. The story memorializes a past defined by the patience and ingenuity of his punishment. When that revenge goes even deeper into memory—fifty years after the murder—the story further memorializes a past defined by Montresor's triumph and vitality. Critics have missed the bril-liance of these temporal maneuvers. For example, when Raymond DiSanza concludes that "Montresor forgets" his immediate motive, he neglects the vagaries of memory.[79] Memories can be vivid or vague, intimate or detached, tormented or tranquil. And, significantly for my purposes, retaliation does memory work: "The objective of vengeance is precisely to forget, or more precisely, to consign to a quieter memory that which rage, guilt, or humilia-tion might otherwise turn into an obsession."[80] The story's closing words and image suggest that Montresor has realized this quieter memory: "Against the new masonry I re-erected the old rampart of bones. For the half of a century no mortal has disturbed them. *In pace requiescat!*" (1263). A "rampart" is both a barrier and a boundary. Fortunato's body lies behind a wall built by Montresor's own hands and fortified by the bones of his ancestors. This stronghold represents an enduring, protective closure. With the honorific, "rest in peace," Montresor promises them all permanent repose.

In Montresor's reprisal, he seizes the possibility that he can entomb his enemy in a bastion of his own design, protected by the talismans of a "great and numerous" family (1259). That would have been a tantalizing prospect for Poe as he shouldered the weight of a bitter past and the derision of increasingly spiteful present. Montresor's perfect revenge would have answered Poe's need for a quieter memory and a similar victory.

RECOGNITION

Some critics have supposed that Montresor finds only an uneasy peace after the murder. G.R. Thompson argues that Montresor has "suffered a fifty-years ravage of conscience" about the killing. Thomas Mabbott suggests that "The Cask of Amontillado" is "perhaps the most moral" of Poe's tales, believing that Montresor feels empathy for his victim in the end (1252). More scholars judge Montresor mad, assuming that the brutality of his crime and his indifference to Fortunato's anguish are the telltale signs of sociopathy.[81]

But such readings neglect the affective recompense of revenge for white nineteenth-century men and the completion—the wholeness—Montresor achieves when he finally tells his story. This section illustrates how carefully "The Cask of Amontillado" locates Montresor and his reprisal within a culture of honor: a culture in which men are duty-bound to vengeance. In the process, it traces the compulsory hold of the insult on the resolve to vengeance. As we shall see, in an honor culture, the insult has the power to empty white masculinity of its dominance. In this context, revenge functions as a way to revive that dominance—to retake its ascendency and manhood. It does this in and through a complex nexus of recognitions. The avenger reconstructs himself in the eyes of his enemy and the eyes of an approving audience.

In an honor culture, men have only and exactly the worth that external measures (i.e., reputation, rank, public perceptions) afford. A man's identity—his character, morality, and value—is entirely socially arbitrated. Bertram Wyatt-Brown confirms that men of honor are made and unmade in the "opinion of others."[82] And Edward Ayers underscores the ubiquity and significance of "dictates of honor" for Southern men. In the American South, women, children, and slaves had no honor. Only adult white men could lay claim to honor, although it had to earned.[83] As Jon Elster clarifies, honor "is achieved or maintained by victories over equals or superiors," and victory might come through silencing a man with insult, raping his wife, or killing him. There is no honor in subduing inferiors—slaves, servants, women, children—but honor can be diminished if insubordination goes unpunished.[84] Thus, a man's honor was inherently insecure. It was an asset that could be gained and lost, and violence was its currency. In Ayers's words, the "heart of honor was the respect of others," and honor could be "purchased with blood."[85] Indeed, Southern honor exalted a certain ferocity, "particularly in the character of revenge against familial and communal enemies."[86] By definition, a culture of honor makes retaliatory violence a masculine imperative. Any threat to status, like the insolence or trespass of a rival, must be answered with reprisal.[87]

With the story's setting and his protagonist's nobility, Poe solidly situates Montresor's revenge in an honor culture. Richard Benton argues convincingly for placing "The Cask of Amontillado" in France, during the years before the French Revolution. Benton also traces Montresor's affinity with Claude de Bourdeille, the seventeenth-century Count of Montresor. Callous and calculating, Bourdeille survived numerous political conspiracies, exile, arrest, and imprisonment. Benton maintains that no other historical Montresor better "fits Poe's vengeful aristocrat in either social position or temperament." Like the Count, Poe's Montresor "is a member of the *noblesse d'epee* and an aristocrat by birth." His familial coat of arms and motto announce "that the men of his family are not to be trifled with."[88] Baraban ventures that Montresor has a "more noble origin" than Fortunato, although Fortunato has more money and influence.[89]

These social markers indicate that Montresor inhabits an old-world system of honor, the same tradition that nourished Southern masculinity. As Ayers explains, elite Southern men adopted the culture of a British and European aristocracy: "Honor and its violence were a part of the culture they regarded as their own, as the only culture worthy of emulation." In addition, lower-class Scottish emigrants—the men of John Allan's world—"carried their own experiences with violence to America, expectations and tendencies that soon combined with aristocratic ideals of honor to spark violence on every level of colonial Southern society."[90] Poe directly invokes this collusion between cultures of honor—Scottish, French, and the American South—through Montresor's family motto: *nemo me impune lacessit*, or "no one attacks me with impunity." This warning was also the motto of the kingdom of Scotland and the knightly Order of the Thistle. With Montresor then, Poe makes a transnational and transgenerational connection to a masculinity bound to honor. As men of honor, Montresor and Poe have a *duty* to vengeance.

They also have a complex responsibility to the insult. Southern men were notoriously sensitive to any offense. Their social and ontological survival—as *men*—depended on their reactivity to issues of honor. As a British traveler observed in 1823, "They must fight, kill or be killed, and that for some petty offense beneath the notice of the law." Refusing the fight was a "stain," a terrible disgrace. More pointedly, ignoring an affront was emasculating, stigmatizing individuals "as less than real men."[91] Jon Elster explains that in an honor culture, the "man who fails to avenge an insult" experiences a

"devastating feeling of shame," an "intolerable loss of honor," and the evacuation of his manhood.[92] Just as tellingly, Southern honor made no distinction between verbal or physical insults. It was as abusive to call a man an
"imbecile" or a "plagiarist" as it was to punch his face. Slurs like "coward"
and "liar" were particularly derogatory: Such language "invite[d] attack." In
this context, there was no minor violation, no inconsequential slight. If it was
intentional, any disrespect required punishment. And if abuse accumulated, it
necessitated a violent resolution. Ayers notes that "Southern newspapers did
indeed relate instances where men killed others over trivial matters, but the
specific incident often seems to have been merely the trigger, after a longer
period of frustration or series of conflicts."[93] In an honor culture, death could
be a reasonable, proportionate, and necessary response to insolence.

This reality illuminates the power of the insult for Poe, Montresor, and
men like them. Baraban observes that "injury" and "insult" are semantically
distinct in Montresor's language, and more resonantly, they are distinct in a
culture of honor. "While 'injuries' presuppose the rivalry of socially equal
enemies, 'insult' involves contempt: that is, treating the other as a socially
inferior person."[94] For Montresor, the word "insult" is a potent cultural
indicator of his commitment to vengeance. With his terminology, Montresor
signals that a man can bear injury—withstand his own pain—but he cannot
tolerate *insult*. Insult carries the force of humiliation.[95] It lowers and degrades.
In consequence, the insult and its perpetrator must be corrected.

Like Montresor, Poe encountered the full force of insult in the War of the
Literati. The offenses against him—from men he considered less talented and
less worthy—were both incendiary and painfully visible. According to Ayers,
a man's honor and his public image were essentially synonymous. Honor
required the approbation of friends, professional associates, newspapers—
any social gaze. Indeed, public recognition was so essential to American
honor that "the published insult constituted the only American contribution to
the ritual of the duel." With this innovation, a man printed his "card," a personal response to insult, in a newspaper "so that as many people as possible,
including strangers, would know of his willingness to defend his honor—and
know also that he possessed honor worthy of defense."[96] Tellingly, both of
English's answers to Poe were "cards." The first was titled, "A Card: Mr.
English's Reply to Mr. Poe"; the second "A Card: In Reply to Mr. Poe's
Rejoinder." Recall, too, that English repeatedly accused Poe of treachery
and cowardice, the worst epithets one could fire at Southern men. In addition, English avowed his own honor in his cards, contrasting it with Poe's
indecency. "My character for honor and physical courage needs no defence
[sic] from even the occasional slanderer," he wrote, and further declared that
"meanness and depravity" rendered Poe "incapable of appreciating the feelings which animate the man of honor."[97] To the nineteenth century, English's

meaning was terribly clear. His cards render Poe a pariah of American manhood: a man with no honor.

Fascinatingly, English also enumerated the aspersions that Poe directed
against him. To illustrate the "style and temper" of Poe's reply, he listed
the words and phrases that slandered him: "'blackguard,' 'coward,' 'liar,'
'animalcula with moustaches for *antennal* [sic],' 'block-heads,' 'quartette
of dunderheads,' *'brandy-nose,'* 'best-looking, but most unprincipled of
Mr. Barnum's *baboons,'* 'filthy lips,' 'rascally carcase [sic],' 'inconceivable
amount of *brass,'* 'poor miserable *fool,'* *'hog-puddles* in which he was wal-
lowed from infancy,' *'by Heaven!'* 'dock-loafers and wharf-rats, his cronies,'
'the *blatherskite's* attack,' 'hound,' 'malignant a villain,' 'wretch,' 'filthy
sheet,' 'hasty pudding by way of brains.'"[98] These passages reinforce the
masculine fixation on the insult as well as its interpersonal violence. Between
men, words were capable of palpable and measurable harm.

In its nastiness, tenacity, and notoriety, the War of the Literati was a blood
feud. The imperatives of honor explain why Poe insisted to men like Godey
and Eveleth that he was *"compelled"* to respond to English's attack. Silence
meant surrender, emasculation, and an unbearable public shame. Indeed,
Poe wrote to William Burton in 1840 after he fired him: "If by accident you
have taken it into your head that I am to be insulted with impunity I can only
assume that you are an ass."[99]

The redemptions of revenge in an honor culture also explain the peace
Montresor finds in vengeance. With his analysis of the significance of "an
eye for eye" in an American logic of justice, Aladjem reinforces the primacy
of recognition in the gratifications of reprisal. Aladjem argues that "an eye
for an eye" expresses a complicated cluster of yearnings: a wish to see and
be re-seen, and "a wish to be recognized at the *expense* of another." In sum,
revenge is consummated in a "play of eyes." The interventions in time and
memory that revenge initiates are only complete when the avenger and the
effects of his vengeance *get seen.* As Aladjem clarifies, "Personal vindication
is best achieved before the eyes of others." Thus, retaliation must "replace
one terrible sight with another." In vengeance's "play of eyes," an avenger
wants to see the violence of the punishment itself and the consequences of
that punishment on the offender's vision. He wants "'to see the offender suffer' and 'to make him see [his trespass].'" The offender must make reciprocal
recognitions, and he must see the avenger's dominance in his own humiliation. This double witnessing has a restorative effect. In the "eyes of his
dying enemy," the avenger's power is returned to him. As Aladjem expounds,
"One's present strength or vitality, displayed in this way before one's enemy,
thus seems to obliterate the ineffectuality or weakness that one has felt
because of him in the past."[100] The enemy's recognition—from the site of his
abjection or death—redeems the wounded subject.

Montresor acknowledges the importance of his enemy's recognition in his conception of revenge. He affirms that retaliation miscarries if "the avenger fails to make himself felt as such to him who has done the wrong" (1256). Montresor holds that Fortunato must "feel him" in the revenge encounter. He must have a sensate experience of Montresor as the retaliator and vindicator. And he must have a sensate experience of his own position as the transgressor, as "him who has done the wrong." There is audible evidence that Fortunato has such an experience. As previously noted, Montresor listens with "satisfaction" to the "furious vibrations of the chains" when Fortunato attempts to free himself (1262). He feels "satisfied" again when, after a "succession of loud and shrill screams," Fortunato has not managed to break the manacles (1262). Implicitly, Montresor revels in the materialization of Fortunato's impotence and fear. Fortunato's dread is so satiating that Montresor expresses his dominance in a jubilant exchange of inchoate screams: "I replied to the yells of him who clamored. I re-echoed—I aided—I surpassed them in volume and in strength. I did this, and the clamorer grew still" (1262). This interaction represents a climax of the felt impact that revenge covets. Fortunato wails in fear and Montresor howls in triumph until Fortunato's distress is silenced, and together, their bodies testify to Montresor's repossession of power. Subsequently, as Montresor puts the terminal stone in place, he hears "a low laugh that erected the hairs upon my head. It was succeeded by a sad voice, which I had difficulty in recognizing as that of the noble Fortunato" (1263). Here, Montresor detects Fortunato's despair, and more importantly, the emptying of his rank and personhood. He does not sound like "the noble Fortunato." He has become the offender, the wrongdoer, the transgressor.

And yet, this play of voices arguably provides only partial recognition, and therefore, an unfinished revenge. Does Montresor *see* enough: of the violence of his punishment and his enemy's suffering? And is he sufficiently *seen*? Is his ascendency adequately beheld? Fortunato offers audible proofs of his powerlessness, fear, and sorrow, but he never begs for his life. He never apologizes. In fact, his final conversation with Montresor introduces troubling ambivalences. Fortunato attempts to reframe the horror as a prank: "an excellent jest" (1263). His laugh in this attempt—a repeated "he! he! he!"—resounds with potential disdain. *The Oxford English Dictionary* stipulates that as a depiction of laughter, "he he" is typically "affected or derisive." Fortunato also reminds Montresor that his wife and friends await them at the palazzo. Indeed, as Montresor testified earlier, Fortunato is "admired" and "beloved," a man who will be missed. Lastly, Fortunato makes an emphatic appeal to religious redemption, *"For the love of God, Montresor"* (1263). This petition is replete with moral condemnation. As Kent Bales asserts, "In a Christian universe no private vengeance can be exacted with impunity, and mortal sin unrepented brings eternal retribution."[101] Thus, an ambiguity emerges in these final moments, one in which Fortunato, by an avenger's standard, retains too much individual, social, and ethical mettle.

This ambiguity is exacerbated by Fortunato's concluding silence: Montresor calls his name twice, but he receives no answer. Montresor registers the affective impact of this irresolution when he admits, "My heart grew sick—on account of the dampness of the catacombs," and he hurries to finish his labor (1263). Critics persistently circle this moment of narrative unease. Charles Nevi maintains that this declaration confirms that Montresor feels no remorse for the murder; only the dankness of the crypt appalls him.[102] Francis Henninger contends that Montresor's heart grows sick because his revenge has failed.[103] David Halliburton maintains that Montresor's complaint indicates that in "victimizing the other," he victimizes himself.[104] DiSanza argues that Montresor sinks in this instant because he finds himself at a "dead end," confronted with the stark reality that he committed an unjustified murder.[105] In my estimation, this heart sickness indicates only that more revenge work remains. Montresor's vengeance will take more time and one final labor.

Recall that revenge is an "attempt to restore the self" and reclaim agency. The promise of revenge thrives in its connection to a "virtually limitless" and voracious power: "An eye for an eye soon gives way to a life for an eye."[106] This promise contributes to how interpersonal the vendetta must become: "In order to restore the self, one cannot let someone else do 'the dirty work.'"[107] Just as importantly, revenge enacts this restoration through the manipulations of memory analyzed above *and* in the eyes of the enemy—through recognition and concession. Punishment is not enough. The enemy's pain is not enough. The avenger's self and its ascendancy are finally restored when his resurrection gets *seen*. Of course, the enemy persists as the first, the most intimate, and perhaps the most pivotal witness of the avenger's revival. As Lopez expounds, "Since the offender has attested so emphatically to my fragility, his attesting to my sovereignty [carries] special weight."[108]

Even so, revenge needs other audiences as well. It needs abetting and ancillary audiences that, in Aladjem's words, also witness "the crime, the perpetrator, the victim, and the punishment in a given way." More pointedly, vengeance requires "an audience that *applauds*," an audience that validates the reprisal and its results.[109] In historical, state-sanctioned spectacles of justice, these audiences have been the citizens summoned to witness an execution, the crowds that gathered at the pillory, or the jury at a trial. In an honor culture, revenge is similarly "triadic": One reclaims honor by punishing an offender in the presence of an observer—a corroborating gaze. As Elster notes, in blood feuds, avengers often publicize their killings; it can actually be considered dishonorable to kill and not to tell the story.[110] The story confers the spoils of honor. Indeed, with retaliation, the avenger "acquires the power to retell the story," and the story itself helps to fix "the reinscription of pain" in history. Similarly, in the archetypal revenge plot, the "catharsis of revenge" is realized through "revelation," through a potent revealing. In the revelations of revenge, the "defeat or subjugation of the offender is demonstrated in such a way that both the victim and the audience seem to look down upon, step over or past the offender into new territory—a destination that would also alter destiny." This destination "reassigns guilt, sharpens blame," and materializes reprisal's most potent effects on time and memory.[111] Revenge realizes its most transcendent and transformative potential in a triumvirate of looks, the moment when an audience recognizes the new reality that the avenger and offender likewise see: the pains of punishment, the redistribution of historical injury, the restoration of the avenger's supremacy.

Montresor's revenge then, is complete when he tells the story, and when his audience receives it. Montresor identifies his audience in the story's opening passage. After declaring that he "vowed revenge," he states, "You, who so well know the nature of my soul, will not suppose, however, that I gave utterance to a threat. *At length* I would be avenged . . . " (1256). This is yet another element of the tale that haunts the critical conversation. As DiSanza notes, most thinkers presume that the "you" Montresor addresses is an arresting police officer, a religious confessor, or psychic projection of Montresor's madness. DiSanza goes on to speculate that the audience might be familial, that "Montresor delivers his tale to descendants in order to demonstrate the lengths that a Montresor should go to defend the family reputation."[112] Certainly a familial audience better aligns with the practices of an honor culture. Lessons in familial vengeance would be essential to the internalization of honor's precepts. Whatever its specific character, the "you" is the audience that applauds, the audience that sanctions, celebrates, and completes Montresor's revenge. Montresor signals that this "you" knows and understands him. They know and understand his approach to vengeance: They know he would never overtly threaten an enemy, they know he would patiently plan and orchestrate a revenge over time. The "you" bears vital witness to the essence of Montresor's "soul" and the truth of his reprisal.

We leave Montresor reveling in the sweet serenity of a vengeance come full circle. He has reordered time, recomposed memory, and reconstructed the past. He has punished the insult and revived his honor, power, and manhood. He has mastered the play of eyes that revenge requires, securing the recognitions of his enemy and a sympathetic audience. He will likewise "rest in peace," and soon enough, his body will be entombed with the remains of his vanquished rival and noble progenitors.

GETTING EVEN

But here we must acknowledge that Montresor achieves a wholeness, a satisfaction, that forever eluded Poe. Within a month of the publication of "The Cask of Amontillado," Poe was destitute, and Virginia was actively dying. They took a cottage in Fordham, New York, thirteen miles outside the city. Poe was already "ill, dreadfully poor and deeply depressed."[113] That winter, their desolation deepened, and newspapers announced their ruin. The *Bostonian* reported in December 1846: "Great God! Is it possible that the literary people of the Union, will let poor Poe perish by starvation and lean faced beggary in New York? For so we are led to believe, from frequent notices in the papers, stating that Poe and his wife are both down upon a bed of misery, death and disease, with not a ducat in the world, nor a charitable hand to minister a crumb to their crying necessities."[114] This was not an exaggeration. Virginia suffered with chills and fever on a straw bed. Poe could not provide blankets, fire, or proper food. He wrapped Virginia in his army coat, and Muddy begged money from New York publishing offices.

Moved by word of Poe's dejection, Nathaniel Parker Willis, editor of *The Home Journal*, published an appeal for aid. On Poe's behalf, he called for a *"retreat for disabled labourers with the brain,"* imagining an "Institution designed expressly for educated and refined objects of charity."[115] A number of papers reiterated Willis's plea, some with sincerity, others with derision. Fuller sarcastically counterproposed an adjoining "asylum for those who have been ruined by the diddlers of the quill," and snarled, "We cannot not call to mind a single instance of a man of real literary ability suffering from poverty, who has always lived an industrious, honest, and honorable life."[116] Still, people sent donations to the Poe household. A newspaper editor collected fifty or sixty dollars at New York's Metropolitan Club. A Brooklyn lawyer raised a similar amount at a trial. John Jacob Aster's grandson gave the family ten dollars.[117] Poe became a celebrity charity case.

Although the money was sorely needed, Poe knew the publicity would further diminish him. Newspapers, including the Saint Louis *Reveille* and the Boston *Evening Transcript*, continued to cover his penury and debility. In response, Poe asked Willis to publish a letter that purported to state "what is true and what erroneous" in the reports of his afflictions. He acknowledged the indignities of the press, saying "the concerns of my family are thus pitilessly thrust before the public." He confirmed that he had "been long and dangerously ill." He testified that from his sickbed, he had been assailed by "personal and of literary abuse." But he denied the extremity of his poverty and isolation. He insisted that he could name "a hundred persons" he could ask for help "with unbounded confidence and with absolutely no sense of humiliation." He prophesied his immediate comeback. "At the very first blush of my new prosperity," he wrote, "the gentlemen who toadied me in the old, will recollect themselves and toady me again." And he closed the letter with a rallying cry: "The truth is, I have a great deal to do; and I have made up my mind not to die till it is done." Later, he confided to Jane Locke that he "thought it prudent to . . . publicly disavow" his financial distress, "since the world regards wretchedness as a crime."[118] Once again, Poe tried to interrupt his descent.

At least two newspapers remarked on the tenor of Poe's statement. In the Philadelphia *Spirit of the Times*, Du Solle said it was "full of this interesting mixture of acerbity and self-confidence. It is Poe-ish all over!" Du Solle also affirmed the writer's grit: "If Mr. Poe had not been gifted with considerable gall, he would have been devoured long ago by the host of enemies his genius has created."[119] Du Solle recognized both Poe's bravado and the wonder of his survival. Likewise, the New York *Yankee Doodle* vouched for the mercilessness of Poe's opposition: "Every mean-spirited cur, who dared not bark when his tormentor had strength, feeds fat his ancient grudge, now that he sees his enemy prostrate and powerless—with heart crushed and brain shattered by the sickness and suffering of those most dear to him."[120]

But Virginia died on January 30, 1847, and the libel trial began the very next day. Tragedy and grief combined with yet more warfare. Indeed, the trial revived the assaults on Poe's person. English testified that "the general character of said Poe is that of a notorious liar, a common drunkard and of one utterly lost to all the obligations of honor."[121] While the verdict ultimately went Poe's way, exonerating him from allegations of forgery and swindling, he was only awarded $225.06 of the $5,000 he demanded. And Fuller proceeded to lacerate Poe for bringing suit. Fuller declared, "No man of character and reputation gained one jot of respectability by a libel suit, for if he cannot by his own efforts rise above the imputation, the verdict of a jury can never buy him the good will of the people."[122] Horace Greeley likewise chastised Poe for litigating the situation, arguing that it was "mistaken and silly" to sue Fuller, "the harmless publisher," rather than his "self-roused castigator." Greeley also minimized the reparations that Poe was entitled to, writing that "$25 would have been a liberal estimate of damages, all things considered, including the severe provocation."[123] By these measures, the verdict was a hollow victory.

Perhaps Poe should have anticipated this emptiness. The precepts of an honor culture devalue the compensations of a legal remedy. Although Southerners were litigious enough, they "believed that injured honor could not receive satisfaction through . . . the state."[124] Indeed, to pursue a lawsuit over a challenge to individual honor meant a man announced his own surrender. As Andrew Jackson's mother famously declared, "The law affords no remedy that can satisfy the feelings of a true man."[125] When honor was at stake, a courtroom was too impersonal. Men of honor exacted their own justice. In the estimations of other men then, Poe had failed to reclaim power, integrity, or status.

Still, scholarship holds tightly to the triumph Poe achieved in "The Cask of Amontillado." Dedmond argues that in writing the tale, Poe "saw himself in a position . . . to silence [English] once and for all—to wall him up."[126] Rust maintains that the story illustrates "Poe's genius and reveal[s] English's weaker literary capacity" and thus, "the story itself punishes perfectly with impunity." More crassly but accurately, Rust asks, "Who . . . reads anything by the once pretentious Thomas Dunn English?"[127] While there is an undeniable preeminence in the story's brilliance and Poe's literary persistence, we should not assume that compensates for Poe's anguish.

In life, Poe's torment, grief, and rage seemed inexhaustible. Five months before he died, he confided to Annie Richmond, "My sadness is unaccountable, and this makes me the more sad. I am full of dark forebodings. Nothing cheers or comforts me. My life seems wasted—the future looks a dreary blank."[128] Poe struggled with the melancholia that plagued so many of his victim-heroes. This terrible sadness could alternate with equally terrible fury. As J. Gerald Kennedy affirms, Poe directed a relentless "angry combativeness" against himself and his enemies.[129] His death, too, was horrific. One of the most plausible theories holds that Poe was "cooped" on an election day. In this violent practice, gangs of political thugs abducted men in the street, drugged them with opiates, forced them to drink to stupefaction, and dragged them from ward to ward, stuffing ballot boxes with their votes. Biographers suggest this partisan mugging instigated Poe's last blackout. Whatever the precipitator, he died from the most severe form of alcoholic withdrawal—delirium tremens—and he was racked with fever, hallucinations, and paranoia.

How do we measure the pain of an individual death or life? What can sufficiently compensate for loss, rejection, deprivation, and humiliation? A critical presumption that Poe rose from the ashes of his infamy with the brilliance of "The Cask of Amontillado" reinforces an organizing fallacy of revenge itself. American ideologies of punishment assume that we can accurately calibrate harm and that we can punish accordingly. Our most formative notions of justice assume that hurt can be "measured and inflicted to effect an exchange that serves some higher purpose—actions deterred; debts repaid, the rage in grief transposed." American culture holds fast to the belief that suffering can be quantified and punishment can compensate for pain. More pointedly, we do not question "the idea that there can be an exacting moral calculus of pain, or that it can be measured or applied without vengeance." But, as Aladjem asserts, pain offers us "nothing intrinsically to determine how much is enough in punishing." Pain eludes our attempts to know and name its dimensions. "The notable thing about pain," Aladjem continues, "is that it is not at all a measurable quantity of experience, but an immeasurable quality of experience—one that threatens, as often as not, to be endless and intolerable." Pain persists as an ineffable element of the human condition. Because it grips us with such urgency, pain "is frequently mistaken for a cause or motive that can be measured and addressed." A calculus of pain gives the lie that harm can be accounted for, that it can be anatomized and alleviated: "It is characteristic of pain that it cannot be explained, but that it demands explanation."[130] Injury sends us into unfathomable chasms of human experience. We hurt, but we can never assess or express how much.

The scholarly relationship with "The Cask of Amontillado" reinforces this need for an exposition of pain. In the critical hope that Poe orchestrated the perfect revenge in "The Cask of Amontillado," we also hope that he got remuneration: meaning, purpose, and justice. We hope to deliver the catharsis of the fictional revenge plot to a posthumous but very real Poe. As Aladjem explains, "A vengeful catharsis comes as the movement seems to precipitate a state of equilibrium—a return to a relative calm of a spent, exhausted state which stands as compensation for the past that has been ruined." This cathartic restoration has historically been the bounty of white men in our culture, reserved for the "masculine, Caucasian" victim-hero that "American audiences so strenuously applaud."[131] Situated in time and place, however—situated in a history of insult, injury, grief, and loss—"The Cask of Amontillado" leaves us only with disequilibrium. We must live, as Poe did, with unbalanced accounts, an ambivalent present, and an unknowable future.

NOTES

1. Joseph Snodgrass, "The Facts of Poe's Death and Burial," *Beadle's Monthly* (May 1867), www.eapoe.org/papers/misc1851/18670300.htm.
2. "The Mysterious Death of Edgar Allan Poe," General Topics About Edgar Allan Poe, last updated October 1, 2020, www.eapoe.org/geninfo/poedeath.htm.
3. John Evangelist Walsh, *Midnight Dreary: The Mysterious Death of Edgar Allan Poe* (New York: St. Martin's Minotaur, 2000), 44.
4. R. W. Griswold, "Death of Edgar A. Poe," *New York Daily Tribune* IX, no. 156 (October 9, 1849), www.eapoe.org/papers/misc1827/nyt49100.htm.
5. J. Gerald Kennedy, "The Violence of Melancholy: Poe Against Himself," *American Literary History* 8, no. 3 (Autumn 1996): 533.
6. Edgar Allan Poe, "The Literati of New York City," in *The Works of Edgar Allan Poe, Vol. VIII: Literary Criticism III*, eds. E. C. Stedman and G. E. Woodberry (1895), www.eapoe.org/works/stedwood/sw0801.htm.

7. Charles Briggs (1804–1877) was a journalist, editor, poet, and novelist. Hiram Fuller (1814–1880) was a journalist, editor, and publisher. Thomas Dunn English (1819–1902) was a physician, congressmen, editor, poet, and novelist.

8. Charles F. Briggs, "The Personality of Poe," *Independent*, XXXII (June 24, 1880), www.eapoe.org/papers/misc1851/cfb18801.htm.

9. Thomas Dunn English, "Reminiscences of Poe [Part 04]," *Independent* XLVIII (November 5, 1896), www.eapoe.org/papers/misc1851/tde18964.htm.

10. Kennedy, "Violence of Melancholy," 535.

11. Mabbot, *Tales & Sketches Volume 2*, 1253, 1252.

12. The Montresor family maxim, *nemo me impune lacessit*, is the national motto of Scotland, John Allan's country of origin. In addition, both John Allan and Fortunato were "rich, respected, admired, beloved"; lovers of fine wine; and members of the Masons (Silverman, *Mournful*, 317).

13. Richard Dilworth Rust, "'Punish with Impunity': Poe, Thomas Dunn English, and 'The Cask of Amontillado," *The Edgar Allan Poe Review* 2, no. 2 (Fall 2001): 38.

14. Elena V. Baraban, "The Motive for Murder in 'The Cask of Amontillado' by Edgar Allan Poe," *Rocky Mountain Review* (Fall 2004): 47.

15. Rust, "Punish," 47.

16. Edgar Allan Poe, "The Cask of Amontillado," in *Edgar Allan Poe Tales & Sketches Volume 2: 1843–1849*, ed. Thomas Olive Mabbot (Urbana: University of Illinois Press, 1978), 1256. Hereafter cited parenthetically in the text.

17. Rust, "Punish," 33.

18. Thomas Dunn English, "Reminiscences of Poe [Part 02]," *Independent* XLVIII (October 22, 1896), www.eapoe.org/papers/misc1851/tde18962.htm.

19. Thomas Dunn English, "Reminisces of Poe [Part 03]," *Independent* XLVIII (October 29, 1896), www.eapoe.org/papers/misc1851/tde18963.htm.

20. Thomas Dunn English, "Reminiscences of Poe [Part 01]," *Independent* XLVIII (October 15, 1896), www.eapoe.org/papers/misc1851/tde18961.htm.

21. English, "Reminiscences [Part 03]."

22. Silverman, *Mournful*, 279, 280, 282.

23. English, "Reminiscences [Part 03]."

24. Meyers, *Edgar Allan Poe*, 191.

25. Baraban writes, "Montresor presents himself as a person who had the right to condemn Fortunato to death; he planned his murder as an act of execution" (Baraban, "Motive," 49). Raymond DiSanza argues that "the one thing we know with absolute certainty about Montesor: he is manipulative" ("On Memory, Forgetting, and Complicity in 'The Cask of Amontillado,'" *The Edgar Allan Poe Review* 15, no. 2 [2014]: 198). Charles Nevi maintains that "Montresor's use of the word 'friend' in reference to Fortunato, a man Montresor hates enough to kill" is a prime example of irony in the text ("Irony and 'The Cask of Amontillado,'" *English Journal* 56, no. 3 [March 1967]: 462).

26. Irwin C. Rosen, "Revenge—The Hate That Dare Not Speak Its Name: A Psychoanalytic Perspective," *Journal of the American Psychoanalytic Association* 55, no. 2 (June 2007): 603, 609.

27. Eugene Goldwater, "Getting Mad and Getting Even," *Modern Psychoanalysis* 29, no. 1 (2004): 31.

28. Judith Shklar, *The Faces of Injustice* (New Haven: Yale University Press, 1990), 93.

29. Miriam Berger, "'Am I My Brother's Keeper': Vengefulness as a Link of Reconnecting," in *Victimhood, Vengeance, and the Culture of Forgiveness*, eds. Ivan Urlec, Miriam Berger, and Avi Berman (New York: Nova Science Publishers, Inc., 2010), 71.

30. Terry K. Aladjem, *The Culture of Vengeance and the Fate of American Justice* (Cambridge: Cambridge University Press, 2008), xiii, 3.

31. Hilary J. Beattie, "Revenge," *Journal of the American Psychoanalytic Association* 53, no. 2 (June 2005): 519.

32. Aladjem, *Culture of Vengeance*, 92.

33. Raymond DiSanza summarizes a number of possible reasons for Montresor's silence on this issue, speculating that he stays quiet "because he fears that his listener will not deem the murder justified," because "there was no insult at all," or because "the specific insult doesn't matter; any insult . . . ought to be punished with the same severity" ("On Memory," 201).

34. Baraban, "Motive," 47, 48.

35. Aladjem, *Culture of Vengeance*, 138.

36. Goldwater, "Getting Mad," 25.

37. Sidney P. Moss, *Poe's Literary Battles: The Critic in the Context of His Literary Milieu* (Durham: Duke University Press, 1963), 190.

38. Moss, *Literary Battles*, 193.

39. As late as May 1846, Walter reprinted "one of the nastiest pieces of vilification she could find," a piece that called Poe "magnificently snobbish and dirty," adding her own observation that Poe was a compulsive liar. Poe battled back, dismissing Bostonians as dull and dimwitted: "The fact is, we despise them and defy them . . . and they may all go to the devil together." But he had few defenders, and his solitary voice could not refute the torrent of bad press (Moss, *Literary Battles*, 206, 207, 203).

40. Silverman, *Mournful*, 291.

41. Meyer, *Edgar Allan Poe,* 192. Meyer goes on to say that in April 1846, the St. Louis *Reveille* reported: "A rumor is in circulation in New York, to the effect that Mr. Edgar A. Poe, the poet and author, has been deranged, and his friends are about to place him under the charge of . . . the Insane Retreat at Utica."

42. Moss, *Literary Battles*, 207.

43. Kennedy, "Violence of Melancholy," 533.

44. Magdalen Wing-Chi Ki, "Superego Evil and Poe's Revenge Tales," *Poe Studies* 46 (2013): 60.

45. Moss, *Literary Battles*, 225.

46. Hiram Fuller, "Mr. Poe and the New York Literati," in *Poe's Major Crisis: His Libel Suit and New York's Literary World*, ed. Sidney P. Moss (Durham: Duke University Press, 1970), 19.

47. Hiram Fuller, "A Sad Sight," in *Poe's Major Crisis: His Libel Suit and New York's Literary World*, ed. Sidney P. Moss (Durham: Duke University Press, 1970), 70.

48. Sidney P. Moss, *Poe's Major Crisis: His Libel Suit and New York's Literary World* (Durham: Duke University Press, 1970), 69.

49. Thomas Dunn English, "A Card: Mr. English's Reply to Mr. Poe," *Evening Mirror* IV, no. 65 (June 23, 1846), www.eapoe.org/papers/misc1827/18460623.htm.

50. George Pope Morris, "Literary Squabble," in *Poe's Major Crisis: His Libel Suit and New York's Literary World*, ed. Sidney P. Moss (Durham: Duke University Press, 1970), 42.

51. Rufus W. Griswold, "Letter to Evert A. Duyckninck," in *Poe's Major Crisis: His Libel Suit and New York's Literary World*, ed. Sidney P. Moss (Durham: Duke University Press, 1970), 43.

52. John S. Du Solle, "Literary Quarrel," in *Poe's Major Crisis: His Libel Suit and New York's Literary World*, ed. Sidney P. Moss (Durham: Duke University Press, 1970), 41.

53. Thomas Dunn English, "A Card: In Reply to Mr. Poe's Rejoinder," *Evening Mirror* IV, no. 82 (July 13, 1846), www.eapoe.org/papers/misc1827/18460713.htm.

54. Edgar Allan Poe, "Poe's Letter to Joseph M. Fields and Field's Article on Poe," in *Poe's Major Crisis: His Libel Suit and New York's Literary World*, ed. Sidney P. Moss (Durham: Duke University Press, 1970), 22, 23. Fields obliged, printing a statement in the *Reveille* that certified "the poet is a figure to compare with any in manliness, while his features are not only intellectual but handsome" (Moss, *Literary Battles*, 22).

55. Edgar Allan Poe, "Letter to Henry B. Hirst," in *Poe's Major Crisis: His Libel Suit and New York's Literary World*, ed. Sidney P. Moss (Durham: Duke University Press, 1970), 44.

56. Edgar Allan Poe, "Mr. Poe's Reply to Mr. English and Others," *The Spirit of the Times* (July 10, 1846), www.eapoe.org/works/misc/18460710.htm.

57. Poe, "Mr. Poe's Reply," www.eapoe.org/works/misc/18460710.htm.

58. William Gimore Simms, "Letter to Poe," in *Poe's Major Crisis: His Libel Suit and New York's Literary World*, ed. Sidney P. Moss (Durham: Duke University Press, 1970), 90, 91.

59. Edgar Allan Poe, "Letter to Louis A. Godey," in *Poe's Major Crisis: His Libel Suit and New York's Literary World*, ed. Sidney P. Moss (Durham: Duke University Press, 1970), 67.

60. George W. Eveleth, "Letter to Poe," in *Poe's Major Crisis: His Libel Suit and New York's Literary World*, ed. Sidney P. Moss (Durham: Duke University Press, 1970), 214.

61. Edgar Allan Poe, "Letter to George W. Eveleth," in *Poe's Major Crisis: His Libel Suit and New York's Literary World*, ed. Sidney P. Moss (Durham: Duke University Press, 1970), 215.

62. Moss, *Major Crisis*, 60, 63.

63. T.F.C, "From Philadelphia," in *Poe's Major Crisis: His Libel Suit and New York's Literary World*, ed. Sidney P. Moss (Durham: Duke University Press, 1970), 66.

64. Edgar Allan Poe, "Letter to Thomas Holley Chivers," in *Poe's Major Crisis: His Libel Suit and New York's Literary World*, ed. Sidney P. Moss (Durham: Duke University Press, 1970), 72, 73.

65. Moss, *Literary Battles*, 232.

66. Hiram Fuller, "A Sad Sight," in *Poe's Major Crisis: His Libel Suit and New York's Literary World*, ed. Sidney P. Moss (Durham: Duke University Press, 1970), 69, 70.

67. For more on Thomas Dunn English's portrait of Poe in his novel, *1844: or The Power of the S. F.* see Leonard B. Hurley, "A New Note on the War of The Literati," *American Literature* 7 no. 4 (January 1936): 376–94.

68. Silverman, *Mournful*, 315.

69. Moss, *Major Crisis*, 111.

70. Francis B. Dedmond, "'The Cask of Amontillado' and the War of the Literati," *Modern Language Quarterly* 15, no. 2 (June 1954): 137, 140.

71. Rust, "Punish," 33.

72. See Dedmond, "War of the Literati," 1.

73. Aladjem, *Culture of Vengeance*, 94.

74. Aladjem, ibid., 41, 42.

75. DiSanza, "On Memory," 194.

76. Aladjem, *Culture of Vengeance*, 44.

77. Roger G. Lopez, "Self-Knowledge and the Elusive Pleasure of Vengeance," *Philosophia* 48 (2020): 293, 292.

78. Aladjem, *Culture of Vengeance*, 43.

79. DiSanza, "On Memory," 201.

80. Aladjem, *Culture of Vengeance*, 46.

81. As Barbaran summarizes, "unable to find a logical explanation for Montresor's hatred for Fortunato, most commentators conclude that Montresor is insane" ("War of the Literati," 47).

82. Bertram Wyatt-Brown, *Southern Honor*, 34.

83. Edward L. Ayers, *Vengeance and Justice: Crime and Punishment in the 19th-Century American South* (Oxford: Oxford University Press, 1984), 11, 13.

84. Jon Elster, "Norms of Revenge," *Ethics* 100, no. 4 (July 1990): 867.

85. Ayers, *Vengeance*, 16.

86. Wyatt-Brown, *Southern Honor*, 34.

87. Hence, Jon Elster considers honor "an intensely interactive" advantage, mediated through direct and violent conflict. Elster maintains that revenge cannot be understood apart from the "phenomenon of honor" ("Norms of Revenge," 868, 883).

88. Richard P. Benton, "Poe's 'The Cask of Amontillado': Its Cultural and Historical Backgrounds," *Poe Studies/Dark Romanticism* 29, no. 1 (June 1996): 22, 25, 26.

89. Baraban, "Motive," 51.

90. Ayers, *Vengeance*, 21.

91. Ibid., 13.

92. Elster, "Norms of Revenge," 872, 870.

93. Ayers, *Vengeance*, 13, 15.

94. Baraban, "Motive," 50.

95. As Richard E. Nisbett and Dov Cohen confirm, "A key aspect of the culture of honor is the importance placed on the insult and the necessity to respond to it. An insult implies that the target is weak enough to be bullied. Since a reputation for

strength is of the essence in the culture of honor, the individual who insults someone must be forced to retract; if the instigator refuses, he must be punished—with
violence or even death" (*Culture of Honor: The Psychology of Violence in the South*
[Boulder, CO: Westview Press, 1996], 5).

96. Ayers, *Vengeance*, 17.

97. English, "A Card: In Reply to Mr. Poe's Rejoinder," www.eapoe.org/papers/
misc1827/18460713.htm.

98. English, "A Card: In Reply to Mr. Poe's Rejoinder," www.eapoe.org/papers
/misc1827/18460713.htm. And again, in his "Reminiscences," English tallied the
worst of Poe's abuses: "'blackguard of the lowest order,' 'coward,' 'liar,' 'the animalcula [sic] with mustaches for antennae,' 'brandy-nose,' 'one of Mr. Barnum's
baboons,' 'poor miserable fool,' 'blatherskite,' 'malignant villain' 'wretch'" ("Reminiscences [Part 01]," www.eapoe.org/papers/misc1851/tde18961.htm).

99. Kennedy, "Violence of Melancholy," 536.

100. Aladjem, *Culture of Vengeance*, 98, 100, 98, 111, 113.

101. Kent Bales, "Poetic Justice in 'The Cask of Amontillado,'" *Poe Studies* 5, no.
2 (1927): 50.

102. Charles N. Nevi, "Irony and 'The Cask of Amontillado,'" *English Journal* 56,
no. 3 (March 1967): 462.

103. Francis J. Henninger, "The Bouquet of Poe's Amontillado," *South Atlantic
Bulletin* 35, no. 2 (March 1970): 39.

104. Quoted in Baraban, "Motive," 48.

105. DiSanza, "On Memory," 202.

106. Rosen, "Revenge," 605, 603.

107. Janne van Doorn, "Anger, Feelings of Revenge, Hate," *Emotion Review* 10,
no. 4 (October 2018): 321.

108. Lopez, "Self-Knowledge," 294.

109. Aladjem, *Culture of Vengeance*, 97, 126.

110. Elster, "Norms of Revenge," 884.

111. Aladjem, *Culture of Vengeance*, 43, 140, 141.

112. DiSanza, "On Memory," 198, 199. DiSanza ultimately concludes that we cannot know the "you" that Montresor confides in because he is "an ironic, manipulative—and perhaps sociopathic—narrator."

113. Meyers, *Edgar Allan Poe*, 200.

114. Moss, *Major Crisis*, 127.

115. Nathaniel P. Willis, "Hospital for Disabled Labourers with the Brain," in *Poe's
Major Crisis: His Libel Suit and New York's Literary World*, ed. Sidney P. Moss (Durham: Duke University Press, 1970), 130.

116. Hiram Fuller, "A Comment on Nathaniel P. Willis's 'Hospital for Disabled
Labourers with the Brain," in *Poe's Major Crisis: His Libel Suit and New York's Literary World*, ed. Sidney P. Moss (Durham: Duke University Press, 1970), 132, 133.

117. Silverman, *Mournful*, 325.

118. Edgar Allan Poe, "Letter to Jane Erma Locke," March 10, 1847 (LTR-251), www
.eapoe.org/works/letters/p4703100.htm.

119. John S. Du Solle, "The Philadelphia *Spirit of the Times* Comments on Poe's Letter in the *Home Journal*," in *Poe's Major Crisis: His Libel Suit and New York's Literary World*, ed. Sidney P. Moss (Durham: Duke University Press, 1970), 158.

120. "Editorial Delicacy," in *Poe's Major Crisis: His Libel Suit and New York's Literary World*, ed. Sidney P. Moss (Durham: Duke University Press, 1970), 160.

121. "J.B.H. Smith Takes Thomas Dunn English's Testimony," in *Poe's Major Crisis: His Libel Suit and New York's Literary World*, ed. Sidney P. Moss (Durham: Duke University Press, 1970), 166.

122. Hiram Fuller, "Three Articles on Poe in the Evening Mirror," in *Poe's Major Crisis: His Libel Suit and New York's Literary World*, ed. Sidney P. Moss (Durham: Duke University Press, 1970), 184.

123. Horace Greeley, "Genius and the Law of Libel," in *Poe's Major Crisis: His Libel Suit and New York's Literary World*, ed. Sidney P. Moss (Durham: Duke University Press, 1970), 188.

124. Ayers, *Vengeance*, 31.

125. Michael Paul Rogin, *Fathers & Children: Andrew Jackson and the Subjugation of the American Indian* (New Brunswick: Transaction Publishers, 2006), 18.

126. Dedmond, "War of the Literati," 146.

127. Rust, "Punish," 48.

128. Edgar Allan Poe, "Letter to Annie Richmond," Poe's Letters, Ltr-311, www.eapoe.org/works/letters/p4904280.htm.

129. Kennedy, "Violence of Melancholy," 540.

130. Aladjem, *Culture of Vengeance*, 15, 22, 76, 77.

131. Ibid., 139, 65.

Epilogue

Ambivalence

In February 2017, Jack Halberstam created a minor media firestorm with a blog post on the Academy Award–winning film *Manchester by the Sea*. Halberstam's review lacerated the movie as an elegy to "white supremacy." Focusing on Casey Affleck's character, Lee Chandler, Halberstam interrogates the film's depiction of white masculine sadness: "Why are white men so sad? Well, in this film, they are sad because women are fucked-up shrews and alcoholics who drag them down, give them heart attacks and, for god's sake, try to talk to them and offer them food." Beyond these sorrows, white men are "also sad because they work for very little money and do the worst jobs in the world. They clean other people's toilets, fix their showers and live in small garrets alone and with very bad furniture. Poor sad white men." Halberstam calls out the cultural and critical empathy with Lee: The film knows that Lee is responsible for the heartbreak that torments him, and yet it still depicts him as "tragic and heroic, stoic and moral, stern but good." Ultimately, Halberstam sees Lee as a shade of a gratuitous "melancholia."[1]

I see the validity of Halberstam's aggravation. I have argued that white masculine melancholia can be particularly insidious. More pointedly, I have argued that the depression of nineteenth-century white men seethes with antagonism, and that it, like other perverse feelings, is an affect of lost privilege and contested dominance. Still, I wonder at the problem of empathy, anger, and grief that Lee Chandler and white men like him represent. Indeed, contemporary white men are more than sad. They are also enraged, alive with the bitterness and antipathy that this book discerns in a historical masculinity. In the early American zeitgeist, white men are miserable with grief, guilt, anxiety, insecurity, and isolation. They are shattered by loss, failure, and betrayal. Time and again, these fallen patriarchs provoke questions like: What should we feel—with or for—the broken, disgruntled white men who haunt our culture? Should we downsize their distress, as Halberstam does, reminding prospective commiserates of the "real" suffering of marginalized people? Should we answer their injury with anger at the white man's narcissism and damage? What if a culture struggles to unfeel the white man's pain? What if a culture knows his privilege and still mourns his losses? What if it even grieves the perdition of the prowess he represents?

SAD, MAD MEN

Mainstream news media swarm with headlines like "White Men's Tantrums" and "There's Nothing More Frightening in America Today Than an Angry White Man." The years 2020 and 2021 saw a legal reckoning with white male harm. Charles M. Blow called these phenomena "a virtual pageant of privilege" as the country watched and waited, wondering if our system of justice would be as merciless with white men as it is with the white man's others.[2] A Michigan appeals court upheld a 175-year prison sentence for Larry Nassar, the physician for the USA gymnastics team who sexually assaulted hundreds of girls in his care. A white police officer, Derek Chauvin, was convicted for the on-duty murder of a black man, George Floyd. Kyle Rittenhouse was acquitted after shooting three men at a racial protest in Kenosha, Wisconsin. The white male organizers of the deadly alt-right rally in Charlottesville, Virginia, were found culpable for twenty-five million dollars in damages. Three white men in Georgia were convicted of killing a young black man, Ahmaud Arbery, for jogging through their suburban neighborhood. The self-proclaimed "Q-Anon shaman," Jacob Chansley, was sentenced to over three years in prison for storming the U.S. Capitol to prevent the inauguration of a lawfully elected president. Ghislane Maxwell was convicted of trafficking scores of young girls for the serial sex offender, Jeffrey Epstein. We seem to be prosecuting white male violence and violation with an unprecedented momentum.

Pundits attribute the crimes behind these trials to the destructive affects of white men, particularly their anger and entitlement. CNN writer and producer John Blake observes, "White male anger has become one of the most potent political forces in contemporary America."[3] *New York Times* columnist Paul Krugman characterizes the "angry white male caucus" that voted for former President Donald Trump—and that rallies for racism, xenophobia, misogyny, homophobia, and transphobia—as a populace "consumed with bitterness driven by status anxiety."[4] Professor and author Ibram X. Kendi argues that white men are fighting mightily to maintain their supremacy, defending an America "where white men can rule and brutalize without consequence."[5]

Of course, one of the central propositions of this book is that sick, sad, angry white men have a history. The perverse feelings of white masculinity—hatred, melancholia, disgust, resentment, and disgust—are integrally tied to centuries of conquest and exploitation. Recent cultural commentators reinforce the signature events of this history. Blake observes, "This angry White man has been a major character throughout US history. He gave the country slavery, the slaughter of Native Americans, and Jim Crow." In addition, Blake declares that "the January 6 insurrection [against the Capitol] wasn't unprecedented. In many ways it was a sequel": a resurrection of the white male extremism that assassinated elected officials, terrorized the Black vote, and toppled state governments in the decades after the Civil War.[6] And, frankly, the plunders of white male antagonism have had many revivals. Kendi writes that the summer of 2021 "compressed 413 years of American history" into the video that recorded George Floyd's death, images "in which anyone could easily see the history for what it always has been: the violent 'self-defense' of white male supremacy." Kendi goes on to enumerate a chronology of atrocities perpetrated by white men purportedly fighting for democracy, liberty, and the pursuit of happiness: "Colonialism, capitalism, slavery and slave trading, Indian removal, manifest destiny, colonization, the Ku Klux Klan, Chinese exclusion, disenfranchisement, Jim Crow, eugenics, massive resistance, 'law and order,' Islamophobia, family separation—all were done in the name of defending life or civilization or freedom."[7] White men are perennially angry, it seems, and especially furious when the spoils of their ascendancy are threatened. As Kai Wright puts it, "Hell hath no fury like a white man scorned."[8]

Although analysts see Donald Trump's election to the U.S. presidency in 2016 as the political apex of white masculine spite, Michael Kimmel chronicled the modern reemergence of the besieged white man in 2013. According to Kimmel, angry white men "feel they have been screwed, betrayed by the country they love, discarded like trash on the side of the information superhighway." In an increasingly global economy, in a world where gay people can get married, black lives matter, and women advocate for wage equality, these men feel persecuted and forgotten. While statistics confirm that white male privilege continues to thrive, the men in Kimmel's study insist on their victimization. The demographic Kimmel tracks are "downwardly mobile lower middle class" men: craft workers, small farmers, independent store owners, and factory workers.[9] Men obstructed by outsourcing, corporate agriculture, discount superstores, and online retail behemoths. But the reality is that, as Krugman reinforces, "white male rage isn't restricted to blue-collar guys in diners. It's also present among people who've done very well in life's lottery," people who are "very much part of the elite."[10] Anger unites white men across professional, class, and regional boundaries.

Kimmel emphasizes the wrath inspired by the cultural demotion of white masculinity, but his angry men also voice intense pain. "Nobody gives a shit about us anymore," says one man. "It's all over." Another man, active in the men's rights movement, explains men's "anger" with a litany of emotional distresses: like losing kids in divorce, fatherhood reduced to child support and miserly custody agreements, and the inability to find a successful long-term relationship. Angry white men also register the "pain" of disappointed privilege. In one man's words, "Look, I thought if I did it right, did everything they asked of me, I'd be okay, you know. Play ball, and you'll get rich; you'll get laid. And I did . . . For thirty years, I've been such a good fucking soldier. And now these new laws about sexual harassment, about affirmative action? And now you're telling me, 'Sorry, but you aren't going to get all those rewards.' Is that what you're telling me? Jesus, I wouldn't have done it if I knew I wasn't going to get those goodies." Kimmel names the psychology of this perceived wounding as "aggrieved entitlement." These men believe themselves "heirs to a great promise, the American Dream," but they have not realized that fantasy of power, control, and wealth. As a result, these men nurse "the injury of losing . . . something valuable, precious." A birthright. A patrimony. Beneath the rage, Carol Gilligan acknowledges, is "immense sadness."[11]

Masculinity studies has been most attuned to this sadness in its analyses of American boys and boyhood. In 1998, psychologist William Pollock roused the nation's consciousness with the publication of *Real Boys*. Pollock warned that boys are "deeply troubled." He cited alarming statistics on boys diagnosed as learning disabled, seriously emotionally disturbed, and depressed; he interrogated the academic achievement gap between boys and girls; and he worried over the disproportionate number of boys who are victims of violent crimes and suicide. Pollock implicated the norms of masculinity in this distress, indicting the distortions of a "Boy Code" for the shame, loneliness, frustration, powerlessness, and anger that boys feel.[12] A year later, psychologists Dan Kindlon and Michael Thompson fueled this cultural confrontation with an afflicted masculinity in *Raising Cain*. Kindlon and Thompson maintained that boys come of age in a "culture of cruelty": an arena defined by boy-on-boy brutality and that schools boys in "domination, humiliation, fear, and betrayal."[13] A cacophony of books and films documenting a disordered masculinity followed, most notably Sut Jhally's *Tough Guise* (1999), Jackson Katz's *The Macho Paradox* (2006), C.J. Pascoe's *Dude, You're a Fag* (2007), Michael Kimmel's *Guyland* (2008), and Niobe Way's *Deep Secrets* (2011). In this media, men and boys are suffering, tormented by a masculinity that acculturates them to silence, invulnerability, and violence. In the last three decades, an entire culture industry attempting to triage a masculinity in crisis has emerged. This crisis is strikingly affective. In it, white men are mad, sad, frustrated, alienated, and psychologically troubled.

CONFLICTED

What does it mean to be a white man in a nation that is wiser to his transgressions? A white man, that as Wright articulates, "looked around and noticed how many of us do not draw their power from proximity to them. In the Obama era, they watched the Dreamers discard the white man's idea of citizenship and demand a fundamentally new conversation about immigrant's rights. They watched black people build a movement on an irrefutable statement of self-worth, one that requires no white person's approval to be true and potent. And now they are watching as millions of women refuse to carry the shame of their male predators."[14] What does it mean to be a white man in this here and now? Do you reject a legacy of anger for an estate of shame? Do you refuse any claim to grievance and instead surrender to humility? Or do you rage against the slow fade of your primacy?

Tellingly, Kimmel contends that American men are "right to be angry." He argues that American men came of age in a system that "promised a lot of rewards if they played by the rules. If they were good, decent, hardworking men, if they saddled up, or even more accurately got into the harness themselves, they would feel the respect of their wives and children; if they fought America's wars, and served their country fighting fires and stopping crime, they'd have the respect of their communities. And, most important, if they were loyal to their colleagues and workmates, did an honest day's work for an honest day's pay, then they'd also have the respect of other men."[15] If men are "right to be angry," does their anger implicitly become a political right? If we better understand the origins of white male anger, does that turn anger into another patriarchal prerogative? What does it mean to extend compassion to reactionary, thwarted assumptions of power? And how do we reconcile Kimmel's scholarly empathy here with allegations against his own sexism, transphobia, and homophobia that will surface in 2018?[16]

In his vacillations, Kimmel embodies a tension—discordant identifications, feelings, and attachments—that troubles much of American culture. The American national consciousness cannot reconcile itself to the malevolence of white masculinity or its punishment. We are conflicted. The conflict is evident in the shockingly lenient sentencing of Brock Turner, the golden-haired Stanford University athlete convicted of rape, despite a thirteen-page victim's statement that began, "You don't know me, but you've been inside me, and that's why we're here today."[17] It is evident in the abiding presence of women among white male nationalists–women who believe that "men have been pushed and pushed and pushed out of spaces where they can . . . express themselves as men"—despite the blatant and unapologetic misogyny of these movements.[18] It is evident in the fatal police shootings of at least 135 unarmed Black men and women since 2015, despite increasing activism against excessive, racialized police brutality.[19] It is evident in Brett Kavanaugh's confirmation to the Supreme Court, despite accusations of sexual misconduct from three women. It is evident in Trump's political sovereignty, despite two impeachment hearings, first on charges of abuse of power and obstruction of justice, and then on inciting a riot. Contrary affects, ethics, and politics war against each other in these incongruities. White men are the nation's villains and victim-heroes.

WOUNDED ATTACHMENT

The truth at the core of this conflict centers on our "wounded attachment" to an anachronistic white manhood. Wendy Brown uses the term "wounded attachments" to describe an identity politics that "becomes invested in its own subjugation": a subjectivity that emerges through assertions of pain, discrimination, and subordination. Brown's critique interrogates identities predicated on the injuries of classism, racism, sexism, and homophobia. In this context, "the real or imagined holdings" of white masculinity are the ultimate "objects of desire."[20] But as this study illustrates, white masculinity is such a tantalizing phantasm that even white men don't have enough of it. Even white men claim exclusion from the abundance their race and gender promise.

How do we make sense of the wounded attachments of a subjectivity that still has more—more money, power, and freedom—than the rest of us? In a later essay, Brown deepens her analysis of an identity premised on suffering and deprivation, an identity that fetishizes the experience of injustice and discrimination. For Brown, wounded attachments translate into a reactionary politics caught in blame and reproach—a politics that can no longer take transformative action. Brown deploys this concept to make sense of the melancholic left and its fixation on the lost utopia of a class revolution. This obsolete radicalism deploys old, tired strategies that have "failed to apprehend the character of" the current era.[21] Heather Love reminds us that these melancholic leftists cling to shattered dreams because of "actual feelings of love, actual desire for radical social change: the problem with their politics is not the attachment but rather the paralyzing effects of melancholic incorporation and disavowal."[22] Remarkably, Brown critiques the melancholic left for the same deficiencies that Kimmel sees in angry white men: "It is a Left that has become more attached to its impossibility than to its potential fruitfulness, a Left that is most at home dwelling not in hopefulness but in its own marginality and failure, a Left that is thus cut in a structure of melancholic attachment to a certain strain of its own dead past, whose spirit is ghostly, whose structure of desire is backward looking and punishing."[23] The sad, angry white man—like the mournful Left—insists on his unviability and erasure. He yearns for a bygone past, punishes the present, and death-knells the future. In queer or feminist contexts, it is relatively comfortable to consider the despair of weary, sad, freedom-loving leftists. But what about the "wounded attachments" of angry white conservatives? What if what's loved is a good ole patriarchy? What if what's desired is a hard-right return to white masculine privilege?

This attachment to white American manhood persists as a bond of what Lauren Berlant calls "cruel optimism." According to Berlant, "a relation of cruel optimism exists when something you desire is actually an obstacle to your flourishing. It might involve food, or a kind of love; it might be a fantasy of the good life, or a political project."[24] And, in my estimation, it might be a fantasy of steady, stable gendered bounties. White men stay optimistically devoted to white American masculinity, despite its dangers and disgraces. Kimmel documents harrowing statistics on depression, suicide, rampage shootings, and addiction in white men. Just as importantly, Kimmel implicates normative masculinity in this despair, particularly its insistence on fearlessness, invincibility, supremacy, and capitalist acquisition no matter the economic odds. Nonetheless, the men in Kimmel's study exhibit "a near infatuation" with traditional masculinity, relying on it for healing and the reclamation of power. Although they are ravaged by manhood, they continue to swear allegiance to regressive notions of manly strength, courage, and success. I am struck by how much Kimmel's men revere—and trust—the early American conception of manhood this book excavates. They exhibit a similar intolerance for insult, failure, or humiliation. They subscribe to archaic notions of honor, revenge, and restorative violence.[25] And they continue to expect unlimited—even unearned—opportunity, wealth, and freedom.

Perhaps they stay faithful to white masculinity because it is all that remains in an era of retrograde capitalism. As Ijeoma Oluo queries, "How do you keep the average white male American invested in a system that disadvantages him? You give them whiteness. You give them maleness."[26] You give them an identity that will provide a chimera of power, status, and respect, even when they are most damaged and defeated. Berlant argues that this tenacity—white masculinity's stubborn hold on the broken promises of supremacy—"enables us to expect that this time, nearness to this thing will help you or a world to become different in just the right way. But, again, optimism is cruel when the object/scene that ignites a sense of possibility actually makes it impossible."[27] White men hope for the rebirth of an old nation, a renascence that will never come.

MIXED FEELINGS

In the current sociopolitical scene, some white men make astonishing and unprecedented claims to victimization. As Sarah Banet-Weiser observes, "While people in positions of privilege have historically claimed to be aggrieved or injured by those who threaten their dominance, we have witnessed a significant shift in the contemporary moment, where individual men publicly and assertively claim to be victims."[28] Contemporary white men identify as victims of feminism, political correctness, affirmative action, economic downturns, false allegations of rape and sexual harassment, prejudicial divorce and child custody laws, gender double standards, and negative media stereotypes.[29] This mentality is a veritable albatross of white American manhood. Tristan Bridges illustrates how white men position themselves as "somehow stigmatized by gender and racial privilege," believing they are unjustly pilloried for their power.[30] More fundamentally, Nancy Dowd's work traces "the odd reality that most men feel powerless rather than powerful, yet that powerlessness does not lead to alignment with other subordinated groups but rather to a defense of potential or actual privilege."[31] For white men, patriarchy does not proffer *felt* potencies and it does not nurture interracial or intergender solidarities. Instead, it exiles them *inside* white masculinity.

I have argued that a victim's identity can be a strategic resource in the traumas of loss, betrayal, and deprivation. I have argued that victimization—with all its moral righteousness and arbitrations of truth—can be a tactical recompense when grief and grievance harden into resentment, threatening the subject with chronic paralysis. I have argued, too, that victimization can subvert the compulsory dominance of white masculinity and expose the violations of male-on-male cruelty.

I need to temper this argument to acknowledge the difference between oppression and disillusionment, subjugation and disappointment. With Judith Butler, Zeynep Gambetti, and Leticia Sabsay, I recognize that claims to victimization resonate differently when powerful actors make them. "When nations advertise their hypervulnerability to new immigrants, or men openly fear that they are now the victims of feminism," or white people see "black people as a threat to their existence," a declaration of vulnerability is a paradoxical reassertion of power. These testimonies of "pain" quickly become a blueprint for the re-oppression of the already oppressed. Butler et al. observe that we exist in a world that distributes precarity unequally: a world where hierarchies of power translate into different allotments of vulnerability. In such a world, it is dangerous to categorize white men as another "vulnerable population."[32] It is equally dangerous to uncritically accept the victimization of sick, sad, angry white men.

In the ataxia of these perils, Heather Love encourages marginalized people to "feel backwards": to "insist on the importance of clinging to ruined identities and histories of injury."[33] Love assures us that if we attend to specific histories of exclusion and violence, we will see structures of inequality more plainly in the present. I am arguing that such clarity is possible now, and that this book contributes to clearer seeing and clearer feeling. In studies like this one, we feel backward through a past rife with the victimization of history's others and the "pain" of their victimizers. This book examines many of the historical events the twenty-first century ascribes to angry white masculinity, including imperialism, slavery, and Indian genocide. It also recovers historical forces that stalked white men with gender-specific jeopardies: the masturbation panic; the medicalization of sex, sexuality, and death; the oedipal shadow of the founding fathers; the economic volatilities of early capitalism; the rapaciousness of Jacksonian masculinity; and the violent imperatives of an honor culture. While these realities had pervasive impacts, nineteenth-century white men *felt* them distinctively and perhaps more intensely. They internalized the pathologies of the manhood that simultaneously gave them an enviable and exclusive power. As this book shows, some men went mad, sickened, or died in the crucible of white American masculinity. Some men became pariahs—deviant outsiders—to the ideal they failed to embody.

The hegemonies of gender, race, and nation damage us all, but our wounds are not the same. I feel backward to a manhood tormented by the pains of supremacy, prohibitions against homosexuality, the brutalities of other men, and their own abuses. I feel forward to a manhood plagued with aggrieved entitlement, the ferocity of its hatreds and phobias, and an emergent culpability. Arriving here, I feel ambivalent. Indeed, I embrace a liberating ambivalence.

Twenty-first-century psychology understands ambivalence as an affect of "mixed feelings," a state in which people feel competing emotions simultaneously: admiration and contempt, attraction and repulsion. As Iris Schneider and Norbet Schwarz explain, ambivalence is different from uncertainty because the conflicting emotions compel us with equal fervor. Ambivalence is also distinct from ambiguity because of what we know and understand: We are not confused about our feelings, and we are not mistaken about their object. In addition, ambivalence is not indifference because we feel too much in its grasp.[34] In ambivalence, we can feel discouraged and hopeful, compassionate and hostile, anxious and detached. In ambivalence, we can feel multiply and concurrently.

Feeling ambivalent about white masculinity means wariness at its propensities for conquest, ownership, and destruction. It means exasperation with its hubris and narcissism. It means rage and grief at its bloodlust and killing. It means concern for men and boys conditioned to impassiveness, predation, and cruelty. It means respect, even awe, for the gender outlaws that defy normative manhood. It means expansive identifications with ideals of freedom, equality, and the right to revolution. It means recognizing that white men, too, can avow their own ambivalence, nurturing a more critical relationship with the afflictions of a gender ideology. It means embracing an "affective disobedience" that Xine Yao associates with disaffection and unfeeling.[35] This affective plurality, happening all at once, enables a more methodical consideration of sociopolitical realities and new political directions. Ambivalence is a mature and thoughtful affect, based on the insights—and complexity—of experience. Hence, I trust my ambivalence, mixed feelings that tangle with a history of sick, sad, angry white men, an untenable present, and a future in the making.

Still, this call to ambivalence may seem counterintuitive. Modern psychology assumes that ambivalence agitates an acute unease that must be resolved. Researchers characterize ambivalence as "an aversive and undesirable state," one that "causes discomfort, anxiety, and tension."[36] This literature sees ambivalence as an affect to avoid. More recently, however, psychologists have begun to recognize that ambivalence can be constructive, that it can enable more creativity and much-wanted change. Taly Reich and S. Christian Wheeler, moreover, note that ambivalence can serve "self-protective purposes": that people summon ambivalence to temper potential disappointment and the caprices of an unpredictable world.[37] Thus, I leave you with ambivalence: an affective intricacy that knows its own wisdom; that protects and steadies us in troubled times; and that kindles imagination and transformation.

NOTES

1. Jack Halberstam, "White Men Behaving Sadly," Bully Bloggers (February 22, 2017), bullybloggers.wordpress.com/2017/02/22/white-men-behaving-sadly-by-jack-halberstam/.

2. Charles M. Blow, "White Men on Trial," *New York Times* (November 17, 2021), www.nytimes.com/2021/11/17/opinion/rittenhouse-trial-bannon.html.

3. John Blake, "There's nothing more frightening in American today than an angry White man," CNN (November 20, 2021), www.cnn.com/2021/11/20/us/angry-white-men-trials-blake-cec/index.html.

4. Paul Krugman, "The Angry White Male Caucus," *New York Times* (October 1, 2018), www.nytimes.com/2018/10/01/opinion/kavanaugh-white-male-privilege.html.

5. Ibram X. Kendi, "The Violent Defense of White Male Supremacy," *Atlantic* (September 9, 2020), www.theatlantic.com/ideas/archive/2020/09/armed-defenders-white-male-supremacy/616192/.

6. Blake, "Nothing more frightening."

7. Kendi, "Violent Defense."

8. Kai Wright, "White Men Have Good Reason to be Scared," *Nation* (November 5, 2018), www.thenation.com/article/archive/white-men-have-good-reason-to-be-scared/.

9. Michael Kimmel, *Angry White Men: American Masculinity at the End of an Era* (New York: Nation Books, 2013), 3.

10. Krugman, "Angry White Male."

11. Kimmel, *Angry White Men*, 118, 18, 27, 23.

12. William Pollock, *Real Boys: Rescuing Our Sons from the Myths of Boyhood* (New York: Henry Holt and Company, 1998), xxiii, xxv.

13. Dan Kindlon and Michael Thompson, *Raising Cain: Protecting the Emotional Life of Boys* (New York: Ballantine Books, 1999), 75, 73.

14. Wright, "White Men."

15. Kimmel, *Angry White Men*, 27.

16. Colleen Flaherty, "More Than Rumors," *Inside Higher Ed* (August 10, 2018), www.insidehighered.com/news/2018/08/10/michael-kimmels-former-student-putting-name-and-details-those-harassment-rumors.

17. Katie J. M. Baker, "Here's the Powerful Letter the Stanford Victim Read to Her Attacker," Buzzfeed News (June 3, 2016), www.buzzfeednews.com/article/katiejmbaker/heres-the-powerful-letter-the-stanford-victim-read-to-her-ra.

18. Seyward Darby, *Sisters in Hate: American Women and White Extremism* (New York: Little, Brown and Company, 2020), 155.

19. Cheryl W. Thompson, "Fatal Police Shootings of Unarmed Black People Reveal Troubling Patterns," NPR (January 25, 2021), www.npr.org/2021/01/25/956177021/fatal-police-shootings-of-unarmed-black-people-reveal-troubling-patterns.

20. Wendy Brown, "Wounded Attachments," *Political Theory* 21, no. 3 (August 1993): 403, 394.

21. Wendy Brown, "Resisting Left Melancholy," *Boundary 2* 26, no. 3 (1999): 20.

22. Heather Love, *Feeling Backwards*, 149.

23. Brown, "Left Melancholy," 26.

24. Lauren Berlant, *Cruel Optimism* (Durham: Duke University Press, 2011), 1.

25. Kimmel, *Angry White Men*, 107. See also 217, 176–79.

26. Ijeoma Oluo, *Mediocre: The Dangerous Legacy of White Male America* (New York: Seal Press, 2020), 23.

27. Berlant, *Cruel Optimism*, 2.

28. Sarah Banet-Weiser, "'Ruined' Lives: Mediated White Male Victimhood," *European Journal of Cultural Studies* 24, no. 1 (2020): 61.

29. Kimmel, *Angry White Men*, 122–23.

30. Tristan Bridges, "Antifeminism, Profeminism, and the Myth of White Men's Disadvantage," *Signs: Journal of Women in Culture and Society* 46, no. 3 (2021): 675.

31. Nancy Dowd, *The Man Question: Male Subordination and Privilege* (New York: New York University Press, 2010), 5

32. Judith Butler, Zeynep Gambetti, and Leticia Sabsay, "Introduction" in *Vulnerability in Resistance* (Durham: Duke University Press, 2016), 4, 5.

33. Love, *Feeling Backwards*, 30.

34. Iris K. Schneider and Norbert Schwarz, "Mixed Feelings: The Case of Ambivalence," *ScienceDirect* 15 (2017): 39.

35. Xine Yao, *Disaffected: The Cultural Politics of Unfeeling in Nineteenth-Century America* (Durham: Duke University Press, 2021), 6.

36. Taly Reich and S. Christian Wheeler, "The Good and Bad of Ambivalence: Desiring Ambivalence Under Outcome Uncertainty," *Journal of Personality and Social Psychology* 110, no. 4 (2016): 494.

37. Ibid., 506.

Bibliography

Ahmed, Sara. *The Cultural Politics of Emotion*. New York: Routledge, 2004.

Aladjem, Terry K. *The Culture of Vengeance and the Fate of American Justice*. Cambridge: Cambridge University Press, 2008.

Allan, Thomas M. *A Republic in Time: Temporality and Social Imagination in Nineteenth-Century America*. Chapel Hill: University of North Carolina Press, 2008.

"An Account of the Dissection of a Young Man, Who Died Dropsical. . . . " *The Philadelphia Medical Museum*, Feb. 4, 1806. search.proquest.com/americanperiodicals.

Anthony, David. "'Gone Distracted': 'Sleepy Hollow,' Gothic Masculinity, and the Panic of 1819." *Early American Literature* 41, no. 1 (2005): 111–44.

de Arrizabalaga y Prado, Leonardo. *The Emperor Elagabalus: Fact or Fiction?* Cambridge: Cambridge University Press, 2010.

Ashworth, Suzanne. "Experimental Matter, Unclaimed Death, and Posthumous Futures in Poe's 'Valdemar,'" *Poe Studies* 49 (2016): 52–79.

Askeland, Lori. *Children and Youth in Adoption, Orphanages, and Foster Care: A Historical Handbook and Guide*. Westport, CT: Greenwood Press, 2006.

Ayers, Edward L. *Vengeance and Justice: Crime and Punishment in the 19th-Century American South*. Oxford: Oxford University Press, 1984.

Baker, Brian. "Gothic Masculinities." In *The Routledge Companion to the Gothic*. Eds. Catherine Spooner and Emma McEvoy, 164–73. New York: Routledge, 2007.

Baker, Katie J. M. "Here's the Powerful Letter the Stanford Victim Read to Her Attacker." Buzzfeed News (June 3, 2016). www.buzzfeednews.com/article/katiejmbaker/heres-the-powerful-letter-the-stanford-victim-read-to-her-ra.

Bales, Kent. "Poetic Justice in 'The Cask of Amontillado.'" *Poe Studies* 5, no. 2 (1927): 51.

Banet-Weiser, Sarah. "'Ruined' Lives: Mediated White Male Victimhood." *European Journal of Cultural Studies* 24, no. 1 (2020): 60–80.

Baraban, Elena V. "The Motive for Murder in 'The Cask of Amontillado' by Edgar Allan Poe," *Rocky Mountain Review* (Fall 2004): 47–62.

Barker-Benfield, G. J. *The Horrors of the Half-Known Life*: *Male Attitudes Toward Women and Sexuality in Nineteenth-Century America*. New York: Harper Colophon Books, 1976.

Bate, Berkowitz Nancy. "I Think, But Am Not: The Nightmare of William Wilson," *Poe Studies/Dark Romanticism: History, Theory, Interpretation* 30, no. 1–2 (1998): 27–38.

Baudelaire, Charles. "Edgar Allan Poe: His Life and Works." In *The Works of Edgar Allan Poe*. Trans. H. Curwen. London: John Camden Hotten, 1873, 1–21. www .eapoe.org/papers/misc1851/1873000m.htm.

Beattie, Hilary J. "Revenge." *Journal of the American Psychoanalytic Association* 53, no. 2 (June 2005): 519–41.

Bendixen, Alfred. "Romanticism and the American Gothic." In *The Cambridge Companion to American Gothic*. Ed. Jeffrey Andrew Weinstock, 31–43. Cambridge: Cambridge University Press, 2017.

Benedict, Barbara M. *Curiosity: A Cultural History of Early Modern Inquiry*. Chicago: University of Chicago Press, 2001.

Benemann, William. *Male-Male Intimacy in Early America: Beyond Romantic Friendships*. New York: The Haworth Press, 2006.

Benjamin, Walter. "Theses on the Philosophy of History." In *Illuminations*. Ed. Hannah Arendt. Trans. Harry Zohn, 253–64. New York: Schockden Books, 1968.

Benton, Richard P. "Poe's 'The Cask of Amontillado': Its Cultural and Historical Backgrounds." *Poe Studies/Dark Romanticism* 29, no. 1 (June 1996): 19–27.

Berger, Miriam. "'Am I My Brother's Keeper': Vengefulness as a Link of Reconnecting." In *Victimhood, Vengeance, and the Culture of Forgiveness*. Eds. Ivan Urlec, Miriam Berger, and Avi Berman, 107–28. New York: Nova Science Publishers, Inc., 2010.

Berlant, Lauren. *Cruel Optimism*. Durham: Duke University Press, 2011.

Bernstein, Jeremy. *Dawning of the Raj: The Life and Trials of Warren Hastings*. Chicago: Ivan R. Dee, 2000.

Blake, John. "There's nothing more frightening in American today than an angry White man." CNN (November 20, 2021). www.cnn.com/2021/11/20/us/angry -white-men-trials-blake-cec/index.html.

Bloom, Clive. *Reading Poe Reading Freud: The Romantic Imagination in Crisis*. Houndsmills: MacMillan Press, 1988.

Blow, Charles M. "White Men on Trial." *New York Times* (Nov. 17, 2021). www .nytimes.com/2021/11/17/opinion/rittenhouse-trial-bannon.html.

Botting, Fred. *Gothic*. 2nd ed. New York: Routledge, 2014.

Botting, Fred. "Reviews." *Erudit* 10. May 1998. www.erudit.org/en/journals/ron /1998-n10-ron422/005797ar/.

Bradbury, Mary. "Freud's Mourning and Melancholia." *Mortality* 6, no. 2 (2001): 212–19.

Bradford, Adam C. *Communities of Death: Whitman, Poe, and the American Culture of Mourning*. Columbia: University of Missouri Press, 2014.

Bridges, Tristan. "Antifeminism, Profeminism, and the Myth of White Men's Disadvantage." *Signs: Journal of Women in Culture and Society* 46, no. 3 (2021): 663–68.

Briggs, Charles F. "The Personality of Poe." *Independent* XXXII (June 24, 1880), www.eapoe.org/papers/misc1851/cfb18801.htm.

Britt, Theron. "The Common Property of the Mob: Democracy and Identity in Poe's 'William Wilson.'" *The Mississippi Quarterly* 48, no. 2 (Spring 1995): 197–210.

Brown, Wendy. "Resisting Left Melancholy." *Boundary 2* 26, no. 3 (1999): 19–27.

Brown, Wendy. "Wounded Attachments." *Political Theory* 21, no. 3 (August 1993): 390–410.

Buckner, Timothy R., and Peter Caster. *Fathers, Preachers, Rebels, Men: Black Masculinity in U.S. History and Literature, 1820–1945*. Columbus: The Ohio State University Press, 2011.

Burns, Stanley B. *Sleeping Beauty: Memorial Photography in America*. Altadena, CA: Twelvetree Press, 1999.

Butler, Judith. *Giving an Account of Oneself*. New York: Fordham University Press, 2005.

Butler, Judith. "Melancholy Gender/Refused Identification." In *The Judith Butler Reader*. Ed. Sarah Salih, 243–57. Malden, MA: Blackwell Publishing, 2004.

Butler, Judith. *Precarious Life: The Powers of Mourning and Violence*. London: Verso, 2006.

Butler, Judith. *Undoing Gender*. New York: Routledge, 2004.

Butler, Judith, Zeynap Gambetti, and Leticia Sabsay, eds. *Vulnerability in Resistance*. Durham: Duke University Press, 2016.

Clewell, Tammy. "Mourning Beyond Melancholia: Freud's Psychoanalysis of Loss." *Journal of the American Psychoanalytic Association* 52, no. 1 (March 2004): 43–67.

Columbus, Christopher. *The Spanish Letter of Columbus to Luis de Sant Angel*. London: G. Norman and Sons, 1893.

Crabtree, Adam. *From Mesmer to Freud: Magnetic Sleep and the Roots of Psychological Healing*. New Haven: Yale University Press, 1993.

Cvetkovich, Ann. *An Archive of Feelings: Trauma, Sexuality, and Lesbian Public Cultures*. Durham: Duke University Press, 2003.

Darby, Seyward. *Sisters in Hate: American Women and White Extremism*. New York: Little, Brown and Company, 2020.

Dayan, Joan. "Amorous Bondage: Poe, Ladies, and Slaves." In *The American Face of Edgar Allan Poe*. Eds. Shawn Resenheim and Stephen Rachman, 179–209. Baltimore: Johns Hopkins University Press, 1995.

Dayan, Joan. *Fables of Mind: An Inquiry into Poe's Fiction*. Oxford: Oxford University Press, 1987.

"The Dead Infant; or, the Agonizing Mother." *New York Weekly Museum* 4, no. 9 (June 29, 1816): 135, proquest.com/americanperiodicals.

Dean, Tim. *Beyond Sexuality*. Chicago: University of Chicago Press, 2000.

Dedmond, Francis B. "'The Cask of Amontillado' and the War of the Literati," *Modern Language Quarterly* 15, no. 2 (June 1954): 137–46.

Deleuze, Joseph Phillipe Francois. *Practical Instruction in Animal Magnetism.* Trans. Thomas C. Hartshorn. New York: D. Appleton & Co., 1843.

D'Emilio, John, and Estelle B. Freedman. *Intimate Matters: A History of Sexuality in America.* New York: Harper & Row, 1988.

DeRochi, Jack E., and Daniel J. Ennis, eds. *Richard Brinsley Sheridan: The Impresario in Political and Cultural Context.* Lewisburg, PA: Bucknell University Press, 2013.

Descartes, Rene. *Passions of the Soul and Other Late Philosophical Writing.* Trans. Michael Moriarty. Oxford: Oxford University Press, 2015.

Dinshaw, Carolyn. *Getting Medieval: Sexualities and Communities, Pre- and Post-modern.* Durham: Duke University Press, 1999.

Dirks, Nicholas B. *The Scandal of Empire: India and the Creation of Imperial Britain.* Cambridge, Mass: Belknap Press, 2006.

DiSanza, Raymond. "On Memory, Forgetting, and Complicity in 'The Cask of Amontillado,'" *The Edgar Allan Poe Review* 15, no. 2 (2014): 194–204.

Douglass, Frederick. *Narrative of the Life of Frederick Douglass.* In *The Norton Anthology of American Literature 1820–1865.* Ed. Nina Baym, 2064–2129. New York: W. W. Norton & Co., 2007.

Dowd, Nancy. *The Man Question: Male Subordination and Privilege.* New York: New York University Press, 2010.

Downing, Lisa. *Desiring the Dead: Necrophilia and Nineteenth-Century French Literature.* Oxford: Legenda, 2003.

Durbach, Nadja. "'Skinless Wonders': 'Body Worlds' and the Victorian Freak Show," *Journal of the History of Medicine and Allied Sciences* 69, no. 1 (January 2014): 38–67.

Edelman, Lee. *No Future: Queer Theory and the Death Drive.* Durham: Duke University Press, 2004.

Elmer, Jonathan. *Reading at the Social Limit: Affect, Mass Culture, and Edgar Allan Poe.* Stanford: Stanford University Press, 1995.

Elster, Jon. "Norms of Revenge." *Ethics* 100, no. 4 (July 1990): 862–85.

Emerson, Ralph Waldo. "Experience." In *The Norton Anthology of American Literature 1820–1865.* Ed. Nina Baym, 1195–1210. New York: W. W. Norton & Co., 2007.

Emerson, Ralph Waldo. "Self-Reliance." In *The Norton Anthology of American Literature, 1820–1865.* Ed. Nina Baym, 1163–80. New York: W. W. Norton & Co., 2007.

Eng, David L., and David Kazanjian, eds. *Loss: The Politics of Mourning.* University of California Press, 2002.

Eng, David L., and Shinee Han. *Racial Melancholia, Racial Dissociation: On the Social and Psychic Lives of Asian Americans.* Durham: Duke University Press, 2019.

English, Thomas Dunn. "A Card: In Reply to Mr. Poe's Rejoinder." *Evening Mirror* IV, no. 82 (July 13, 1846), www.eapoe.org/papers/misc1827/18460713.htm.

English, Thomas Dunn. "A Card: Mr. English's Reply to Mr. Poe." *Evening Mirror* IV, no. 65 (June 23, 1846), www.eapoe.org/papers/misc1827/18460623.htm.

English, Thomas Dunn. "Reminiscences of Poe [Part 01]." *Independent* XLVIII (October 15, 1896), www.eapoe.org/papers/misc1851/tde18961.htm.

English, Thomas Dunn. "Reminiscences of Poe [Part 02]." *Independent* XLVIII (October 22, 1896), www.eapoe.org/papers/misc1851/tde18962.htm.

English, Thomas Dunn. "Reminisces of Poe [Part 03]." *Independent* XLVIII (October 29, 1896), www.eapoe.org/papers/misc1851/tde18963.htm.

English, Thomas Dunn. "Reminiscences of Poe [Part 04]." *Independent* XLVIII (November 5, 1896), www.eapoe.org/papers/misc1851/tde18964.htm.

Esquirol, E. *Mental Maladies: A Treatise on Insanity*, Classics of Medicine Library. Trans. E.K. Hunt. Philadelphia: Lea and Blanchard, 1845.

Feldman, Michael. "Grievance: The Underlying Oedipal Configuration." *International Journal of Psychoanalysis* 89, no. 4 (2008): 743–58.

Fischer, Agneta, Eran Halperin, Daphna Canetti, and Alba Jasini. "Why We Hate." *Emotion Review* 10, no. 4 (October 2018): 309–20.

Flaherty, Colleen. "More Than Rumors." *Inside Higher Ed* (August 10, 2018). www.insidehighered.com/news/2018/08/10/michael-kimmels-former-student-putting-name-and-details-those-harassment-rumors.

Folks, Jeffrey. "Poe and the *Cognito*," *Southern Literary Journal* 42, no. 1 (Fall 2009): 57–72.

Foote, Lorien. *The Gentleman and the Roughs: Manhood, Honor, and Violence in the Union Army*. New York: New York University Press, 2010.

Foreman, Gabrielle P. "New England's Fortune: An Inheritance of Black Bodies and Bones." *Journal of American Studies* 49, no. 2 (May 2015): 287–303.

Foucault, Michel. *Abnormal: Lectures at the College de France 1974–1975*. Trans. Graham Burchell. New York: Picador, 1999.

Foucault, Michel. *The History of Sexuality: An Introduction*, Volume 1. New York: Vintage Books, 1978.

Frank, Adam. "Valdemar's Tongue, Poe's Telegraphy," *ELH* 72, no. 3 (2005): 635–62.

Frank, Lucy E., ed. *Representations of Death in Nineteenth-Century US Writing and Culture*. Burlington, VT: Ashgate, 2007.

Freccero, Carla. *Queer/Early/Modern*. Durham: Duke University Press, 2006.

Freeman, Elizabeth. *Time Binds: Queer Temporalities, Queer Histories*. Durham: Duke University Press, 2010.

Freud, Sigmund. "Mourning and Melancholia." In *The Standard Edition of the Complete Psychological Works of Sigmund Freud*, Volume XIV. Trans. James Strachey, 243–58. London: Hogarth Press, 1964, www.sas.upenn.edu/~cavitch/pdf-library/Freud_MourningAndMelancholia.pdf.

Freud, Sigmund. "The Uncanny." In *The Standard Edition of the Complete Works of Sigmund Freud, Volume XVII*. Trans. James Strachey, 219–52. London: Hogarth Press and the Institute of Psychoanalysis, 1958, uncanny.la.utexas.edu/wp-content/uploads/2016/04/freud-uncanny_001.pdf.

Fuller, Robert C. *Mesmerism and the American Cure of Souls*. Philadelphia: University of Pennsylvania Press, 1982.

Gaylin, Willard. *Hatred: The Psychological Descent into Violence*. New York: Public Affairs, 2003.

Gilmore, Paul. *The Genuine Article: Race, Mass Culture, and American Literary Manhood*. Durham: Duke University Press, 2001.

Gilson, Erinn Cunniff. "Vulnerability and Victimization: Rethinking Key Concepts in Feminist Discourses on Sexual Violence." *Signs* 42, no. 1 (Autumn 2016): 71–98.

Gleig, G.R. *Memoirs of the Life of the Right Hon. Warren Hastings*, Volume 3. London: Richard Bentley, 1841, play.google.com/books/reader?id=7IlUAAAAcA AJ&pg=GBS.PP4&hl=en.

Glover, Lorri. *All Our Relations: Blood Ties and Emotional Bonds among the Early South Carolina Gentry*. Baltimore: Johns Hopkins University Press, 2000.

Glover, Lorri. *Southern Sons: Becoming Men in the New Nation*. Baltimore: John Hopkins University Press, 2010.

Godbeer, Richard. *The Overflowing of Friendship: Love Between Men and the Creation of the American Republic*. Baltimore: Johns Hopkins University Press, 2009.

Goddu, Teresa A. "The African American Slave Narrative and the Gothic." In *A Companion to the American Gothic*. Ed. Charles L. Crow, 69–83. Hoboken, NJ: John Wiley & Sons, 2014.

Goddu, Teresa A. *Gothic America: Narrative, History, and Nation*. New York: Columbia University Press, 1997.

Goldwater, Eugene. "Getting Mad and Getting Even." *Modern Psychoanalysis* 29, no. 1 (2004): 23–36.

Graham, Sylvester. *Lectures to Young Men on Chastity*, 2nd edition. Boston: Light & Stearns, Cocker & Brewster, 1834, collections.nlm.nih.gov/catalog/nlm:nlm uid-7704062-bk.

Greenburg, Amy S. *Manifest Manhood and the Antebellum American Empire*. Cambridge: Cambridge University Press, 2005.

Gregg, Melissa, and Gregory J. Seigworth, eds. *The Affect Theory Reader*. Durham: Duke University Press, 2010.

Greven, David. "'The Whole Numerous Race of the Melancholy among Men': Mourning, Hypocrisy, and Same-Sex Desire in Poe's *Narrative of Arthur Gordon Pym*," *Poe Studies* 41, no. 1 (2008): 31–63.

Griswold, R. W. "Death of Edgar A. Poe." *New York Daily Tribune* IX, no. 156 (October 9, 1849), www.eapoe.org/papers/misc1827/nyt49100.htm.

Haggerty, George E. *Gothic Fiction/Gothic Form*. University Park: The Pennsylvania State University Press, 1989.

Halberstam, Judith. *The Queer Art of Failure*. Durham: Duke University Press, 2011.

Hartley, Lucy. *Physiognomy and the Meaning of Expression in Nineteenth-Century Culture*. Cambridge: Cambridge University Press, 2001.

Hendershot, Cyndy. *The Animal Within: Masculinity and the Gothic*. Ann Arbor: University of Michigan Press, 1998.

Henninger, Frances J. "The Bouquet of Poe's Amontillado." *South Atlantic Bulletin* 35, no. 2 (March 1970): 35–40.

Herndon, G. Melvin. "From Scottish Orphan to Virginia Planter: William Galt, Jr., 1801–1851." *Virginia Magazine of History and Biography* 87, no. 3 (1979): 326–43.

Herz, Rachel. *That's Disgusting: Unraveling the Mysteries of Repulsion*. New York: W. W. Norton, 2012.

Hogget, Paul. "Ressentiment and Grievance." *British Journal of Psychotherapy* 34, no. 3 (2018): 393–407.

Horn, Andrew. "Poe and the Tory Tradition: The Fear of Jacquerie in 'A Tale of the Ragged Mountains.'" *ESQ* 29, no. 1 (1983): 25–30.

Horowitz, Helen Lefkowitz. *Rereading Sex: Battles Over Sexual Knowledge and Suppression in Nineteenth-Century America.* New York: Vintage Books, 2003.

Hubbs, Valentine C. "The Struggle of Wills in Poe's 'William Wilson.'" *Studies in American Fiction* 11, no. 1 (Spring 1983): 73–79.

Hurley, Leonard B. "A New Note on the War of The Literat.," *American Literature* 7 no. 4 (January 1936): 376–94.

Hutchisson, James M., ed. *Edgar Allan Poe: Beyond Gothicism.* Newark: University of Delaware Press, 2011.

Icks, Martin. *The Crimes of Elagabalus.* Cambridge: Harvard University Press, 2012.

Isani, Mukhtar Ali. "Some Sources for Poe's 'Tale of the Ragged Mountains.'" *Poe Studies* 5, no. 2 (1972): 38–40.

Jackson, Stanley W. *Melancholia and Depression: From Hippocratic Times to Modern Times.* New Haven: Yale University Press, 1986.

Jaros, Peter. "A Double Life: Personifying the Corporation from *Dartmouth College* to Poe." *Poe Studies* 47 (2014): 4–35.

Jefferson, Thomas. "Report of the Commissioners for the University of Virginia to the Virginia General Assembly," 1818, founders.archives.gov/documents/Madi son/04–01–02–0289.

Johnson, David. *John Randolph of Roanoke.* Baton Rouge: Louisiana State University Press, 2012.

Kaplan, Louise J. "The Perverse Strategy in 'The Fall of the House of Usher.'" In *New Essays on Poe's Major Tales.* Ed. Kenneth Silverman, 45–64. Cambridge: Cambridge University Press, 1993.

Katz, Jonathan. *Love Stories: Sex Between Men Before Homosexuality.* Chicago: University of Chicago Press, 2001.

Kelly, Daniel. *Yuck!: The Nature and Moral Significance of Disgust.* Cambridge: MIT Press, 2000.

Kendi, Ibram X. "The Violent Defense of White Male Supremacy." *Atlantic* (September 9, 2020), www.theatlantic.com/ideas/archive/2020/09/armed-defenders -white-male-supremacy/616192/.

Kennedy, Gerald J. *A Historical Guide to Edgar Allan Poe.* Oxford: Oxford University Press, 2001.

Kennedy, J. Gerald. *Poe, Death, and the Life of Writing.* New Haven: Yale University Press, 1987.

Kennedy, J. Gerald. "Poe, 'Ligeia,' and the Problem of Dying Women." In *New Essays on Poe's Major Tales.* Ed. Kenneth Silverman, 113–29. Cambridge: Cambridge University Press, 1993.

Kennedy, J. Gerald. "The Violence of Melancholy: Poe Against Himself." *American Literary History* 8, no. 3 (Autumn 1996): 533–51.

Kett, Joseph F. *Rites of Passage: Adolescence in America, 1790 to the Present.* New York: Basic Books, 1977.

Kimmel, Michael. *Angry White Men: American Masculinity at the End of an Era*. New York: Nation Books, 2013.

Kimmel, Michael. *Manhood in America: A Cultural History,* 3rd ed. Oxford: Oxford University Press, 2012.

Kindlon, Dan, and Michael Thompson. *Raising Cain: Protecting the Emotional Life of Boys*. New York: Ballantine Books, 1999.

Koch, Peter O. *Imaginary Cities of Gold: The Spanish Quest for Treasure in North America*. Jefferson, NC: McFarland and Company, Inc., 2009.

Kolnai, Aurel. *On Disgust*. Eds. Barry Smith and Carolyn Korsmeyer. Chicago: Open Court, 2004.

Korsmeyer, Carolyn. *Savoring Disgust: The Foul and the Fair in Aesthetics*. Oxford: Oxford University Press, 2011.

Kristeva, Julia. *Powers of Horror: An Essay on Abjection*. Trans. Leon S. Roudiez. New York: Columbia University Press, 1982.

Krugman, Paul. "The Angry White Male Caucus." *New York Times* (October 1, 2018), www.nytimes.com/2018/10/01/opinion/kavanaugh-white-male-privilege .html.

Kushner, Howard L. "Suicide, Gender, and the Fear of Modernity in Nineteenth-Century Medical and Social Thought." *Journal of Social History* 26, no. 3 (Spring 1993): 461–90.

Laderman, Gary. *The Sacred Remains: American Attitudes Toward Death, 1799– 1883*. New Haven: Yale University Press.

Langmade, Lynn. "The Wilson Duplex: Corporatism and the Problem of Singleton Reading in Poe's 'William Wilson' (or, Why Can't You See Twins?)." *Poe Studies* 45, no 1. (2012): 5–39.

Laqueur, Thomas W. *Solitary Sex: A Cultural History of Masturbation*. New York: Zone Books, 2003.

Lawlor, Clark. *From Melancholia to Prozac: A History of Depression*. Oxford: Oxford University Press, 2012.

Lepore, Jill. "The Humbug; Edgar Allan Poe and the Economy of Horror." *New Yorker* (April 27, 2009), www.newyorker.com/magazine/2009/04/27/the-humbug.

Leverenz, David. "Spanking the Master: Mind-Body Crossings in Poe's Sensationalism." In *A Historical Guide to Edgar Allan Poe*. Ed. J. Gerald Kennedy, 95–128. Oxford: Oxford University Press, 2001.

Lind, Sidney E. "Poe and Mesmerism." *PMLA* 62 (1947): 1078–85.

Lopez, Roger G. "Self-Knowledge and the Elusive Pleasure of Vengeance." *Philosophia* 48 (2020): 289–311.

Love, Heather. *Feeling Backward: Loss and the Politics of Queer History*. Cambridge: Harvard University Press, 2007.

Luciano, Dana. *Arranging Grief: Sacred Time and the Body in Nineteenth-Century America*. New York: New York University Press, 2007.

Macaulay, Thomas Babbington. "Warren Hastings." In *Critical, Historical, and Miscellaneous Essays*. New York: Sheldon and Company, 1860, https://www.gutenberg.org/files/55905/55905-h/55905-h.htm.

Mallipeddi, Ramesh. "'A Fixed Melancholy': Migration, Memory, and the Middle Passage." *The Eighteenth Century 55*, no. 2/3 (Summer/Fall 2014): 235–53.

Maxwell, Lida. *Public Trials: Burke, Zola, Arendt and the Politics of Lost Causes.* Oxford: Oxford University Press, 2014.

Mayer, Ruth. "Neither Life Nor Death: Poe's Aesthetic Transfiguration of Popular Notions of Death." *Poe Studies/Dark Romanticism* 30, no. 1 (June 1996): 1–8.

McCormack, Patricia. "Necrosexuality." *Rhizomes* 11, no 12 (Fall 2005–Spring 2006), http://www.rhizomes.net/issue11/maccormack/index.html.

McGinn, Colin. *The Meaning of Disgust.* Oxford: Oxford University Press, 2011.

McWhorter, Ladelle. *Racism and Sexual Oppression in Anglo-America: A Genealogy.* Bloomington: Indiana University Press, 2009.

Melville, Herman. *Moby-Dick.* Eds. John Bryant and Haskell Springer. New York: Pearson Longman, 2007.

Menninghaus, Winfried. *Disgust: The Theory and History of a Strong Sensation.* Albany: SUNY Press, 2003.

Meyers, Jeffrey. *Edgar Allan Poe: His Life and Legacy.* New York: Charles Scribner's Sons, 1992.

Miller, William Ian. *The Anatomy of Disgust.* Cambridge: Harvard University Press, 1997.

Mills, Bruce. *Poe, Fuller, and the Mesmeric Arts: Transition States in the American Renaissance.* Columbia: University of Missouri Press, 2006.

Moores, D. J. "'Oh Gigantic Paradox': Poe's 'William Wilson' and the Jungian Self." *The Edgar Allan Poe Review* 7, no.1 (2006): 31–48.

Moreland, Clark T., and Karime Rodriguez. "Never Bet the Devil in Your Head': Fuseli's The Nightmare and Collapsing Masculinity in Poe's 'The Black Cat,'" *The Edgar Allan Poe Review* 16, no. 2 (2015): 204–20.

Morrison, Toni. *Playing in the Dark: Whiteness and the Literary Imagination.* New York: Vintage Books, 1992.

Moscoso, Javier. "The Shadows of Ourselves: Resentment, Monomania, and Modernity." In *On Resentment: Past and Present.* Eds. Bernardino Fantini, Dolores Martin Maruno, and Javier Moscoso, 19–36. Newcastle: Cambridge Scholars Publishing, 2013.

Moss, Donald, ed. *Hating in the First-Person Plural.* New York: Other Press, 2003.

Moss, Sidney P. *Poe's Literary Battles: The Critic in the Context of His Literary Milieu.* Durham: Duke University Press, 1963.

Moss, Sidney P., ed. *Poe's Major Crisis: His Libel Suit and New York's Literary World.* Durham: Duke University Press, 1970.

Mukherjee, Mithi. *India in the Shadows of Empire.* Oxford: Oxford University Press, 2010.

Munoz, Jose Esteban. *Cruising Utopia: The Then and There of Queer Futurity.* New York: New York University Press, 2009.

"The Mysterious Death of Edgar Allan Poe." General Topics About Edgar Allan Poe. October 1, 2020, www.eapoe.org/geninfo/poedeath.htm.

Nelson, Dana D. "The Haunting of White Manhood: Poe, Fraternal Ritual, and Polygenesis." *American Literature* 69, no. 3 (September 1997): 515–46.

Nevi, Charles N. "Irony and 'The Cask of Amontillado.'" *English Journal* 56, no. 3 (March 1967): 461–63.

Ngai, Sianne. *Ugly Feelings*. Cambridge: Harvard University Press, 2005.

Niebuhr, G. B. *The History of Rome*, Volume 3. Trans. William Smith and Leonhard Schmitz. Philadelphia: Lea & Blanchard, 1844.

Nietzsche, Friedrich. *On the Genealogy of Morals and Other Writings*. Trans. Carol Deith. Ed. Keith Ansell-Pearson. Cambridge: Cambridge University Press, 2017.

Nisbett, Richard E., and Dov Cohen. *Culture of Honor: The Psychology of Violence in the South*. Boulder, CO: Westview Press, 1996.

Nussbaum, Martha. *From Disgust to Humanity: Sexual Orientation & Constitutional Law*. Oxford: Oxford University Press, 2010.

Nussbaum, Martha. *Hiding from Humanity: Disgust, Shame, and the Law*. Princeton: Princeton University Press, 2004.

Oluo, Ijeoma. *Mediocre: The Dangerous Legacy of White Male America*. New York: Seal Press, 2020.

Oppenheim, Janet. *Shattered Nerves: Doctors, Patients, and Depression in Victorian England*. Oxford: Oxford University Press, 1991.

Percy, M. "On the Dangers of Dissection." *Eclectic Repository and Analytical Review, Medical and Philsophical* (January 1819), search.proquest.com/american periodicals.

Person, Leland S. "Outing the Perverse: Poe's False Confessionals." In *The Oxford Handbook of Edgar Allan Poe*, Eds. J. Gerald Kennedy and Scott Peeples, 252–68. Oxford: Oxford University Press, 2019.

Person, Leland S. "Poe's Philosophy of Amalgamation: Reading Racism in the Tales." In *Romancing the Shadow: Poe and Race*, 205–24. Eds. J. Gerald Kennedy and Liliane Wiessberg. Oxford: Oxford University Press, 2001.

Person, Leland S. "Queer Poe: The Tell-Tale Heart of His Fiction." *Poe Studies* 41, no. 1 (2008): 7–30.

Peyser, Thomas. "Poe's 'William Wilson' and the Nightmare of Equality." *Explicator* 68, no. 2 (2010): 101–03.

Pike, Judith E. "Poe and the Revenge of the Exquisite Corpse." *Studies in American Fiction* 26, no. 2 (Autumn 1998): 171–92.

Pinel, Phillipe. *A Treatise on Insanity*. Classics of Medicine Library. Trans. D. D. Davis. London, 1806.

Pisano, Frank. "Dimmesdale's Pious Imperfect Perverseness: Poe's 'Imp of the Perverse' and *The Scarlet Letter*." In *Poe Writing/Writing Poe*. Eds, Richard Kopley and Jana Argersinger, 143–58. New York: AMS Press, Inc, 2013.

Pitts, Geo R. "Hints on Melancholy." *American Medical Recorder* (Oct 1823): 596, American Periodicals.

Pitts, Jennifer. *A Turn to Empire: The Rise of Imperial Liberalism in Britain and France.* Princeton: Princeton University Press, 2005.

Poe, Edgar Allan. *Edgar Allan Poe Tales & Sketches, Volume 1: 1831–1842*. Ed.Thomas Ollive Mabbot. Urbana: University of Illinois Press, 1978.

Poe, Edgar Allan. *Edgar Allan Poe Tales & Sketches, Volume 2: 1843–1849.* Ed. Thomas Ollive Mabbot. Urbana: University of Chicago Press, 2000.

Poe, Edgar Allan. "Instinct vs Reason." *Alexander's Weekly Messenger* 4, no. 5 (January 29, 1840), www.eapoe.org/works/essays/ivrbcata.htm.

Poe, Edgar Allan. The Letters of Edgar Allan Poe. Edgar Allan Poe Society, www .eapoe.org/works/letters/index.htm.

Poe, Edgar Allan. "The Literati of New York City." In *The Works of Edgar Allan Poe, Vol. VIII: Literary Criticism III*. Eds, E. C. Stedman and G. E. Woodberry (1895), www.eapoe.org/works/stedwood/sw0801.htm

Poe, Edgar Allan. "Mr. Poe's Reply to Mr. English and Others." *The Spirit of the Times* (July 10, 1846), www.eapoe.org/works/misc/18460710.htm.

Poe, Edgar Allan. *The Selected Writings of Edgar Allan Poe.* Ed. G. R. Thompson. New York: W.W. Norton & Co., 2004.

Pollock, William. *Real Boys: Rescuing Our Sons from the Myths of Boyhood.* New York: Henry Holt and Company, 1998.

Porter, Susan L. "A Good Home: Indenture and Adoption in Nineteenth-Century Orphanages." In *Adoption in America: Historical Perspectives*, 27–50. Ed. E. Wayne Carp. Ann Arbor, MI: University of Michigan Press, 2002.

Poyen, Charles. *Progress of Animal Magnetism in New England.* Boston: Weeks, Jordon & Co., 1837.

Pugh, David G. *Sons of Liberty: The Masculine Mind in the Nineteenth Century.* Westport, CN: Greenwood Press, 1983.

Quinn, Arthur Hobson. *Edgar Allan Poe: A Critical Biography.* Baltimore: Johns Hopkins University Press, 1998.

Rabelais, Francois. *Gargantua and Pantagruel.* Trans. Burton Raffel. New York: W. W. Norton, 1990.

Recalcati, Massimo. "Hate as a Passion of Being." Trans. Ramsey McGlazer. *Qui Parle* 20, no. 2 (Spring/Summer 2012): 151–82.

Reich, Nicholas Tyler. "Bottom Terror in Poe's 'William Wilson,'" *Edgar Allan Poe Review* 21, no. 1 (2020): 86–108.

Reich, Taly, and S. Christian Wheeler. "The Good and Bad of Ambivalence: Desiring Ambivalence Under Outcome Uncertainty." *Journal of Personality and Social Psychology* 110, no. 4 (2016): 493–508.

Reynolds, David S. *Beneath the American Renaissance: The Subversive Imagination in the Age of Emerson and Melville.* New York: Alfred A. Knopf, 1988.

Rogin, Michael Paul. *Fathers & Children: Andrew Jackson and the Subjugation of the American Indian.* New Brunswick: Transaction Publishers, 2006.

Rosen, Irwin C. "Revenge—The Hate That Dare Not Speak Its Name: A Psychoanalytic Perspective." *Journal of the American Psychoanalytic Association* 55, no. 2 (June 2007): 595–620.

Rosenheim, Shawn, and Stephen Rachman, eds. *The American Face of Edgar Allan.* Baltimore: Johns Hopkins University Press, 1995.

Rotundo, E. Anthony. *American Manhood: Transformations in Masculinity from the Revolution to the Modern Era.* New York: Basic Books, 1993.

Rozin, Paul, Jonathan Haidt, Clark R. McCauley. "Disgust." In *Handbook of Emotions*. Eds. Michael Lewis and Jeannette M. Haviland, 575–94. New York: Guilford Press, 1993.

Ruby, Jay. *Secure the Shadow: Death and Photography in America*. Cambridge: MIT Press, 1995.

Rushdy, Ashraf H. A. *After Injury: A Historical Anatomy of Forgiveness, Resentment, and Apology*. Oxford: Oxford University Press, 2018.

Rust, Richard Dilworth. "'Punish with Impunity': Poe, Thomas Dunn English, and 'The Cask of Amontillado.'" *Edgar Allan Poe Review* 2, no. 2 (Fall 2001): 33–52.

Salisbury, Laura, and Andrew Shail, eds. *Neurology and Modernity: A Cultural History of Nervous Systems, 1800–1950*. New York: Palgrave MacMillan, 2010.

Sandler, Matt. "Poe's Survival Stories as Dying Colonialism." In *The Oxford Handbook of Edgar Allan Poe*. Eds. J. Gerald Kennedy and Scott Peeples, 269–85. Oxford: Oxford University Press, 2019.

Sappol, Michael. *A Traffic of Dead Bodies: Anatomy and Embodied Social Identity in Nineteenth-Century America*. Princeton: Princeton University Press, 2002.

Sbriglia, Russell. "Feeling Right, Doing Wrong: Poe, Perversity, and the Cunning of Unreason." *Poe Studies* 26 (2013): 4–31.

Scheler, Max. *Ressentiment*. Trans. Louis A. Coser. Milwaukee, WI: Marquette University Press, 1994.

Schneider, Iris K., and Norbert Schwarz. "Mixed Feelings: The Case of Ambivalence." *ScienceDirect* 15 (2017): 39–45.

Sedgwick, Eve Kosofsky. "Jane Austen and the Masturbating Girl." *Critical Inquiry* 17, no. 4 (Summer 1991): 818–37.

Sedgwick, Eve Kosofsky. *Tendencies*. Durham: Duke University Press, 1993.

Sheridan, Richard Brinsley. "At the Trial of Warren Hastings." In *World Famous Orations, Volume VI, Ireland*. Ed. William Jennings Bryan, 77–98. New York: Funk and Wagnalls, 1906, ia800705.us.archive.org/28/items/worldsfamousorat190 67brya/worldsfamousorat19067brya.pdf.

Shklar, Judith. *The Faces of Injustice*. New Haven: Yale University Press, 1990.

Shookman, Ellis, ed. *The Faces of Physiognomy: Interdisciplinary Approaches to Johann Casper Lavater*. Columbia, SC: Camden House, 1993.

Silverman, Kenneth. *Edgar A. Poe: A Mournful and Never-ending Remembrance*. New York: Harper Perennial, 2008.

Smith, Adam. *The Theory of Moral Sentiments*. Ann Arbor: University of Michigan Library, 2005, name.umdl.umich.edu/K111361.0001.001.

Snodgrass, Joseph. "The Facts of Poe's Death and Burial." *Beadle's Monthly* (May 1867), www.eapoe.org/papers/misc1851/18670300.htm.

Spooner, Catherine, and Dale Townshend, eds. *The Cambridge History of the Gothic*, Volume 3. Cambridge: Cambridge University Press, 2021.

Spooner, Catherine, and Emma McEvoy, eds. *The Routledge Companion to the Gothic*. New York: Routledge, 2007.

Stadler, Gustavus T. "Poe and Queer Studies." *Poe Studies/Dark Romanticism* 33, no. 1–2 (2000): 19–22.

Stannard, David E., ed. *Death in America*. Philadelphia: University of Pennsylvania Press, 1975.

Steiner, John. "Revenge and Resentment in the 'Oedipus Situation.'" *International Journal of Psychoanalysis* 77, no. 3 (1996): 433–43.

Steiner, Michael J. *A Study of the Intellectual and Material Culture of Death in Nineteenth-Century America*. Lewiston, NY: Edwin Mellon Press, 2003.

Stern, Julia. "Double Talk: The Rhetoric of the Whisper in Poe's 'William Wilson.'" *ESQ* 40, no. 3 (1994): 185–218.

Stern, Megan. "'Yes:—no:—I have been sleeping—and now—now—I am dead': Undeath, the Body, and Medicine," *Studies in History and Philosophy of Biological and Biomedical Sciences* 39, no. 3 (2008): 347–54.

Sternberg, Robert J., ed. *The Psychology of Hate*. Washington, D.C.: American Psychological Association, 2005.

Stott, Richard. *Jolly Fellows: Male Milieus in Nineteenth-Century America*. Baltimore: Johns Hopkins University Press, 2009.

Strawson, P. F. "Freedom and Resentment." In *Freedom and Resentment and Other Essays*. New York: Routledge, 2008, www.ucl.ac.uk/~uctytho/dfwstrawson1.htm.

Swedlund, Alan C. *Shadows in the Valley: A Cultural History of Illness, Death, and Loss in New England, 1840–1916*. Amherst: University of Massachusetts Press, 2010.

Terry, Jennifer. *An American Obsession: Science, Medicine, and Homosexuality in Modern Society*. Chicago: University of Chicago Press, 1999.

Thompson, Cheryl W. "Fatal Police Shootings of Unarmed Black People Reveal Troubling Patterns." NPR (January 25, 2021), www.npr.org/2021/01/25/956177021 /fatal-police-shootings-of-unarmed-black-people-reveal-troubling-patterns.

Thompson, G. R. "Is Poe's 'A Tale of the Ragged Mountains' a Hoax?" *Studies in Short Fiction* 6 (1968–1969): 454–60.

Thompson, G. R. *Poe's Fiction: Romantic Irony in the Gothic Tales*. Madison: University of Wisconsin Press, 1973.

Thoreau, Henry David. "Resistance to Civil Government." In *The Norton Anthology of American Literature, 1820–1865*. Ed. Nina Baym, 1857–72. New York: W. W. Norton & Co., 2007.

Thoreau, Henry David. *Walden*. In *The Norton Anthology of American Literature, 1820–1865*. Ed. Nina Baym, 1872–2046. New York: W. W. Norton & Co., 2007.

Tissot, Samuel August. *A Treatise on the Diseases Produced by Onanism*. New York: Collins & Hannay, 1832, archive.org/details/57110430R.nlm.nih.gov.

Townshend, Chauncey Hare. *Facts in Mesmerism with Reasons for a Dispassionate Inquiry into It*, 2nd ed. London: T. G. Wiegel, 1844.

Van Doorn, Janne. "Anger, Feelings of Revenge, Hate." *Emotion Review* 10, no. 4 (October 2018): 321–22.

Walsh, John Evangelist. *Midnight Dreary: The Mysterious Death of Edgar Allan Poe*. New York: St. Martin's Minotaur, 2000.

Ware, Tracy. "The Two Stories of 'William Wilson." *Studies in Short Fiction* 26, no. 1 (1989): 43–48.

Weinauer, Ellen. "Race and the American Gothic." In *The Cambridge Companion to American Gothic*. Ed. Jeffrey Andrew Weinstock, 85–98. Cambridge: Cambridge University Press, 2017.

Weinstock, Jeffery Andrew. "Introduction: The American Gothic." In *The Cambridge Companion to American Gothic*. Ed. Jeffrey Andrew Weinstock, 1–14. Cambridge: Cambridge University Press, 2017.

Weintrobe, Sally. "Links Between Grievance, Complaint, and Different Forms of Entitlement." *International Journal of Psychoanalysis* 85, no. 1 (2004): 83–96.

Weitzel, Shelby. "On the Relationship Between Forgiveness and Resentment in the Sermons of Joseph Butler." *History of Philosophy Quarterly* 24, no. 3 (2007): 237–53.

Whalen, Terry. *Edgar Allan Poe and the Masses: The Political Economy of Literature in Antebellum America*. Princeton: Princeton University Press, 1999.

White, Dana. *National Manhood*. Durham, NC: Duke University Press, 1998.

White, Paul. "Acquired Character: The Hereditary Material of the 'Self-Made Man.'" In *Hereditary Produced: At the Crossroads of Biology, Politics, and Culture, 1500–1870*. Eds. Staffan Müller-Willie and Hans-Jörg Rheinberger, 375–97. Cambridge: MIT Press, 2007.

Williams, Michael J. S. "Poe's Ugly American: 'A Tale of the Ragged Mountains.'" *Poe Studies* 34, no. 1–2 (2001): 51–61.

Williams, Timothy. *Intellectual Manhood: University, Self, and Society in the Antebellum South*. Chapel Hill: University of North Carolina Press, 2015.

Willis, Martin. *Mesmerist, Monsters, and Machines: Science Fiction and the Cultures of Science in the Nineteenth Century*. Kent: Kent State University Press, 2006.

Wing-Chi Ki, Magdalen. "Superego Evil and Poe's Revenge Tales." *Poe Studies* 46 (2013): 59–77.

Winter, Alison. *Mesmerized: Powers of Mind in Victorian Britain*. Chicago: University of Chicago Press, 2000.

Wright, Kai. "White Men Have Good Reason to Be Scared." *Nation* (November 5, 2018), www.thenation.com/article/archive/white-men-have-good-reason-to-be-scared/.

Wurmser, Leon. "The Superego as of Herald Resentment." *Psychoanalytic Inquiry* 29, no. 5 (2009): 386–410.

Wyatt-Brown, Bertram. *Southern Honor: Ethics and Behavior in the Old South*. Oxford: Oxford University Press, 2007.

Yao, Xine. *Disaffected: The Cultural Politics of Unfeeling in Nineteenth-Century America*. Durham: Duke University Press, 2021.

Zwarg, Christina. "Vigorous Currents, Painful Archives: The Production of Affect and History in Poe's 'Tale of the Ragged Mountains.'" *Poe Studies* 43, no. 1 (2010): 7–33.

Index

About the Author

Dr. Suzanne Ashworth teaches early American literature, LGBTQ literature, film, queer theory, and gender and sexuality studies at Otterbein University in Columbus, Ohio. She is a recipient of multiple teaching, advising, and leadership awards, including *Ohio Magazine*'s Excellence in Education and the Ohio LGBTQ Leadership awards. Her published work centers on nineteenth-century writers and historical conceptions of the body, gender, desire, sex, and sexuality.

www.ingramcontent.com/pod-product-compliance
Lightning Source LLC
Chambersburg PA
CBHW022311280326
41932CB00010B/1058